KT-103-336

Beyond Supervet

How Animals
Make Us
the Best We
Can Be

Also by Noel Fitzpatrick

Listening to the Animals: Becoming the Supervet
How Animals Saved My Life: Being the Supervet

For younger readers
Vetman and His Bionic Animal Clan

NOEL FITZPATRICK

Beyond Supervet

How Animals
Make Us
the Best We
Can Be

TRAPEZE

This book contains references to child abuse and suicidal ideation.

Some of the names of those featured in the book have been changed to protect their personal information.

First published in Great Britain in 2022 by Trapeze
an imprint of The Orion Publishing Group Ltd
Carmelite House, 50 Victoria Embankment
London EC4Y 0DZ

An Hachette UK Company

1 3 5 7 9 10 8 6 4 2

Copyright © Fitz All Media Limited 2022

The moral right of Noel Fitzpatrick to be identified as
the author of this work has been asserted in accordance
with the Copyright, Designs and Patents Act of 1988.

All rights reserved. No part of this publication may be
reproduced, stored in a retrieval system, or transmitted
in any form or by any means, electronic, mechanical,
photocopying, recording, or otherwise, without the
prior permission of both the copyright owner and the
above publisher of this book.

A CIP catalogue record for this book is
available from the British Library.

ISBN (Mass Market Paperback) 978 1 3987 0649 1
ISBN (Export Trade Paperback) 978 1 3987 0648 4
ISBN (eBook) 978 1 3987 0650 7
ISBN (Audio) 978 1 3987 0651 4

Typeset by Input Data Services Ltd, Somerset

Printed and bound in Great Britain by Clays Ltd, Elcograf S.p.A.

MIX
Paper from
responsible sources
FSC® C104740

www.orionbooks.co.uk

For all the innocents

CONTENTS

All buttoned up

It was one of those spring mornings in Ireland where your breath hung in front of you like smoke. As I pulled the calving jack out of the boot of my rusty, but trusty, Mazda 323 in the freezing drizzle, the metal of its long shaft felt like an icicle. A bleary sun blinked through banks of grey clouds above. It being not long into the morning, after a late night before, I was somewhat bleary myself.

I heard the sound of wellingtons sploshing in muddy puddles and looked up and as I did so I bashed my head on the boot of the car.

'Ye'd be better wearing yer cap now then, wouldn't ye?' said a man dressed in muck-caked green overalls who was sauntering across the yard with the unmistakable air of someone who had been left in charge while the man and woman of the house had gone off to Mass on a Sunday morning. I'd actually bought a tweed cap with a view to making me look wiser than my twenty-three years, because generally when a farmer has a serious problem with one of their animals, they'd rather have an experienced old hand on the scene, not the new kid on the block. But my boss had despatched me, so here I was.

I could tell straight away he enjoyed the thought of having someone else to boss around.

'Oh, ya won't be needing that now,' he muttered, gesturing to the calving jack in my hand. The 'jack' is a T-shaped device constituting a long shaft rail with three hooks which are attached to the legs and head of the emerging calf with ropes, and moved using a ratchet handle down the rail. The short saddle part at the top of the T is braced up against the buttocks of the cow, thus 'jacking' the calf out of the mother. Think of it as like pulling a cork.

I didn't understand what he meant until I looked beyond the gate, half its green paint flaked away, into the yard beyond. When the call came in, I'd been told only that it was a cow in trouble calving. But now the nature of the problem became clear. She was down in the corner of the yard, lying in a splattering of muck, and groaning from her difficult labour. The most the farmhand had been able to do was let the other cows out of the yard, so at least she wasn't being bothered by the throng. Already beside this particular cow, there was a calf trying to nuzzle for milk, still matted with some birth fluids. It had found its feet well, and so I guessed it had been out in the world for a while.

'Oh, sure she's calved a few hours now . . .' my companion confirmed. 'We didn't see this one comin'.'

I quickly donned my flat tweed cap and squelched over to her side. 'This one comin'' was a uterine prolapse. The poor cow probably had a rough time forcing the calf out and continued to push thereafter.

I must have muttered something sympathetic under my breath, but the farmhand didn't seem all that concerned.

'Ah, yeah, 'twas a rough ride for the wee *lao* . . . poor crater,' he said, as he stood there doing exactly nothing. *Lao* is 'calf' in Gaelic and I understood it must have been a difficult calving, only achieved with some considerable brute force a few hours earlier.

Uterine prolapse is not an uncommon complication of calving, and I'd seen more than my fair share. When a cow is straining to deliver a big calf for some time, particularly if mum has a lack of calcium, the womb and foetal membranes can follow the calf.

There are basically two ways to try to get a prolapsed uterus back in when a cow is down. Most people nowadays try to put the cow in the 'New Zealand' position, which is her lying on her chest, with legs splayed out behind like a frog. However, the poor cow was down and out, exhausted from straining, and it was by no means clear how I might get the uterus back in again.

I took control immediately as only a supremely over-confident young veterinary graduate can, asking him to go to the main house and bring supplies: a couple of sheets, some kind of blanket, a towel, and two buckets of warm water.

'. . . Oh, and a big bale of straw. And some sugar.'

He made one final unhelpful remark: 'Well, there'll be sugar but no straw in the house, yer'll find,' and then turned on his mucky heels before he could miss my dirty look. When he returned after a few minutes, without the straw, he had more details on what had happened.

'Ah, sure meself and the boss man were pullin' before dawn . . . taut we'd never get 'im out . . . head down . . . big fella he is . . . sure what can ya do? . . .' He trailed off, lost in his own thoughts.

I snapped him out of it pronto and beckoned him to help. This would be at least a two-person job. We tried for several minutes, from several positions, and failed. The cow was in no mood to help. I like to think, as we fell back sweating, that my new friend and I had found some mutual respect in the endeavour.

He found some straw in a shed nearby and we set about spreading it around her, to try to at least soak up some of the muck and give us a kind of bedding to roll the cow onto. I spread the rug he'd brought out on the straw and then put one of the sheets over it.

I carefully pulled the foetal membranes and most of the muck off the uterus and then washed, disinfected and doused it with sugar, which is *hypertonic*, and as such helps to reduce the oedema or swelling of the womb. Then I used a blade to shave some hair off the rump above the base of the tail.

'Are ye gonna chop it off with the blade, den?' asked my helper.

No, I most certainly wasn't. That would be a very last resort.

I drew up lidocaine into a syringe and administered the anaesthetic into the lower spine (an epidural).

Having failed with 'New Zealand' positioning, I decided to attempt the old 'roly poly Irish special', as I called it – which requires a team of three strong men at the best of times. No matter, two blokes of mediocre strength, but with great willingness, would have to do. We were in the middle of nowhere, so getting more help quickly wasn't possible and anyways, the nearest neighbour was probably at Mass too. So we decided we'd give it our best try on our own.

Now, I'd grown up on a farm in Ballyfin, in County Laois in the Republic of Ireland, so I'd seen it all before since I was knee-high to a grasshopper. I'd had my first hand inside a sheep aged eight and I'd lost count of the number of animals since. I knew the score. It certainly wasn't the first or last time I would have birth fluid, blood and shite all over me. I had experienced the excreta of calving many times in my life, but this was next level. Grunts emanated from the farm helper, who'd rolled up his sleeves to hoist the legs of the cow up onto a large bale of straw. His heavy breathing mingled with my own, and drifted in vapour trails from the yard where we toiled and over the ragged stone walls of the farmyard. We spoke in grunts and curses, with the odd instruction thrown in.

'Hold her! Hold that leg. For God's sake, hold on . . . Don't let her fall now.'

We grunted and groaned, huffed and puffed, slid and slipped, until we finally got her back end rolled up a ramp of straw onto a bigger bale, so that her hind legs were in the air, with her on her back, and my new pal precariously perched on the precipice, holding her legs with the ropes normally used for pulling the calf out. But as I tried to push the uterus back where it belonged, I found I simply didn't have enough limbs to hold one section in while moving to the next. My accomplice did his part, gripping the legs, but I just couldn't maintain the pressure needed with only two hands.

So I did what anyone in my situation would have done and used my head. Literally. I was thankful I'd worn the hat.

It didn't escape me how weird this actually was, or how

ironic. Just three years earlier to make a bit of extra cash in vet school, I'd modelled some knitwear and some tweed. I was the proud face of Kilcarra wool knitting patterns and I'm quite sure there's a picture of me somewhere, with a beaming smile, proudly wearing a very fashionable tweed flat cap. Well, I wasn't smiling now. After much heave-ho-ing, things were finally looking good and my friend let out a huge sigh of relief and let a rope go. As one of the legs hit me straight in the forehead, I yelped and then quick as a flash, probably with my own sigh of relief, blurted, 'Well my hat didn't save me from that one, now, did it!'

We both laughed. But too soon. The cow heaved again and I had to push again. 'Grab those legs,' I shouted, as I got wrist-deep, then elbow-deep, then near shoulder-deep. I was wearing waterproofs, but at this point, all concerns for clothing were out of the window.

'Do you think you could get me a wine bottle?' I asked.

'Are ye out o' yer mind? ... There's no wine drinkin' 'round here.'

'No, no, no – for pushing the last bit!'

He gently lowered the legs this time, as I kept my right arm shoulder-deep inside her. She lay there panting but otherwise motionless. My friend trotted off to the farmhouse and before long returned with a bottle of whiskey and a jug. He took off the cap and poured the whiskey into the jug, as if showing me the lengths he was prepared to go to to help me and the cow in our moment of need. Then he proudly screwed the cap back on and handed me the empty bottle.

I got him to lather it in disinfectant, then held it by the neck and used it to return the uterine horn to where it belonged. And so, it was done. My friend stood back, but I kept my arm in place, just in case she felt the urge to push again.

I was still in that position when, shortly after, we heard the sound of a car pulling into the yard beside the farmhouse. The farmer and his wife were back from Mass. They rounded the corner on foot in their Sunday finest and he leaned on the gate. 'All right, lads?' he called over. 'Are ya here, veterinary? Sure, I calved her hours ago.'

As if to hammer home the obvious, he nodded to the calf, which was now gambolling around the yard, no doubt somewhat confused in her search for her mother, who was still incapacitated.

'Yeah, I am,' I replied, from my compromised position shoulder-deep in the cow. The farmer's eyes passed over the scene and settled on his helper, looking on with the jug of whiskey in his hand. He spoke before I had a chance to say any more, stammering, 'A prolapse . . . She only went and had a prolapse, didn't she.' He looked at me for some kind of reassurance. I nodded, as I somewhat self-consciously withdrew my arm from the poor cow and stood up from my crouched position, whiskey bottle in hand.

There followed a moment of what, looking back, must have been comical silence, which I'm quite sure the cow didn't find funny at all as she lay there somewhat forlorn and still panting from the effort. Then the woman of the house just mumbled, 'Oh, for goodness' sake . . . What are yous like?' I walked to the gate and handed her the whiskey bottle. My friend sheepishly did the same with the jug. Not a word more was said.

We turned to try to haul the poor cow into some kind of an easier position for her, but it was clear that between us we didn't have the manpower. The farmer took off his Sunday coat and hung it on the gatepost. 'Ah, me bloody shoes,' he muttered, as he hightailed it to the small outhouse by the back door and promptly returned with overalls and wellingtons on. He marched into the yard. 'What a palaver! What a thing now.'

All three of us rolled the cow up a bit so she was a little more comfortable. I still had a close eye on her. It's a bit controversial nowadays whether you use stitches, but back then that was how I was taught to do it, and it's still often done today. So, I just said out loud, as the thought came to mind, 'Do you have any big buttons?'

I could see the farmer's wife washing the whiskey bottle under the outside tap by the back door of the house. She heard me and shouted back, 'Just a minute.' We all turned around to see her take the top off the bottle and pour the whiskey from the jug back into it again, then lift the bottle to her eyeline and check the whiskey was all there, before heading back into the house, screwing the cap back on as she went.

Less than a minute later she trundled back out again, skirt billowing over her newly donned boots, with a big pair of what looked like blade shears for shearing sheep in her hand. These were like giant scissors that I recognised well from wielding them myself, very ineffectively it must be said, whilst the shearer on the farm I grew up on tried and failed to impart the skill to me. Our shearing scissors had been rusty and a bit blunt in spite of regular rubbing of the edges with a sharpening stone, but these looked well maintained, with shiny silver bows and rivets at the handle end. I had no idea why she'd brought them out though.

'Where's yer coat?' she asked her husband. 'Der's no big buttons in da house.'

A peculiar look of resignation and consternation washed across the poor farmer's face. He darted a look towards where his coat was hanging on the gatepost.

'Ah, now . . . sure dat's me Mass coat,' he protested, in a rather plaintive tone which was more of an acquiescence to the inevitability of what was about to happen than an actual objection. But his wife was a formidable woman – and clearly not to be argued with. Sure enough, she ignored him, grabbed his coat, then turned with a squelch of her big boots and marched back across the yard. With a sharp flick of the shears, she made short work of snipping four very large black buttons out of each side of the double-breasted coat, eight in all.

My 'Thanks' must have sounded like a meek whimper as I instinctively held out my hand and she placed the buttons in my palm, one by one.

'Der ya go now . . . on wit ya,' she announced with another rapid twirl of the floral skirt and off she tromped, coat in hand, back into the house. I looked at the buttons, then up at the face of the farmer which by now was a curious mixture of bewilderment and just a little trickle of intrigue. I walked over to the gate, climbed over it yet again and fumbled in the boot of my hatchback. Finally, I found it – a big spool of nylon that I used for stitching up cow Caesareans.

I pulled the sheet out a bit from the straw and knelt on it. The poor cow was calmer now, just taking long breaths and beginning to notice that she had just brought life into the world, her head twitching towards her calf. The anaesthetic I'd previously injected would be sufficient to reduce any pain. As I picked up the giant curved stainless-steel needle in my right hand, her calf gave her a gentle tap on the nose with his, as if to say, 'Thanks, Mum, for bringing me into the world – I'm sorry for all the hassle . . .'

The farmer, our helper and I stood back and admired the four rectangles of heavy-duty nylon I had placed through eight large black buttons, four on each side, sealing the aperture in an effort to prevent further prolapse. I jabbed her with a broad-spectrum antibiotic and an anti-inflammatory painkiller, then we rolled her up onto her haunches. I raised the jugular vein in her neck with my fist until it was bulging, then instructed the farmhand to keep it up with pressure, held the tip of a large sharp needle over the skin with the finger and thumb of my left hand and then rammed it in with the palm of my right. Blood spurted out and I rapidly attached an orange tube 'flutter valve', connected to a big brown bottle of calcium, which I trickled into her bloodstream, since it may well have been this deficiency that had predisposed her to the prolapse in the first place.

Then we helped her up to her hooves. Unsteady as she was at first, she had her newborn to keep her preoccupied. I marvelled, not for the first time, and certainly far from the last, at how much I have to learn from cows about resilience, and even love, as she propped herself up against the wall of the yard, legs close to buckling as her calf gratefully suckled.

Thirty years later and 400 miles east across the Irish Sea, I again used the button mattress technique, but this time to help one of the great loves of my life – Ricochet, a black Maine Coon cat who allows me to be in his life and brings me an indescribable amount of love on a daily basis. He's my greatest animal friend in the world today, roaming around my office and jumping up on my knee, flinging his big panda paws around my neck to pull my head closer, so he can press his muzzle into my chin and eye socket. It's his way of telling me about his day, and empathising with mine. I can't even describe in words how much I adore him. He smells of sunshine, albeit with an undertone of 'poo-foot' (from fastidious scooping in the litter tray), or fresh rain on grass, depending on the day.

As a kitten, he had a big polyp which grew from the membrane on the inside of his inner ear. We drilled into the base of his skull and pulled out this chunk of tissue with tentacles which was growing up behind his nose and through his eardrum into his ear canal. After removing it, he was fine for a while until he got an infection in his ear canal, a common occurrence thereafter. He's a secretive bugger though and clearly didn't let me see him scratching his ear at all until I awoke one morning to his nose in my eye socket and a giant swollen earflap bashing my forehead. He'd scratched and shaken his head to the point that he had ruptured the small blood vessels between the skin and the thin cartilage of his ear flap.

Ricochet has such amazingly beautiful ears, with spiky hair that sticks bolt upright from his lion-tufted head, as if permanently struck by lightning. He always looks startled because he has a squinty eye, which can happen when the nerves are affected by the polyp and surgery.

Now, though, his magnificent ear flap was bloated with blood. I jumped out of bed and took a closer look. I'm a vet – how could I not have noticed he had an ear canal infection? My bedroom is four feet from my bathroom, and ten feet through a door to my desk. I rang the team . . . 'Ricochet has an aural haematoma – we cut after consults.' The operation would be very simple by comparison with the other procedures that we normally perform, but everyone was on tenterhooks, because this was the boss's baby.

With slightly more trepidation than normal, I held my boy whilst the intravenous line was put in place, and I kissed his forehead as the general anaesthesia kicked in. I had performed surgery on aural haematomas many times in my early career – but that was more than twenty years previously and my expertise lay in a different area now. For more than two decades, the tools of my trade had been drill, saw, hammer and screws. I studied my arse off to earn my degrees, but I've only ever seen the exams and coursework as hoops of fire that have to be jumped through in order to get the real juice that fuels a good clinician and surgeon – experience. My degree certificates don't hang on my wall, but rather a sign that says 'Always be yourself unless you can be Batman, in which case always be Batman.' Mammy always said, 'Pride takes a fall,' and my daddy, 'You're only as good as your next job.'

Now, I'm a neuro-orthopaedic specialist, or so the pieces of paper say. That means I know nothing at all about diarrhoea or kidney or liver problems, no matter how many queries I get on such things. To the average person – and I can't blame them – I'm a vet. But the day Ricochet needed his surgery, I needed to revert to being a general vet again, because I wasn't ready to trust anyone else. It was time to delve back into my twenties to resurrect the old button technique.

Following induction of general anaesthesia, I cleaned Ricochet's ear flap with disinfectant, and then sliced the skin open on the inside of the thin ear cartilage. The blood came gushing out. To stop the many tiny blood vessels bleeding, I'd need to stitch the skin back on to the cartilage flap. But here's the kicker – I'd have to squish the skin down at multiple spots using some kind of pressure pads. You can buy such things from medical suppliers, but there's nothing wrong with the tried-and-tested button method.

I could have asked a nurse to brave rooting through the cupboards in my office, but there was another more readily available source – the clothes rack that stands in the small kitchen next to my office bedroom. I found a scruffy old shirt that I really didn't mind losing and with a few snips collected eight buttons in total, just like for the prolapsing cow thirty years earlier. This particular operation was supervised by the other Maine Coon cat I'm lucky enough to have in my life, Excalibur, who lives with me at the practice when I'm there (which is most of the time). Excalibur is a glorious giant silver tabby and Ricochet's best friend. He smells permanently of fresh linen and so it was appropriate that he sat on my stripy Paul Smith shirt and held it still for the delicate button-snipping procedure.

I placed one sterilised button on each side of the cartilage of the ear flap, outside and inside, and stitched them with nylon suture in a mattress fashion, pulling them down tight against the skin, and thus distributing the force at four separate points – a button sandwich, just as I had done for the cow many years earlier. Then we cleaned out poor Ricochet's ear canal and stuck a needle through his eardrum, which had already been significantly damaged by the previous polyp, to flush and suck infection from what was left of his inner ear.

Perhaps Paul Smith himself would have been proud of my sartorial creation, but the patient wasn't best pleased. Few animals like the cone of shame, and Ricochet proceeded to hiss and spit at Dada as I carried him back to the wards. I was shocked and just slightly amused, as I'd never seen his temper before. It has to be said that he looked embarrassed after each hiss-spit, and with time just cuddled into me and fell asleep. Eventually I had to move my hands because they were needed for the next patient in the operating theatre. But when I finished work at 2 a.m., I curled up for a while with Ricochet in the wards, before trudging down the corridor to my own bed.

He was fine for a few days and then disaster struck – more bleeding. It seemed Mr Smith's buttons were too small for the task, and there was breakthrough bleeding on the top and bottom ends of the slash – the ear flap was filling again. It was time to call in the big guns.

Fortunately, my colleague, nurse Carly, who helps run my surgical theatres, once had a very promising career in teddy-bear making, and it turns out that teddy-bear button eyes are the absolutely perfect tension absorbers of appropriate size for Maine Coon ear flaps. I sat down and gingerly poured all of the multi-coloured buttons onto the table, carefully selecting the right diameter, and those that had a flat, rather than convex or concave surface that wouldn't distribute the load equally; and of course – most important of all – the right colour scheme. Ricochet couldn't be doing with garish, mismatched button pairs. With the complex button triage selection process complete, I set about our business again. Poor Ricochet! This time he had five pairs of buttons equally distributed around the periphery of the slash wound, in fetching blue and yellow pairs.

I was taking no chances this time and left the buttons in

for four weeks, after which I removed them a pair at a time over five days. He sat on my knee, prodded my eye socket with his muzzle, talking to me in miffed and impatient throaty purrs, until finally it was done. Ricochet's celebrations at being button-free involved his favourite game of running from office to bedroom to kitchen feverishly, knocking over as many things as possible. I could hardly blame him. He looked even more cute, with his squinty eye and his slightly scrunched up bent right ear – one ear pointing up, the other slightly wilted.

I thought back to how, thirty years before, I had returned to the yard with the ragged stone walls. This time the muck was covered with a thin layer of crispy ice. I had crunched my way over to the cow, now looking much healthier and munching on a bag of hay held by the same farmhand, whilst the 'boss man' himself held the halter on her head. They were happy to see me and the calf was skidding around happily, clearly full of nutritious milk. All was well. I donned a long plastic glove, lifted the tail, scraped the shite off the buttons and then plucked the stitches out one by one with a blade.

As I removed the buttons, the farmer's wife's bare and hard-worked hand was held out beside me, gratefully receiving each one, like a cashier counting change. When I'd finished, she clenched all eight tightly in her fist and muttered, 'Waste not want not,' as she sauntered back to the farmhouse.

A few weeks later, the helper reliably informed me that the buttons 'scrubbed up fine' and were stitched firmly back into the farmer's Sunday coat in two nice rows of four.

As I put the teddy bear eye buttons into a little plastic bag in my office cupboard, I thought about those two sets of buttons, and about the thirty years in between. I could see that I had carried the farmer's wife's message through to my present world (to the chagrin of anyone who has ever tried to tidy my office). I have collected tons of junk, aka 'potentially very useful items' over the years in two cupboards which are always in danger of overflowing into my office. These treasure troves are affectionately known by my team and me as 'Narnia'. Like that thrifty farmer's wife, I waste little, because you never know when something might come in handy. Should I need a piece of titanium mesh to fix a hole in bone, some high-density foam to build a support bandage for a dog, an old plastic shoe to put on the bottom of an external skeletal fixator – whatever it might be, there's a decent chance it can be found in the 'organised chaos' of Narnia. I still have the small green pouch of surgical instruments from my time in vet school. My father was the same, so my instinct to hoard might be a genetically inherited Irish farmer's trait. My daddy held up his trousers with the same bit of baler twine for months, and when it wouldn't tie his pants any more, he used it to tie a gate closed. But it's not just useful objects; I have also collected experiences and knowledge along the way too in the cupboards of my mind, to be pulled out when needed.

My career in large animal practice in Ireland had ended one night whilst I was paring a cow's hooves by the lights of a Massey Ferguson tractor and she shat on my head. As it poured down my hair and into my ears, I figured that life just wasn't for me. But those days showed me what hard work really was and what resourcefulness and tenacity looks like – experiences I have drawn on time and again in later life.

I could see that the desire to do whatever it took to alleviate the suffering of an animal was a thread that stretched unbroken from then to now. Through all those years of studying, training, exams and qualifications, building two large veterinary referral centres and starting filming *The Supervet*, I'd been guided and driven on the journey by a single simple idea – unconditional love.

I thought of the thousands of animals I had attended and the humans who loved them and relied on them. I thought of how much I had learned about failure and what it had taught me about success. And I thought of the calf nuzzling its mother, of Ricochet nuzzling his head against mine, of how love really is absolutely everything that's important in the world.

I set out to change the world through this love, one animal at a time. But sadly for me, the world was about to shit on my head. Just as I thought I had it 'all buttoned up', the fabric of my world was about to unravel in ways I could never have imagined.

A wise person once said, 'Be the person your dog thinks you are.' And of course it doesn't just apply to dogs. I'll bet that the animal you love thinks you are the best human in the world . . . because you *are*. You just maybe don't believe it.

Our animal companions are there for us through thick and thin, through the death of our loved ones, through divorce, losing a job, illness and accidents. They share every tragedy and epiphany with us. They are molten reservoirs of love, bathing us in the warmth of unconditional affection wherever they go.

Imagine for a minute how irritated you are with your

puppy for chewing your favourite socks, when just a minute later, he is forgiven and cuddled. Could you do this with your neighbour who keeps parking across your drive? Your co-worker who annoys you? Your friend who was a total arse last week? This book is my attempt to translate the love I have shared with animals and humans over the past thirty years into a currency for compassion for the world. If we felt the same about each other as our animal friend does about us, we would be awesome humans. Do you ever feel anxious, uncertain, inadequate, misunderstood, mistreated or lonely? Are you running away from fear, corruption, discrimination or persecution? Are you running towards something that you never quite reach in the sense of emotional, spiritual or deep inner fulfilment?

I have been running all of my life, and I've met others who sublimate whatever pain they carry with something or other – alcohol, drugs, sex, material stuff. I'm particularly lucky because my primary addiction is work. Otherwise, I'd have been hooked to one of those other things or I'd be dead. I have had issues, which I've been open about. Nobody's life is ever really as it appears on the outside, if they're honest. But I do think when we tear aside the masks we put on to meet the world – be they virtual, on social media, or the facades we wear in the flesh – then it rapidly becomes apparent the reason why we love an animal so deeply is that they give us sanctuary, a place of peace where we can truly be ourselves. The story we tell the world is rarely who we really are. Our animal friends give us permission to give a more honest account – to ourselves and to others.

I have seen this miracle many times: how the love of a dog has deterred a boy from a life of peer pressure and knife crime; how a cat has rescued a heroin addict from the depths of a life-crushing habit. I have seen the love of some chickens make criminals in jail want to be better people when they get out. I have seen a horse help a girl to overcome the trauma of sexual assault, I have seen the love of a rabbit give solace in the aftermath of an abusive relationship, and the love of a tortoise comfort a woman who worked in a hospital cancer ward for terminally ill patients. For decades I have witnessed first-hand how the love of an animal makes us the best we can be and heard it from others many times. My dream is to translate these small miracles into a kind of love that might just change the world for the better.

Our animal friends do not judge us; they accept us for who we are. Most of the dogs and cats I know prefer it when I haven't shaved my chin for weeks, and when I am sweaty or smelly. They do not care where we're from or the colour of our skin. This is all completely irrelevant to them, for unconditional love transcends all boundaries. What they mean to us becomes apparent when, inevitably, they die all too soon. The price we pay for that intense love is intense pain, a tragedy I have seen more times than I can count. When the companion animal we love might not pull through, all the things we think are so important fade to insignificance and the things we didn't even realise about ourselves suddenly come into sharp focus. The power of truly unconditional love is impossible to understand or believe in unless you've been lucky enough to feel it. As the guardian of a puppy said to me recently, 'He has unlocked a little bit of my heart I didn't know I had.'

I really want to find a way to be a messenger for the love that I see for an animal in my consulting room into an expression of love for animals on the planet generally. I wish there was a greater sense of responsibility for wild animals across the world, from the humble hedgehog to the mighty rhinoceros. Could we become the guardians and advocates for animals that are not part of our family? Wouldn't it be wonderful if we saw the whole world as our house and all animals as our companions? During my fifty-something years to date, 50 per cent of all vertebrate species on planet earth have become extinct. Our world as we have come to know it will not be here in one lifetime from now unless we get better – better as humans, better as guardians, better as custodians of the planet. Our children will not forgive us if we get the next bit wrong.

Will humanity survive? Only if animals do.

The animals I have been blessed to know have tried to make me the best I can be too. Sometimes I falter and sometimes I fail. This book is a story of how repeated failure leads to success, and the thirteen traits that I feel were most important in helping me on that journey. I hope they might help you too. I call them the 'thirteen traits of triumph'. Thirteen because Border terrier Keira, the love of my life, lived to her thirteenth year. Thirteen, because I was born on 13 December 1967.

Five months before my birth, John Lennon and Paul McCartney, two of my heroes, had written 'All You Need is Love'. They were so right. About 400 million people watched The Beatles sing those five words on the very first live global television link, *Our World*. Four satellites beamed four lads from Liverpool into living rooms in twenty-five countries across the globe. These lyrics have been written in big capitals on the wall behind my desk for years. John Lennon said, 'My art is dedicated to change.' So is mine. But I can't sing, I can't write a tune and I can't broadcast to 400 million people. My mission is to bring the medicine of unconditional love as a beacon of hope to the world. Maybe I don't have to sing in tune with the rest of the world or even the rest of my profession; in fact, maybe it's better if I'm not in tune at all.

The dog or cat on our sofa is trying to tell us, just as John and Paul did, that love really is all you need. I hold their life and death in my hands daily, and to those who don't know them, they might be 'only a dog' or 'only a cat'; but to me and to the family who put their trust in me, it's the unconditional love shared with this animal that can make us most human.

Other than music and medicine, I also love comic books. Captain Marvel was born the same as me in December 1967. My favourite Captain Marvel quote comes from an issue where he's telepathically explaining to an alien that 'Before you can change, you must wish to do so. You must see why there must be a change for the good of the entire galaxy.' Like John Lennon, his life was also dedicated to change and he followed this brilliantly insightful observation with another gem: 'Look once again into your soul's eye and see that which no mortal has ever been privileged to witness.' I think that's the molten core of love inside all of us, for which animals are a direct conduit. If we allow them to, the animals we passionately care about can conduct this love like vibrant electricity to everyone around us. All I ever wanted to do was to get animals out of pain and in so doing to show the very best that humanity can be, freeing ourselves from pain too. The love of a companion animal plugs directly into what makes us human at all – our ability to feel, care and love deeply.

Man's inhumanity to animals on this planet is dwarfed only by our inhumanity to ourselves. The central tenet of my big dream is to somehow translate the love I see between a human and an animal into a currency of 'oneness' to make humanity kinder to each other.

As long as mankind has existed, there has always been war – for money, greed, power – and fuelled by discrimination and prejudice. Right now, there is still war all over the globe, and amidst those conflicts, acts so heinous that it's unbearable to think of. We can all feel like a tiny speck in the enormity of it all. Yet I really do believe that if each and every one of us could radiate the connected love of 'oneness' that we feel for our companion animal friends out into the world, we really can change the world for the better – for all the innocents – and animals can show us the way.

If I've still not convinced you of the power of love, let me take you back to June 2017 when I was standing in a field of dogs for DogFest, an event I founded. I had wanted to build a community of compassion through the same kind of love I felt as a boy, hiding in a cowshed and hugging our farm dog Pirate during difficult times. The young girl who approached me that day had just listened to a talk I had given about my dream – to make us better custodians of the planet for animals and ourselves and to make us strive for peace and not war by becoming better people. She was holding her dog very tightly, tears streaming down her face. She had been at a concert in Manchester Arena, where the singer Ariana Grande was performing, when a suicide bomber killed several young people. Stammering more than a little, she thanked me for my talk and asked me if I could try hard to 'talk to the people who do bad things . . . and show them how much I love Rupert'. Then she and her dog were gone in the blink of an eye with someone pulling her away one way and my team pulling me another.

This might seem impossible, but is it really? Should we not try? There was a time when it would have been thought impossible to give a cat two bionic legs. Someone who suggested it would have sounded quite mad. But I tried, and I will continue to do so at each new frontier. I might fail. Failure in surgery is woven inexorably and inevitably into each and every day of my existence. I have been both the one to tell someone the news they were desperate to hear and the very worst thing they could hear in that moment.

It weighs heavily on my shoulders.

On an average day, entirely by choice, I roll out of bed in the room that adjoins my office, having finished too late the night before to drive home. I play with the cats Ricochet and Excalibur for a few minutes, usually while they try to stop me putting on trousers and shoes by grabbing the legs or chewing on my laces. I drink a coffee while Ricochet dunks his head under the dribbling tap – we call it a 'drink-shower'. I consult with clients until about 1 p.m. I answer emails and phone queries as I grab something to eat and change into scrubs. I operate from about 2 p.m. until whenever we finish, interspersed with emails and phone calls and meetings about all kinds of matters, be they clinical management, financial, implant design, academic projects, media endeavours or whatever. Often I don't have time to eat. Sometimes I don't even have time to send a text. Weeks go by and I haven't acknowledged the message of a good friend. I often finish operating late, though late nowadays is between 8 p.m. and 9 p.m., when in the good old days it used to be one or two in the morning. Working hours regulations quite rightly stipulate what can be expected of my colleagues, who are on shift patterns, and I am deeply grateful to all of them, but there are no such limits on my labour, just like there weren't for my father on the farm. I emphasise that all of this is entirely my choice. The only reason I describe my day is to explain that I am doing this for a big reason, which I think is incredibly important, and I hope you will too.

Afterwards, I have client phone calls, queries to answer, implant design to consider for new patients, and then hours of reviewing all the radiographs, CT scans and MRI scans of that day, integrating them with clinical histories from other vets that can be many pages long. I'll dictate a report for my long-suffering secretary Emma to type up the following day, which will need to be read and corrected for legal due diligence.

Three nights a week I try to go to the gym or for a run between 10 p.m. and 2 a.m. Weekends I do more paperwork, management, seeing outpatients operated on that week, changing bandages, answering phone and email queries, doing more implant design, writing academic papers and lectures and dealing with all of the things I didn't get around to during the week, including writing this book. I have serious envy for professional authors who have time set aside to write. I have to squeeze it in between midnight and 4 a.m. For a very long time I thought all of this was a price worth paying, but I'm beginning to reassess in the light of everything you're about to read, and that's why I've titled this book *Beyond Supervet*. If I live until I am eighty-two like my father, I have roughly 1,450 weeks left – and that's if I'm lucky. So, I need to decide what is worth fighting for in that time – and what isn't.

So that is the purpose of this book – to look backwards at

the journey so far, but only so I can chart the future. I want to change how business is done in medicine and how that impacts animals, our families and our planet. I want to alter government policy, to expose complacency, apathy and vested interest. I want a world which is fair for animals through a philosophy called 'One Medicine' and through conservation of species – and a world which is fair for humans too, where we realise our potential for 'One Love'. I have written scores of scientific papers about success and failure over twenty years that hasn't changed anything tangibly very much at all. I care deeply about my profession, and the animals I signed up to protect and advocate for – both in *our* homes and in *their* homes on Planet Earth. I care about the human families, who love their animal friends very much. However, none of these may be much better off when I die than when I started unless we all consider our future in a radically different way. That is why I have written this book – for the innocents.

The dream I have outlined are the reasons I exist. I am going to be brutally candid in these pages about things I have never talked about before. I'm aware that this could place me directly in the cross-hairs of some who may wish to pull the trigger. I suppose if someone, somewhere, isn't upset, I'm probably not trying hard enough. Since my mother and my dog Keira died and I myself am getting on in years, I have nothing to lose if I tell the truth, but a great deal to lose if I don't – my soul.

Give me a few hours of your time and I promise you'll be entertained and maybe gain a few insights too. I do not take one second of your light or your love for granted. Long may you shine.

Let's go.

CHAPTER 1

Dreams

I was sitting at my desk in my underpants, answering urgent emails, when the office phone rang with news that Keira had collapsed in the hydro pool and was on her way to prep. My stomach fell away. I was mid-dressing already for the afternoon's cutting. I grabbed my scrub trousers, slipped on my theatre shoes which sat under the desk, and rushed down to the preparation area. My beautiful Border terrier, Keira, was already on one of the tables at the hub of prep, several of my colleagues huddled over her. I nudged in. She was gasping for air, mouth open, membranes going rapidly blue. The team grappled for intravenous access and gave some drugs. My fingers fumbled on her little hairy chest, frantically searching for a heartbeat. With the stethoscope, it came through, faint and fading.

No, no. Please, God, no . . .

I was screaming inside, but I said little to the others. The team knew what they were doing. The crash trolley was always to hand, and various bits and pieces of potentially life-saving equipment were methodically grabbed. Drugs were sequentially injected, as was the designated protocol. Everyone worked in synchrony, but all I could hear was the sound of life ebbing away, the receding *thud, thud . . . thud* of her slowing heart. I looked at the ECG trace, as the bounding squiggles of cardiac activity flattened to a line. My baby was dying.

My own heart was racing as compressions of her chest continued. Nothing. No response. The team looked at me. I looked at them. I grabbed a pair of sterile gloves from the trolley and, almost in a whisper, said, 'Cut down now.' I sliced into the side of her thorax between the ribs over her heart and stuck in my index finger, while a colleague tried to inflate her lungs via a tube placed into her trachea to deliver oxygen. At first there was no beat at all. I compressed her little heart manually with my finger, feeling for movement and watching the monitor at the same time. The line sprang up again. The soft thumps of recovery. But it was erratic, and not accompanied by spontaneous breathing. Keira's mucous membranes remained pale and blue, with her eyes rolled back. Another solitary *thud*, then Keira's heart stopped beating in my hand. Nothing. Nothing. Nothing. Flatline. I felt life leave her. The silence echoed.

We all knew it was over. The seconds passed as we stood in silent grief and reluctant acceptance. Then the assembled team peeled away as if in slow motion, each with a hand to my shoulder, a mumbled word of comfort. I was oblivious to all. I crumpled down over Keira's small, motionless body, wrapping my arms around her, as if to form a human shield against the darkness closing in. I scooped her to my chest, aching, ripped open, bleeding tears. Slowly, carefully, instinctively, I lifted her from the table. I cradled her precious lightness and left the room, one foot, then the next, shuffling. I carried her to the garden one last time, then collapsed, still clutching her, next to the chestnut tree I had planted for my dear friend and former drama teacher Philip in the hedgerow outside my office window. It was Philip's wise words, that I had to find my 'reason big enough' in life, that helped fuel my path to where I am today. I leaned against the trunk, imagining Philip himself there, holding me up.

Keira, like most dogs, had liked the taste of salt. If she had still been able, she would have licked the tears from my face to tell me everything was going to be okay. But not this time. This time nothing was going to be okay. I huddled there for more than an hour, sobbing, until Keira's human family arrived: her mum Amy and brother Kyle, Amy's partner Liam, and my then girlfriend Michaela. All utterly devastated and beyond consolation. Keira had been our co-parented baby and the light of our lives for nearly fourteen years. My darkest nights had been illuminated by cuddling her, she had seen Amy progress in her nursing career and she'd watched Kyle grow from boy into man.

I dug a grave between Philip's chestnut tree and the cherry blossom I had planted for my other dear friend, Malcolm, who was a television casting director, and he believed in me even when I didn't believe in myself, giving me my first job on TV. We laid her in the soil, wept and hugged.

Before I folded the soil in on top of her, I crossed the yard in a daze. There was something in my office that we needed. Keira had chosen it herself the previous evening when she had unearthed a small box filled with straw from a pile of clothing on my office floor. She'd only wanted the straw

3

packing in the box, but the object it cradled was a candle in a glass holder. It had been sent to me as a gift by Ballyfin Demesne hotel – the new incarnation of the school I once attended, and where I had studied to get the grades to go to vet college. Keira had played with the straw and left the candle on the floor. I picked it up, carried it outside, then fumbled and dropped it because I was still crying. The glass container smashed, but the candle was undamaged. I lit it, said a prayer, then placed it in the grave before heaping soil over the top. With the quenching of its flame, Keira's own light drifted off into the 'oneness'.

A few days later, on what would have been her fourteenth birthday, I said a few words for all of my Fitz-Family at the practice and we placed a gravestone with the following inscription.

Keira. 16-09-07 to 07-09-21.
To our beautiful baby girl.
May you run in the stars forever.
Your light remains inside us
and you are forever by our side.
Love you. xxx

I'm grateful to have had that final year with Keira. She could have died just a couple of weeks short of a year before, when she was hit by a van in the practice yard. That she survived at all was due to our proximity to the clinic, the valiant efforts of my practice colleagues and her own will to pull through. Now, though, old age had taken her.

I shall forever be grateful to the incredible clinical teams that looked after her at the two practices I had founded. My own base in Eashing, Surrey, took care of orthopaedics, neuro-surgery, advanced bionics and regenerative medicine, and we built a second hospital specifically for cancer and soft-tissue surgery in Guildford a few miles down the road. These four pillars of surgery were the culmination of a dream I'd had since 1978, the night I watched a lamb die in a frozen field on our family farm. Back then I determined I would become a veterinary surgeon and thereafter I strove to provide the best care in the world in the four major surgical disciplines.

I am very glad I did have the determination, tenacity and opportunity to pursue my dreams and I'm very grateful for the blessings in my life, of which Keira was among the greatest. She had been by my side through thick and thin during the building of my dream hospitals. She was my very best companion in the world, and I still think of her every day, especially when I hear a song that she and I listened to together in my office or on our walks. 'Born to Run' by Bruce Springsteen was a favourite of ours that we'd play while we ran the country lanes of Surrey together, covered in mud – 'tramps like us . . . born to run'.

As I listen to Springsteen and my other musical heroes, I often also think of how things could have been very different for me, for Keira and for thousands of other animals, had two particular incidents in my life played out in a different way.

As a child I sometimes walked with my mother from our house to a river with a man-made waterfall about three miles away called Barkmills. She enjoyed the air and the freedom of the birds she saw there. I annoyed her endlessly along the route, bashing trees with a stick, because I liked the different noises I could make. The holy grail was to find a hollowed-out log to whack at the waterside. Oh, my goodness – the racket

I could produce! I was annoying Mammy as usual, walking too near the water's edge, nimbly hopping across the slippery rocks to her fearful consternation, when I suddenly slipped and fell into a bed of bull reeds. She rushed over muttering how stupid I was and that I was going to be the death of her. I emerged from the shallow water covered in mud, proudly clenching a bull reed in each hand and proceeded to bash their giant, soggy, cigar-shaped heads off a piece of bark that had been trapped in the rocks by the lapping of the water. It was absolutely magnificent. In my head, I was like one of the drummers I'd seen on our black-and-white television. But even in my rapture I couldn't miss the fact that my mother's face was less than impressed. On the walk back to the house I was quiet for the longest time, scuffing my wellies on the rough road surface. Finally, Mammy asked what was wrong with me. I was quiet again. After a few more steps I looked up at her and said, 'You didn't think I was any good on the drums, did you?' She just smiled, and innocently said, 'Now, I don't think that's for you now, Noel, is it? There's enough clattering about, without you adding to it.' As we walked back down the lane, I walked away from my drumming aspirations.

My dream of being a guitarist died not long after. I was probably about eleven. It was a magical day of hazy sunbeams. We had cut the grass in the fields out the back of the farmhouse, turned it with a hay rake on the back of the tractor twice a day for a few days, and now the tractor and baler were crawling up and down the neatly heaped rows of dried grass. Out the back of the baler every few yards dropped a neatly compacted bale of hay, with two tidy twine binders. Great feed for the cattle and sheep in winter. Daddy was in the next field over and we were both supposed to be 'stacking' the hay. We generally didn't have the tractor power to bring the hay home to a shed straight away, and it needed to dry out anyway, so instead the bales were turned up on their ends and leaned against each other in groups of four like a wigwam. That way the inevitable rain could flow off the top side of the bale, not soaking into the dried grass within.

I was behind one such structure and peeped through the gap in the nearby hedgerow. Daddy was at the opposite end of the next field. The coast was clear. I grabbed a discarded plastic fertiliser bag from the hedgerow where it had drawn my attention earlier in the day, and slipped it onto a bale of hay, threaded beneath the two twines. I grabbed two further twines from a pile in the gap and wrapped them too around the bale, pulling them taut. I now had a four-stringed hay-bale guitar, and I started to pluck the strings enthusiastically. Their short, sharp, smacking twang against the plastic made me quiver with delight as I played in my band of one in the Ballyfin sunshine.

I had, not long before, found an old Sony radio on a scrapheap in Mountmellick, the local town, and had built an aerial out of a coat hanger. It was on this simple device that I heard Led Zeppelin's 'Stairway to Heaven', the very first song that I had found by myself. I could not believe that this beauty existed in the world, having only heard hymns, Celtic music and the occasional pop song on the television or some other radio before. I was instantly and firmly hooked. Music was mine and mine alone – the only thing that I had all for myself – and the only thing that was beyond corruption, no matter the trauma that churned in my head and heart. Music had the ability to transport me to a place outside of Ballyfin, away from the travails of my childhood. It became my secret obsession. So secret, that none of my siblings ever knew, and still don't to this day, where I hid my secret radio – a place where I could lie on the ground, looking up at the stars in the night sky, and float away on a dream in which I was someone other than me. The tunes were like silken tendrils woven to earth from heaven. Jimmy Page, Phil Lynott, David Bowie, Keith Richards, Eric Clapton, The Edge, Rory Gallagher, Angus Young, Mike Rutherford, Brian May – gods amongst men – melodic magicians who cast their spells.

The highlight of any week was *Top of the Pops*, but whether I managed to get to watch it depended on my income. Our wind-up black-and-white television was coin-slot operated. So if I had earned fifty pence for getting in sheep for Mr Lewis, or for helping some farmer load calves or cattle or sheep at Mountrath market, the chart show was my reward. I'd put the coin in the slot and tingle with excitement as I turned the key and heard the coin drop into the collection box for the TV man.

That day when I should have been bale stacking, I was probably imagining myself as Jimmy Page or Brian May, when my father emerged from the other side of the gap in the hedge.

'What are you playing at?'

'Ah, er, ah . . . nothing!' I stammered.

'C'mon, it'll be dark in a minute. You do that side and I'll do this.' He beckoned me to a section of the field to stack as the dust plumed from the hay baler machine a hundred yards away. I had hoped the noise had hidden my musical transgression.

As the staccato clickety-clack sound of the baler finally shut down and dusk closed in around us, we stacked for another hour or so before converging mid-field. My father never talked much when working, be it weeding turnips, making silage or walking cattle, other than to bark orders or criticise. The only times he'd impart information of any use was when we were sheltering from the rain somewhere. And even then, he rarely talked about anything except farming. There would be very few paternal life lessons for me. I knew it only too well. And so, having stacked all the hay, I seized my chance and just blurted it out.

'Daddy, do you think maybe that I could have you know . . . one of those . . . Do you think I could have a guitar? Not a proper one . . . Maybe one that someone else is throwing out. An old one. And if it has no strings, I could make some . . .'

For a brief moment, my father paused above a half-completed haystack as the last motes of dust danced in the dusk breeze. My hopes hung in the air too – maybe he could hear how much it would mean to me to have my own guitar and make my own music. Then Daddy looked up and said, 'I'll give you the saw tomorrow. You can sharpen it and help me cut the horns off the bullocks.' That was it. Nothing more. Daddy didn't even acknowledge the question. I may as well have asked for a magic carpet for all the notice he took. His mind, right or wrong, was on the farm and what needed to be done. He didn't have time for my dreams when it came to music and the instrument known as 'a guitar' wasn't any-where in his spectrum of appreciation.

De-horning cattle was a brutal but necessary job, now thankfully relegated to history in favour of 'disbudding' calves shortly after birth, using a caustic paste or hot iron applied directly to the blood vessels on the horn buds. Back then, one couldn't take the cattle to market with horns as they would fight and gore each other. First, the cattle were ushered into a 'crush', which was a long chute between parallel metal fences, forming an alley in which they could only go forwards and not turn around. Then the head of the first young bullock in line was trapped in a sliding gate, which locked the neck in place. Then one grappled to secure the animal's nose with tongs, which resembled rusty fire tongs that looked to belong in the Middle Ages. Then one pulled the head around the gatepost, with one foot on either the post or the skull of the struggling animal. Anaesthetic was injected from Daddy's decade-old syringe in an effort to numb the cornual nerve, which was a hit-and-miss job, and then one literally sawed and sawed as the bullock screamed.

I generally got spattered with the spurting cornual artery as I tried to use a pair of tweezers to prevent it recoiling elastically into a tiny hole in the skull. When I asked if the procedure hurt the bullocks, Daddy said, 'You have to be cruel to be kind.' I think he applied the same logic to me, wanting to harden me up by exposing me when just a boy to the cold realities of farm life. I'm not sure his lesson had quite the effect he imagined, given where I've ended up. This kind of brutal 'surgery' is clearly no longer for me, but I do have that exact same saw, with the tweezers and the syringe in a mounted glass case on my office wall – a permanent reminder of how one's dreams are as much determined by one's circumstances as they are by natural interest, talent or determination. I became a surgeon and not a guitarist or a drummer.

I might not have had the opportunity to touch someone's life with a song I've written or performed in the way some of my musical heroes touched my young life, like someone reaching out to me personally and taking my hand, but I have been lucky enough to see the look in someone's eyes when they learn the animal they adore is going to be okay. I have held the hand and the paw of many humans and animals, helping them to have longer together, to sustain their love and to have a better life. Throughout my life, I have seen both music and medicine consistently weave their not dissimilar magic. They can both be a currency for love and transformation, albeit in a different language. Lyrics and a good tune can elevate us to an ethereal state transcending the humdrum of daily life and give us hope or remind us of a happier time. Medicine preserving the bond between us and an animal companion can do the same, taking us out of ourselves and connecting us to a very pure state of unconditional love and belonging. In this way, the love of both music and animals can and does change the world. At the concert of our favourite musical artist, we feel revitalised and in love with life once more regardless of what's going on in the world, and it's that exact same currency I feel in my consulting room in the presence of unconditional love every single day. I feel so incredibly blessed that medicine for animals has been my music, and as I share these feelings with you in this moment, I sense that we are in perfect tune, transcending time and place. In this moment we can be who we really are, the world is 'love' and things are going to be okay. I remember the first time I saw Prince in concert. He was right. 'Nothing compares to you.'

My dreams in veterinary medicine have certainly changed shape, but I reckon if I could go back and tell my story to that boy with the hay-bale guitar, he'd have understood that it all very much turned out for the best.

As I buried Keira, I was right in the middle of the most traumatic period of my professional life. I had lost the love of my life and hope seemed very far away. I could hear no music at all, just the dull thud of my dreams crashing to dust. Sadly, my company, Fitzpatrick Referrals, had fallen on hard times due to various factors, including the SARS-CoV-2 pandemic, when some surgeons and nurses left for many reasons and it was difficult to recruit, meaning we couldn't treat as many animals, but the overheads remained the same. Meanwhile, corporate consolidation of practices across the country also had a dramatic effect on our business model, since we depend entirely on patients being referred to us by primary care clinicians. You cannot walk in off the street to a specialist referral centre seeking treatment for your cat or dog; according to the current regulations and precedent in the UK, you have to be referred. As such, my entire dream was and is dependent on GP vets being willing to send patients to us for treatment, or for the families of animals to actively seek out our services and ask for a referral.

As more and more primary care practices have been bought by one of several large companies, they have tended to recommend the referral centres that they themselves own for understandable business reasons, rather than me and my colleagues. This is especially true for the more routine procedures, which a practice like mine needs in order to survive, since we do the ordinary things extraordinarily well for the animals and they pay the wages for my team, but GP vets don't send us enough of these cases. In the months preceding Keira's death, it had become apparent that Fitzpatrick Referrals would need to undergo dramatic transformation or we would not survive. I had borrowed heavily to fund the practice over the years, and the debt was growing quicker than I could make the repayments. My surgeon colleagues had left for different geographic locations, different lifestyles or different experiences, which were all good and understandable life choices, for the benefit of themselves and their families – I love them all and I wish them well. For someone else in my position, the answer might have been to sell up, but the thought was complete anathema. The practice is *me*. My home. My soul. I'm no more able to give up my practice than a tortoise is their shell. I would find it ethically unacceptable not to have control over what could or could not be offered as possible solutions when my animal friends are in pain.

As I pushed a little cross of twigs into the ground above Keira's grave, I felt acutely the weight of the journey I had chosen for myself more than forty years earlier when that lamb perished on my watch. It felt like the end of an era when Keira died and yet I knew that dreams evolve, so while change was completely inevitable, progress in the midst of that change was entirely up to me. Back when I was ten years old, I lay there on the frosted dew in our field and howled at the night sky. My eyes found the brightest star in heaven and I made a wish – that I would one day be good enough, strong enough and clever enough to be better able to help animals. My life changed forever in that moment and I was thenceforth determined to heal their injuries and take away their pain. I created a fictional mentor, Vetman, with his 'Bionic Bunker', where impossible feats of surgical ingenuity would be undertaken to restore my animal friends to health and happiness. My dream was to become Vetman in real life. And now it seemed that I needed him more than ever.

Dreams like mine can be grand in their scope, but the journey we take towards them often consists of many small, and sometimes even backward, steps. At secondary school, I realised I had a long way to go. I couldn't read or write at anything like the level of my peers. The other boys knew about things like maths and girls, but both were a mystery to me. So, I became obsessed with studying to the exclusion of all else except some work on the family farm. As a result, I was mercilessly bullied, beaten up physically and mentally every day. My only friend in those hard times was Pirate, who was chained to the wall in a cowshed on our farm. To everyone else he was 'just' the farm dog, but to me he was my dearest companion. I cuddled him and made up stories where he and I flew around the world together with Vetman, saving all the animals with the help of a lion who had a very big heart. When I cried he licked my face, as Keira would nearly forty years later. I studied day and night, seven days a week, even during holiday breaks, and finally, to cut a long story short, was offered places to study both human and veterinary medicine. It wasn't a hard decision. I didn't much like people then, whereas animals were my friends. Plus, funding was available from the Irish Government to go to vet school if one got the necessary grades. I did – so off I went.

Inside my heart, the flame of other dreams also continued to burn. The inspiration which music gifted me was soon joined by an intrigue for the drama I saw in the black and white movies on our television. I was fascinated by how both music and drama could communicate in an inexplicable way and could actually make people think differently. Though I probably couldn't have explained it to anyone at the time, I knew that their magic offered a glimpse at a life so much bigger than my own, and I saw how they could change the world. Music was my salvation and comfort blanket in the silent moments of loneliness in my childhood and teenage years. And meanwhile, the boy who could barely read had become an ardent lover of literature too and I developed an avid interest in how the written word sprang to life in the hands of talented actors and film-makers. I wanted to be a part of it, and I wanted to learn how to use words to change the world. My parents wouldn't have understood, which wasn't their fault, and I certainly couldn't get funding for drama school, so I parked my secret dreams of music and drama, promising myself I would try to come back to it after vet school. I was desperate to get to America, choosing Philadelphia because it was the home of the fictional boxer Rocky Balboa, whom I'd seen on our television, and if he could achieve his dreams against the odds, then so could I. (For me at the time he was far from fictional and his dreams were real.) I earned a scholarship to the University of Pennsylvania School of Veterinary Medicine. The start was not propitious. When I arrived, I got mugged on the first night and spent the next few nights sleeping in a broom cupboard. It was all great in the end though and I was working towards my dreams.

I worked as a waiter, a gardener and a model whilst in college in Ireland and America. I studied every hour I could, sometimes cycling over thirty miles a day there and back to the vet school. My love life was slow to blossom – I didn't have a girlfriend until I was in my twenties, and upon graduation I was so busy that she could see me only if we went on farm calls together, which she did, God bless her. On those calls, I calved and lambed hundreds of cows and sheep; I treated countless cases of pneumonia; I held up bottles of calcium, magnesium and cocktails of salt and soda boiled up on farmers' stoves and poured them into the veins of hundreds of cows affected by milk fever, tetany and mastitis. Large animal practice was arduous and never-ending; I never had a day where I had completed all the calls that needed doing. Sleep was on an 'as needed' basis.

After vet school, I worked in large animal practice in three different parts of Ireland, and applied for further training internships in Ireland, the UK and the USA, but nobody felt I was good enough. So, I got a job as a general practice primary care vet in Guildford, Surrey, mainly because the town had three theatres and a drama school, for which I was determined to audition. I did, but with no success. I started attending day and night courses at the Royal Vet College, the University of Cambridge Vet School and Bristol Vet School and I studied first for a Certificate in Veterinary Orthopaedics and then a Certificate in Veterinary Radiology, both of which I achieved in the early nineties. Simultaneously I attended classes at the London Academy of Music and Dramatic Arts and earned a gold medal. I applied, and wasn't accepted, for residency training to become a specialist surgeon.

I decided, therefore, to build my own destiny. I flew over and back from America constructing my own training programme with the best people I could find in each of the sub-specialities of imaging, orthopaedics and neurosurgery. My mentors have become friends for life and I am indebted to them for teaching me so kindly and graciously and helping me towards my dreams. I continued in clinical practice, at first mixing farm and companion animal, and then focusing on companion animal only. I carried a pager so that my acting agent could contact me for auditions, and I made the calls to her in the darkened radiograph processing room which was in a small wooden hut beside a bigger hut which was preparation room, X-ray room and operating room all in one. I acted in some plays, several TV shows like *London's Burning*, *Casualty*, *The Bill* and *Heartbeat*, plus a few small-budget films. During this time, I met the only people apart from my mother who ever really believed in me: Philip and Malcolm. They gave me permission to dream and supported me emotionally all the way through.

By the late 1990s I was practising only orthopaedics and neurosurgery as a veterinary surgeon, first in the huts beside a domestic dwelling and later in a small practice next to a kebab shop. From there, to keep the dream alive, I borrowed some money to start a practice in the woods outside Guildford. I wanted to borrow more, but the bank wouldn't take the risk. I was open seven days a week, fifty-two weeks a year and saw every case I was asked to see. I never turned an animal away, being prepared to work however long it took. On a Friday night at 2 a.m. I plugged in an MRI truck that came from Scotland; on Saturday we scanned spinal cases and on Sunday I operated on them. At our busiest, we scanned twenty-one patients one weekend and I operated on nine spinal patients that same weekend with only four nurses. Back then, working hours regulations weren't foremost in people's minds. I slept on the floor of the office and did the night duties myself – changing drips, giving injections and emptying urinary bladders. We didn't have night nurses and the place was tiny anyway, so my mattress on the floor was only a dozen yards from the inpatients themselves. We had three walk-in kennels and sixteen smaller cubicles. Most of the patients went home by 2 a.m. on a Sunday night or on Monday morning. Soon though, alongside my wonderful colleague, Sarah, who still works with me to this day, we built enough of a track record to borrow more money and to start converting old farm buildings, nearby in the village of Eashing, into a state-of-the-art animal facility.

I ran out of money and changed banks three times. I felt that I could force my dream into existence if only I worked hard enough, with integrity of purpose. Eventually I bought the ground footprint of today's practice, which cost another few million pounds borrowed from the bank. Everything was perpetually on the line, and I was often extremely stressed to the point of despair, but I kept going. As I've mentioned, my dream was to build four pillars of surgical excellence – orthopaedics, neurosurgery, soft tissue surgery and oncology (cancer), just like the Mayo brothers had done with the Mayo Clinic for humans in the USA. I wanted to build the greatest hospitals that ever existed on the planet for companion animal care, to offer the same level of care as human patients would get, with ethics and compassion at the core of the practice. I converted three of the four old farm buildings into Fitzpatrick Referrals Orthopaedics and Neurosurgery Team (FRONT). Soon I had about 150 highly motivated professionals around me.

I wasn't allowed to sit the examinations for specialist status in veterinary orthopaedics for twenty-three years due to my lack of a formal residency training, but twenty-three years after I graduated as a vet I worked by day and studied by night to attain specialist status in orthopaedic surgery and in sports medicine and rehabilitation. I helped to found the Veterinary School at the University of Surrey, became a professor and stayed up many late nights writing lectures which I delivered at symposia around the world. I contributed to the publication of more than one hundred academic papers and book chapters, each of which took many hours, days, weeks and months of time, and I was awarded two honorary doctorates.

I explain all of this journey in summary, not out of egotism but rather to highlight that huge dreams demand huge effort. There are no shortcuts to sustainable success, and if you choose to follow the path of your dreams, then you have to commit absolutely to them. The bottom line is that there are no free rides on the way to real fulfilment of your dreams. You can have quick fixes and quick flurries of success, but they will ultimately prove empty if you don't put in the work and earn the title. Recognition is a means to an end. I need it to change the world – but other than that, all praise and all criticism are equal as long as you know you're doing the right thing. I offer you this litany of tiny steps to illustrate that you too can achieve your dreams if you are prepared to keep going no matter what. The real challenges for me in the end would have more to do with what other people wanted to do than what I myself wanted and this is a salutary warning on the road to your dreams – if you are in a team sport, the team need to want to be on the journey with you or you will not succeed, and you'll need to find a different way to realise your dreams.

As examples of some other small steps with which I came a cropper and needed to change, I founded VETFest as an education event for veterinary surgeons which would combine my love of music and veterinary medicine by having an education festival in a field of tents alongside a live music event. It was absolutely fantastic. I also founded DogFest which was a field of fun and compassion for dog lovers everywhere. It was awesome. I started the Humanimal Trust charity, which aims to converge human and animal medicine for the greater good of both, a concept called 'One Medicine'. To raise money for this charity, I founded One Live, a music festival. It was spectacular. But, in due course, each and every one of these event initiatives would lose an unmanageable amount of money. Dreams fuelled by passion and one's own money can often fail, but that doesn't mean one should give up.

I wanted to combine my twin passions of media and medicine, and I tried to pitch a TV show to several production companies. Finally I met the radio DJ Chris Evans – who has since become a dear friend – when I operated on his dog, Enzo. He pitched a TV show called *The Bionic Vet* on my behalf to the BBC. With my friend, Jim, we made six episodes which broadcast in 2010. It wasn't recommissioned because the broadcaster felt it didn't want a show about animal science. I tried to explain it was really a show about unconditional love, but they didn't understand. My approaches to other production companies were ignored too. But as is the way of such failures, if you really believe in your dream, you keep going.

I'd flown to LA to pitch to National Geographic. I chose to stay in the same hotel where one of my musical heroes, Dave Gahan from Depeche Mode, had taken a mixture of cocaine and heroin, then flatlined for two minutes before paramedics had brought him back from the brink of death. I asked a concierge in the hotel to try to get me Dave's exact room, and whether he did or he didn't, I believed I was meeting with National Geographic in that exact room, and it was to be the location of my resurrection too. The merger of music and medicine was a valuable currency after all! National Geographic didn't want the show, but through a contact, someone at Channel 4 heard about the idea and expressed an interest. I bought a RED digital cinema camera – the first of its kind in the UK – so that Jim and I could shoot a pilot. Channel 4 duly optioned it, and it was on that station that my show *The Supervet* launched. Jim, a friend and man of extraordinary talents, has since gone on with that same production company to win a BAFTA. Such is the way with dreams – there's a ripple effect – but only if one works like there are no measurable hours in the day – or night. As Dave himself sang, you'll stumble in your footsteps, but don't ever come to any conclusions until you try 'walking in my shoes', or indeed the shoes of anyone who has dreamed big before you. You can't win any race if you don't train hard and run hard. Dreams are easy, success is hard.

The Supervet started the same year I sat my specialist exams and tried to borrow another tranche of money to build premises for the next two pillars of the dream – the soft tissue surgery and oncology hospital. The bank I was with at the time were reluctant, objecting that 'cancer doesn't make money'. Given I wasn't making enough at my existing practice to fund the project, I jumped on the train into London countless times to visit private equity firms in an effort to raise the capital. I hated those journeys. I hated begging for money, cap in hand, because I knew I couldn't promise the returns such potential investors required and that ultimately they didn't share my values. Eventually I changed bank a fourth time and they loaned me the money with a personal guarantee – the liability for the new hospital rested with me personally. No one forced me to sign those papers, and perhaps I was naive, but I still felt that if I just put in the hours, single-mindedness and hard work would carry me through. I paid for the hospital build and, with my clinical partners, we started Fitzpatrick Referrals Oncology and Soft Tissue Surgery Team (FROST). My mammy was present for the cutting of the ribbon in 2015. It was her last public outing in her wheelchair.

My daddy by this time had been dead for seven years. He'd only ever seen me operate once, in the late nineties, when he watched me fuse the broken wrist of a dog, a pancarpal arthrodesis. At that time, I didn't have any proper tools – just a wood drill on a long electrical cable to remove cartilage from bone, and a mechanic's hand drill with a bit to make holes in the bone for screws, both covered in sterile cloth drapes. I performed this operation in that large wooden gardener's hut. I had always hoped that Daddy might one day say he was proud of me. He never did. He came back one more time just as I was building the hydrotherapy pool at FRONT. I could see that he was a bit impressed – and undoubtedly would talk about it to anyone who would listen when he returned to Ballyfin, but to me he never said the words 'well done'. I don't blame him. He was a man of his generation and upbringing. To this day, I have never said that I am proud of a single one of my achievements. I just keep dreaming as big as possible, even when they are dreams that are deemed impossible.

Along the way I had founded Fitzbionics to design and manufacture customised implants that would forever change the paradigm of surgery for companion animals. Together with my wonderful colleague, Jay. There would have been no *Bionic Vet* or *Supervet* without engineer Jay Meswania, whom I first met in 2006. Jay is the kindest, most genuine, gracious and dedicated colleague I have ever had the good fortune to be on my journey with. I admire him and I love him as a mentor, colleague and dear friend. I invented dozens of new techniques which have saved many limbs, and many lives, of dogs and cats. We made the impossible possible. Then I set up FitzRegen to create a reliable system for processing and delivering stem cell technology for my patients. Together these would form the backbone for my final tranche of bank borrowing to convert the fourth building on the Eashing site into a state-of-the-art surgical facility to be called the Fitzpatrick Institute for the Restoration of Skeletal Tissue (FIRST). This centre would facilitate operations hitherto considered impossible by fusing together the power of bionics and regenerative medicine.

By this stage, I employed more than 250 people. We all worked hard and there were ups and downs as there are in any business, but we were doing okay. Then the worldwide SARS-CoV-2 pandemic reached our shores. As the initial waves receded and the country began to open up, our problems were just getting started. Following the departure of surgeons and nurses, I couldn't rebuild quickly enough to stem the financial challenges. My dreams were unravelling, and it took its toll. I became a different person, psychologically and behaviourally, which is a shame for me and those around me too. Hitherto I would have simply worked harder, trying to keep the flame alive through sheer force of will and graft, the captain who grits his teeth and sails on into the storm. But not this time. The waters were about to get very choppy indeed.

To perform the kind of surgery I do, one needs a huge team of people. Nurses and interns to help admit, sedate and work up the patient. A gait analysis person to objectively measure lameness so that we can have sequential follow-up to provide evidence of efficacy. An advanced diagnostic imaging team for CT and MRI scans. Interns and nurses to help with radiography. Theatre auxiliaries to prepare theatre and surgical kit, and to clean up afterwards. Ward auxiliaries, rehabilitation practitioners and hydrotherapists to look after the patients alongside day and night nursing teams. A surgical team of nurses and vets, including anaesthetists. Then interns and residents to help the senior clinicians to look after the patients, day in, day out. Building maintenance people to keep the facilities in tip-top condition. And of course, reception, accounts and clinical communication colleagues who speak to clients daily. In addition to a huge bill for disposables, implants, cleaning and lighting, to name a few costs, there is a giant wage bill. It's a far cry from the old days with me and one nurse and a wood drill. I simply could not even consider the kinds of surgeries I perform without this massive team.

The price of my dreams has been significant in both financial and personal costs. I was married to the dogs and cats of 'strangers' rather than to a woman. Not that my clients seem like strangers to me, and nor do the animals – they're like family. This might be a weakness as well as a strength, and we can be victims of our success and reputation. Sometimes the demands of clients can be overwhelming for me and my colleagues. Ironically, we give them and their animal friends so much love that they can take it for granted. In spite of our best efforts, things don't always go to plan, and we occasionally bear the brunt of disgruntled clients. For me, this really did chasten my dreams since it was taking a significant toll on my mental health and the wellness of some of my colleagues around me. I had always wanted to build my own 'Fitz-Family' at the practice – a team to share the dream with – but as the strange Covid years receded, some of those brothers and sisters would also leave. That's the nature of life, work and careers. I had contributed to their dreams, but they have other dreams thereafter too. Now, with the change of circumstances, I knew I'd have to recalibrate mine. Was there something I could do to help animals in a different way, rather than working every hour God sent? Or should I be prioritising a different life, settling down to start a family? That would be selfish, not to mention impractical, without big changes. I was caught at a crossroads, unsure which way to travel. And meanwhile, I was putting myself and others under unbearable pressure.

Some people pay for therapy sitting across from another human being. I've done it and for the most part it's not for me. It exposes all of my rawness and the next day I feel so naked and vulnerable that I just want to hide. One can't hide when there are sick, broken and dying animals. So instead, I escape into music or performance, sliding into a state of ethereal 'oneness' with the rest of the audience. I can honestly say that without the therapy of music or theatre (of the drama kind) in my life, I would not have pulled through or achieved any of these dreams. Whenever I can I dash from work, hop on a train and escape into the welcome arms of a gig or theatre show where I can be invisible, lose myself and escape the pressures of my own mind. There I get the hug I need to keep me going and there I can keep dreaming without boundaries. As Bono wrote in the U2 song 'Acrobat', 'dream out loud' so that you 'don't let the bastards grind you down'.

Having dreamed of being a drummer or a guitarist as a child before the vocation of being a vet became, in the best way possible, all-consuming, I thought maybe I could do both. But most guitar teachers, no matter how patient, get bored waiting for me to come out of my operating theatre, and who could blame them? So, though dreams are essential fuel for a life well lived, one has to acknowledge that to be really great at something, whether that's a career, marriage, sport or vocation, 'something's gotta give' – and that's the price of dreaming big. Our dreams drive us to change the world, but the world in turn changes us. In the early part of my life, my mammy, Rita, had supported me in striving for my dreams of becoming a vet. Later it was Keira by my side through the trials and tribulations of making Fitzpatrick Referrals a reality. Now they are both gone and my dreams are shifting too.

Vetman had been born in my imagination as my saviour when I was ten years old. I had now built his bionic bunker in real life and I had made impossible things possible. In my imagination as a child, he had been born in 2021 BC in Mesopotamia, and so it was vitally important for me that he be born into our real world in AD 2021. I achieved that dream against all the odds and his first adventure was published last year. As I said earlier, I need him now more than ever before, as he and I fashion new dreams and maybe even a new world. As I sat by Keira's grave that fateful night, I looked to the brightest star in heaven, just as I did as a child, and again wished I could be good enough, strong enough and clever enough. But this time my dream was bigger than ever. I want to help all of the animals in the world, both domesticated and wild. Through the love we share with animal companions in our homes, I dream of being a messenger for love of animals in our bigger home of planet earth. Then through this currency of compassion, I hope to show how we can be kinder to each other as humans, regardless of country, ethnicity, religion or gender. My dream now is to shine the love I have been blessed to share with animals as a beacon of hope for the world – to make all of us more 'human'.

CHAPTER 2

Readiness

When I first met Bran, a seven-and-a-half-month-old German shepherd puppy, he was crawling along on his front legs. When he was seven weeks old, one of his hind legs had been removed because of a fracture and he had dislocated the opposite hip when he was allegedly kicked down a staircase. He could not stand or walk. But mentally it was clear to me that he was ready for anything. He was a boisterous puppy desperate to live life to the full. However, not everyone felt the same. The vets he saw had recommended euthanasia, because 'nothing could be done'. They meant well, since it was perceived he was suffering and wasn't fixable. Bran was indeed ready for anything, but my profession was not.

Bran's shin bone (tibial) fracture would have been absolutely fixable when he was a few weeks old, but there had been no money and the limb was placed in a splint. That wasn't anyone's fault. He had been bought from a puppy farm at four weeks old and then reportedly suffered at the hands of people, which absolutely was their fault. Casts can be fine for puppies if managed correctly, but his wasn't. His muscles became contracted and the bandage caused pressure sores. The rescue centre amputated his limb because that was the only option open to them. Rescue centres do a magnificent job and look after the welfare of as many animals as possible with a very limited budget. Surgery, alas, cannot be done for free as equipment, wages and facilities need paying for.

However, that doesn't mean that we should say 'it's not possible' to fix the fracture in a four-legged dog or the hip dislocation in a three-legged dog just because we're not ready to open our minds or the practical and financial resources aren't there to do so. Willingness does not always translate to readiness if there is a lack of opportunity.

This is true for so many of us in our lives – we all have infinite potential, but perhaps personal circumstances or the environment in which we grow up makes it hard to reach that potential. One can't be ready for a better future in adverse circumstances unless one is amazingly strong and can find opportunities along the way. There are some people who have overcome incredible hardships but that doesn't mean that everyone can. However, readiness really does count when a magnificent opportunity arises. If you're not ready it will pass on by.

The opportunity for Bran came when the rescue centre put a picture of him on their website and a young lady called Kasey fell in love with him instantly. Bran was so ready! Perhaps in him Kasey saw herself. Like me, she had suffered anxiety in secondary school and was badly bullied. She escaped with her mother and younger brother in the night from her violent father. She cared desperately about animals and brought Frankie the ferret with her. She suffered from post-traumatic stress disorder, couldn't use her legs some days and, following a diagnosis of myalgic encephalomyelitis, she didn't leave the house for two years. Eventually she got a job in a pet store where she gave her all, but her joint pain got the better of her and because she then couldn't do manual work, she lost her job. Finally, a rheumatologist diagnosed her with the connective tissue disorder, Ehlers-Danlos syndrome. Like me, she struggled to make bonds with people and escaped into comic books and superheroes, and she wanted to save all the animals in the world because they were her friends. She told her rescued raccoon, Cody, all about these adventures, as I had done with my friend, Pirate.

Kasey's health problems spiralled downwards. She had surgery for a thyroid tumour, haemorrhaged from an ovarian cyst and ended up with endometriosis. With constant pain, her mental anxieties and panic worsened and she was diagnosed with dysthymia, a persistent depressive disorder which can cause mood swings, a lack of energy and appetite, feelings of hopelessness, isolation and lack of self-esteem. Counselling and therapy helped, but her readiness for anything at all was stymied by her self-perception. Then, her magnificent opportunity came in the form of Joey, whom she met when working in a video store and they bonded over the game Dungeons and Dragons. Joey was kind and sensitive and was ready to love her for who she was. Perhaps this is close to what true love is all about, such that together you can become more ready for anything than you ever could alone. Love unlocks readiness every time.

This was never more true than when Kasey and Joey loved Bran even more for his resilience and readiness to seize every day with a loud bark and extraordinarily long wagging tongue in spite of his injuries. Bran made them smile every day, but as it became apparent how much pain he was in, depression, frustration and pain were all that Kasey felt and nobody seemed ready to help. He whimpered incessantly, unable to stand up, dragging himself along with his front paws. Kasey knew what it felt like to be in severe physical pain and she could relate to him trying to enjoy his life no matter what pain he was in. Sometimes she had felt cursed because no matter how much she was ready to live a normal life, her circumstances prevented it.

Radiographs revealed that the head of Bran's thigh bone (femur) was rubbing on a very shallow socket (acetabulum) and he screamed loudly when anyone touched it. Kasey was distraught because the well-meaning vet said that they didn't feel that she should have been allowed to adopt Bran, that he should have been put to sleep earlier and recommended putting him to sleep on that day because he 'didn't have a chance'. This vet meant well. One can have endless potential and be ready for anything, but never get a magnificent opportunity. I think of this often. I wonder how many internationally renowned figures were high achievers at school, whose tutors told them they had great potential versus how many overcame adversity and had to be ready to seize their 'chance' when it came? Therein lies the fundamental challenge with 'readiness' for all of us. We won't all be handed the same opportunities but we have to be ready to grab hold of good grace when it happens. As the singer Stormzy says in his song, sometimes we feel 'not worthy' when the universe holds out a hand to fix us, but we have to be ready to be 'blinded by' its 'grace'.

Kasey didn't accept that Bran had no chance and she fervently sought the grace she felt he was worthy of. She asked the primary care vet if Bran could be referred to Fitzpatrick Referrals because she had seen 'this guy on the telly' fix complicated cases. The vet, for whatever reason, didn't feel that I was the right surgeon for Bran and suggested another specialist centre, but warned they were likely to recommend putting Bran to sleep too.

Bran was referred to a different practice who performed a CT scan. She and Joey had no money, so Joey had worked overtime for weeks to raise the funds. In my opinion, a relatively inexpensive radiograph was all that was required for the diagnosis of Bran's dislocated hip and one would only need a CT scan if specific measurements were needed for a custom implant to be manufactured. (As an aside, I encourage everybody to ask the question of whether the test they are paying for is value for money and will advance the opportunity for treatment.) Kasey didn't know any of this at the time or that she had any power herself to determine where Bran might be referred to, when euthanasia was again recommended.

Many people told Kasey that she was 'being cruel' for not putting Bran to sleep, but she persisted for many weeks and was finally referred to Fitzpatrick Referrals. As she wrote to me, 'Without a true insight into what is wrong with him, how can I just kill him?' All she ever wanted for him was that he might be able to have a run on the beach and into the sea, rather than just looking at it longingly from the car window.

A total hip replacement for Bran's remaining diseased hip joint was entirely possible and I had performed it before on three-legged dogs, but because of the tilting of Bran's pelvis and profound disease of the joint, I felt that keeping a new head securely in the socket would be best served by using a customised implant system. I had invented such a system and had already used it on scores of patients successfully, but nobody else had. I got the idea from an ice-cream scoop. The handle of the scoop was screwed to the wing of the pelvis (ilium), whilst the scoop would form a well-anchored shell within which one could position a new plastic cup for the new metal ball head on the femur.

As often occurs, this meant that it would be a procedure that no other vet would have carried out before and I had learnt that meant some vets might complain or even accuse me of malpractice, because they weren't ready for it and didn't agree with it, even if they had never themselves performed advanced total hip replacement. These are other sorts of readiness that are important – on the one hand, readiness to relinquish recalcitrance to change and, on the other, resolute readiness to stand up for what you believe in, despite your critics. I submitted a detailed review to the Royal College of Veterinary Surgeons (RCVS) in the hope of helping Bran, whilst protecting myself and my colleagues from any potential accusation of wrongdoing. The irony was that anyone could perform a standard hip replacement on Bran with no challenges, but I didn't feel it would work. RCVS replied that at that stage they didn't have the capacity to deal with ethics approval for individual cases. Therefore, I was aware that if I was to try to help Bran, I could leave myself open to accusations of malpractice.

Of course, the Hippocratic oath resonates: 'primum non nocere' – 'first, do no harm'. But which was the greatest harm – to give Bran a chance, to leave him in pain or to put him to sleep?

My willingness to help or the readiness of Kasey and Joey

for Bran to be helped would not be enough. I completed a few hours of paperwork and found a group of vets that were willing to offer an opinion on whether Bran deserved a chance or not. Just because he was ready did not mean that Bran would be saved. His magnificent opportunity might never be offered.

Bran literally and figuratively didn't have a leg to stand on, in the sense that he couldn't stand up and also the vets he had thus far seen felt that euthanasia was the favoured option. I very much empathised with him, also both literally and figuratively. There is enormous push-back by some vets who feel that I 'over-treat' animals with surgery because they don't agree with the options I offer, as I strive to get veterinary medicine ready for next-level animal care in the UK. I genuinely passionately feel that everything I do is absolutely only ever in the best interests of my patients, but vets who disagree because of what they see as 'over-treatment' on my TV show feel that I 'don't have a leg to stand on', figuratively speaking. In the words of the song 'November Rain' by Guns N' Roses, 'it's hard to keep an open heart when even friends seem out to harm you'. It appeared that the Supervet TV show contributed to the reason why Bran was denied access to see me by vets in the first place, because of prejudice, the reason that I was advised to seek ethics approval because of criticism and the reason that Bran might have any opportunity at all, because otherwise Kasey would never have heard of what I do.

Like Bran, I too have had periods in my life when I could not actually stand on my legs at all. I don't really remember the first time I damaged my right ankle, but my older sister Mary has told me the story. I was three or four years old and sitting on the back carrier of the bicycle she was riding.

Apparently, my dangling foot got caught between the spokes and the upright of the carrier, ripping off my skin and causing the joint to swell up. The second time, I remember vividly. I was kicking someone's head in the University College Dublin Shotokan Karate Club. I made impact inadvertently, harder than intended. My sparring partner ended up with a very sore jaw, and I managed to sprain my ankle. The third time I was standing on a bale of straw trying to get my arm deep enough into the womb of a cow to pull up the head of a calf that was twisted downwards beneath its front legs and under its mother's pelvis. The cow's legs buckled and my forearm was trapped between the calf's head and her pelvis as she went down. On the brink of breaking my arm, I tumbled off the bale and, needless to say, the weak rubber of an Irish welly boot was not nearly enough to prevent a horrendous popping noise as I subluxated my tibiotarsal and subtalar joints – a very bad sprain indeed. The pain was something I hadn't experienced before and the swelling was impressive. It didn't help that I was limping around mucky farmyards for a month in a big plaster cast, covered with a boot fashioned from an old rubber sole and a heavy-duty cement sack.

My ankle weakness [again] reared its ugly foot in most dramatic fashion during a short stint as a crack cocaine dealer. I should add that this was part of a dramatic role in the UK TV police show *The Bill*. The scene in question called for my character to drive his car, skidding to a halt on a rain-glazed warehouse forecourt, before jumping from the door and sprinting down an alley between two brick walls. The stuntman did the driving, before a cut to me once the car had stopped. The script said 'Suspect runs erratically, brandishing gun and looking around frenetically, confused, scared', followed by 'Suspect hits the wall at the end of the alley and tries to scale it with a single jump, grabbing the top with his fingers and dragging himself upwards, as PC Tony reaches up and drags him to the ground.' So, I gamely performed the jump from the stationary car and sprinted down the alley, whereupon I slipped in a puddle, sprained my right ankle again, along with tearing my hamstring muscles and straining my calf muscle badly as I slid onto my backside. Recovering for the sake of the scene – the show must go on after all – I stumbled up and ran erratically, brandishing said firearm and looking around frenetically, confused, very much scared and also in considerable agony. I threw myself at the wall at the end of the alley with a thud, and clawed upwards on the dry grouted bricks, until PC Tony duly apprehended me. And . . . 'Cut'. I think I took 'method acting' to a whole new level! My drug-dealing days were over, and any thoughts of going for the occasional run, as I'd always like to do, were again on indefinite suspension.

When I had tried to run in the years since, I always experienced niggling right ankle pain. Sometime in the noughties I was running on a dirt track, stumbled, and in an effort to protect my right ankle, sprained my left. I did the exercises recommended by physios, for proprioception and balance, but over time my right ankle got more and more painful, eventually hurting even when I was standing for surgery. Sometimes I stand for twelve hours and, with all my focus on the animal in front of me, my posture is the last thing on my mind. An MRI scan revealed multiple subchondral bone cysts. Joint fluid was leaking into cysts under the cartilage surface of my talus bone, the major moving bone of the ankle, and the hydraulic pumping motion was not only enlarging the cysts gradually but also causing significant pain. Something would have to be done.

I would have operated on myself, if it were legal. Luckily, I knew a wonderful surgeon called Mike. He did his best to fill the holes using artificial bone graft. Just as I give my recovering patients strict instructions, the 'Fitz Rules' – no running, no jumping, no slipping, no sliding – Mike told me not to operate afterwards and to keep my leg elevated on a stool as much as possible to promote rehabilitation. I tried to follow his advice, but after a couple of weeks, I met a puppy called River who was affected by a condition whereby the head of the radius bone in her elbow didn't fit properly, and the poor fit was getting worse as she grew. She was in a lot of pain and surgery would involve a very specific kind of bone-cutting procedure, which was time-critical. Even in a few weeks, the elbow bones would become so misshapen that surgical correction would become impossible. The family had little money and their young boy loved River like a sister. I could see a lot of myself in him. There wasn't anyone else experienced in performing this particular surgery.

First, I tried to operate sitting down with my foot on a stool. That didn't work. So I drew upon my wheelchair skills, developed for a movie role in which I played a paralysed character who learns to walk again (spoiler alert for those of you who haven't yet seen 2001's *Ghost Rig*; i.e. *all of you*). But trying to operate from a wheelchair also proved impossible for me. Next, I built a Thomas-Schroeder extension splint, a support mechanism that had originated in the First World War, where it was devised to keep soldiers with broken legs standing and shooting in the trenches. I'd used such a method to fix the fractured femur of a dog in my first ever orthopaedic procedure on a farmer's kitchen table. In my personal version, my foot, in a plastic support boot, was anchored in a large split-open trainer that I taped to the bottom of two upright iron bars to the outside and inside of my leg. These in turn were affixed to a child's toilet seat at the top of the leg. The objective was to keep my foot supported while I stood on the other leg, with my bum cheek resting on the seat and metal rods. That worked pretty well, but it didn't take long for my glutes to ache as much as my foot. I am of course a deplorable hypocrite for not listening to Mike, but in my defence, I don't think my lack of rest and recuperation was the only reason that I didn't heal properly. The artificial bone graft placed in my cysts wasn't as effective as it could have been. A few months later I was back to square one.

From the beginning, I had favoured drilling into my pelvis, to take some marrow and transplant it, as I have done in hundreds of animals. And that was indeed what Mike would do next. That's the nature of being a surgeon – one is always ready to get back on the bicycle and ride again. He was ready.

However, I was not ready for the second operation in any way. It had to be moved forward quickly because otherwise my talus bone was liable to collapse and then I'd end up with an ankle fusion, a likely limp, and worst of all from my point of view, I wouldn't be able to run again. With the sudden rush to operate urgent cases, to finish off filming for *The Supervet* TV show at the end of a run of 256 days for the rig cameras at the practice, and to deal with reports and management responsibilities, I was delighted finally to lie on the bed for the propofol anaesthesia that would initiate my own procedure. Afterwards, I slept nearly constantly for three days, with a patient-controlled analgesia pump unit strapped to a catheter in my left hand and a tube in my right pelvis (from which the graft came) delivering local anaesthetic. It was messy, with blood leaking out, but great because it killed all the pain. My euphoric oblivion was interrupted only by nurses coming and going to check on me, and the occasional kind text from my team at work, who very wisely had been advised not to ask my advice on anything for a couple of days. However, as usual, my friend Chris Evans didn't get the memo and got his radio show to call me to ask something about animals live on the show. I have no idea what he asked me, and I have no recollection of the call, but apparently under the influence of class A drugs, I offered the most direct and lucid answer I've ever given him in the many years we have known each other. Maybe the subconscious mind is ready for anything if we allow it to flow.

The so-called 'meth-bubble', delivered legally, was fantastic. It was as if my body was screaming for more sleep juice after a lifetime of deprivation. My cells must have been yelling at my brain, 'Hang on a minute. You never told us this kind of blissful existence was possible. You never told us we could rest for more than a few hours at a time. You've been holding out on us, you cheeky monkey, and we all vote to shut you down for as long as possible, thank you very much.' And so, they did. Finally, I woke up in a kind of daze, part of my brain tumbling towards the stress waterfall of needing to immediately go to work, and the rest of my cells saying, 'Take it easy, brother. There's no work today. We're all good here. Now how about a little more sleep?' Eventually I woke up enough to turn on my phone and the email deluge began. Dozens of work-related messages all marked urgent. 'Yikes,' went my half-asleep brain as it realised the consequences of a few days of shutdown. I struggled to focus, but sat bolt upright in bed as a single thought electrified my synapses – the following week I was due to have lunch with the Queen. More of which later, but I was very far away from being ready for that.

I thought I was ready to resume normal life, but my body had other ideas. My first outing away from the practice after my operation was to CarFest – the hybrid outdoor music and motor show Chris Evans has run for several years. I'd seen that the Irish band The Corrs were playing and, having a lifelong crush on all of the sisters equally, I asked if I could introduce them. Chris kindly said yes. I got so incredibly overjoyed that I jumped in the air in front of 40,000 assembled car-festers as I welcomed the band onto the stage. I left the ground an excited small boy, but somewhere during my flight, my grown-man brain kicked in with a warning: 'Do not land on your weak right ankle, you stupid Irish eejit!' And so, predictably, I came down hard on the left ankle instead, heard the loud crack which accompanies the snapping of ligaments and fell to the ground in agony. I wish I could say I 'styled it out', but instead I dragged myself stage-side to tumultuous applause as The Corrs began to play. And so I watched the band, ankle in an ice bucket for beverages, enthralled as always by their pulchritude and enraged by my profound stupidity. However, there was one upside. I was sitting backstage afterwards feeling sorry for myself, awaiting a car back to the train station to go home and ascertain the new damage. I was struggling to put on a bandage which I'd purloined from a first-aid kit when something quite extraordinary happened. Andrea Corr herself, noticing my plight, went down on one knee and bandaged my ankle. I have to say . . . the pain was worth it!

Secretly, I'd always wanted to run a marathon, and thought

it could never happen now, but I loved running and was determined to get back some level of fitness. I began to take a few short runs on the Surrey lanes around the practice in the darkness after work. To begin with, my ankle throbbed a bit and I sometimes hobbled in through the back door of the practice, but I was gradually doing better.

When I say, 'I'd never run a marathon,' that was before a magnificent opportunity arrived that forced me into readiness. Chris Evans announced live on air in January 2019 that I was running the London Marathon with his little team. At some point I must have muttered a vague notion about my secret aspiration, and he decided to tell everyone. But friends are friends, so I forgave him for landing me in it. My initial thought was that the very idea was ludicrous. I hadn't run more than a few miles for years, with my exercise confined mainly to the gym I've built at the practice. Not finishing work until 2 a.m. most days doesn't leave a lot of time for pounding the pavements. Other friends and acquaintances seemed to agree it was ill-advised, with one asking whether I'd yet completed a will, such was the likelihood of me dying somewhere on the twenty-six-mile route. In short, I wasn't ready. As it turned out, I didn't perish, because the marathon was cancelled in 2019 and 2020 due to Covid, thus providing ample time for Chris to forget all about it and for me to carry on operating on dogs and cats. Or so I thought. But Chris's memory is often too good for my liking, and he repeated again to his listeners that I was running with him in 2021.

That spring, then, I had a decision to make – to get ready to run a marathon or to somehow extricate myself from the commitment Chris had made on my behalf for later that year. There were a million excuses not to do it, the foremost being the loud voices in my head telling me that I was in no physical condition to run that far and that I absolutely did not have time for training. Despite all this, a whisper told me otherwise. There was one very good reason – faith.

I needed faith at that particular point because I was having significant challenges in my personal and professional life, and battling self-esteem issues. Faith is integral to readiness, since one can never be ready unless one has the faith that practice and preparation are actually worthwhile. Tactical decision-making and managing risk are also crucial to readiness. I have grown accustomed to this as a surgeon, since intra-operative challenges, of which there are many, are only ever conquered through readiness born of years of study and practical experience. Being prepared is everything for a good surgeon.

The same, I learnt from studying army manuals, is true for a good soldier. I suppose this is because of the stakes involved, when not being ready can mean the difference between life and death – both your own and that of others. I was once invited to speak to the armed forces at the Royal Military Academy Sandhurst. I explained to my audience what I've learned about the importance of prioritising readiness, and making sacrifices to be prepared. To maintain focus, I ask myself how I'd like to *feel* when a goal is accomplished, and this forces me to prepare to the best of my ability. There's nothing like the anticipation of future satisfaction to sharpen the mind and body in the present. In the past – however I might try to dress it up to myself or others – that future satisfaction was inexorably tied up with gratification of my ego, or proving myself to others. I have met some veterinary surgeons down through the years who were similarly deluded and in danger of losing true compassion for their patients in becoming clinical scientists. It's easy to enjoy the back-slapping indulgence of scientific meetings if my achievements or lectures become about me and not so much about my patients and my profession. At the height of my ego as a surgeon, I never got to the point of not deeply caring about my patients, but I certainly really did mind what people thought of me. Over time, though, I've come to value my work more as a contribution to the animals and to the field that will outlive me, rather than any plaudits the work might bring or indulgence derived from giving a lecture. For a soldier, I have no doubt that there is an element of self-esteem and ego in proving oneself amid competition with one's contemporaries, but to protect and serve one's country must surely be a more noble and sustaining goal.

I had come across the same conflict when I was an actor. Both the acting and music businesses are really tough. Both can involve years of getting ready – the practice, rehearsals, perfecting technique to no audience or applause. And even after all the toil of readiness, success is by no means certain. You may never get a chance to shine. I've seen amazingly talented young actors and musical artists never getting a lucky break, whilst folks with what I consider less talent and dedication being really successful. It can be really hard to find delight with the journey, when the destination seems forever out of reach, and the good fortune of reaching it so arbitrary and random. Throughout my life though, I have found time and again if I focus only on the destination or look for shortcuts, I'm doomed to ongoing unhappiness. Many I've met miss the joy of the here and now because they're thinking about being at the right social gatherings, or what's being said about them on social media. Readiness is about

42

living in the moment and taking joy in the serendipitous discoveries that the world throws your way. Art has its value, whether it's delivered to a stadium crowd or the back room of a pub, a packed-out theatre or the stage of a regional town hall. Surgery does too if you're attentive, grateful and have integrity – whether it's in a garden hut operating theatre as mine once was, or a state-of-the-art theatre as I have now. Attaining 'readiness' can either be a drag, or an exhilarating journey of discovery. I'm with the 'discoverers' all the way. In my view the biggest enemy of readiness is complacency, or as Pink Floyd once put it – becoming 'comfortably numb'.

That would be the greatest thing about running the marathon, I thought – the journey. If I could somehow get myself remotely ready, I really didn't give a damn what people thought, how long it might take, or whether I could actually finish it and claim a medal. The thing was, I would be doing it as something entirely personal just for me. I'd be discovering something about myself. Maybe this was a little selfish, because I knew I'd have to set aside time for training, and at that point in my life, I couldn't even find time for a relationship. But I needed headspace. And maybe this was the best way to get it.

To achieve anything at all worthwhile in life, you need readiness. Luck can open doors, but you need to be prepared to jump through them at the right moment and deliver whatever is expected of you on the other side. If you're ready, you make the most of the opportunity; if you're not, your luck can run out very quickly indeed. It's often said by the envious that the most successful people had plenty of luck on the way. But it's interesting to me that the successful people always seem to be the hardest working too. They had a modicum of natural flair or talent and then worked their arses off to be ready when a lucky break came, such that they continue to thrive afterwards. You have to put yourself in the right place, at the right time. And then you have to fight to stay there. Wishing on a lucky star but making no definitive decisions to take action does not make you either ready or successful.

I believe that both fate and destiny are the product of recognising 'signs' – being open to the moments of decision when a single definitive action can set you on a different path: one of those 'sliding doors moments' in life. I have experienced these moments many times: a flash of inspiration when the perfect invention to solve a problem comes to mind; a sudden, unprompted thought about an old friend you'd forgotten to call; being drawn to approach some stranger who will change your life. Sometimes even tragedies can offer inspiration to future triumphs. I'm no idealist though. I've seen enough talented and hard-working people *not* make it to realise that success is not inevitable, even with all the will and talent in the world. But I've seen very few truly successful people who weren't prepared in some way through hard work, who didn't have the willingness to keep improving their craft, developing their talent, paddling to remain on the crest of the wave. There's no easy fix.

Worshiping at the altar of the self in the hope of fame and fortune is an empty religion in my view, which is true in any form of expression, including social media. It's the opposite of readiness, and a pale facsimile of hard work. I've seen time and again how the pool of success may appear deep and satisfying when one observes others from outside, but it may drown some even in the shallowness of their façade, as they float on a tide of make-believe adulation for a little while, but haven't put in the effort to learn how to swim.

William Shakespeare, in his play *Twelfth Night*, wrote, 'Some are born great, some achieve greatness and some have greatness thrust upon them.' I do feel that it's possible to be born with a genuine genetic gift for something, to be passionate about it and succeed, but I can absolutely promise you that I have seen more people succeed in all walks of life without sublime talent, simply by making a choice to be 'ready' to seize that 'moment' and especially if you're also ready to contribute to the greater good and, in so doing, get what you need for yourself.

What do you think the chances are of a farm boy from the Republic of Ireland, who couldn't read and write properly aged ten, becoming the 'Supervet', with a show broadcast in this and many countries across the world? Close to zero, I'd have thought. But armed with my dreams, and a will to succeed, I was determined to be ready. Of course, the biggest reason that people don't get ready is that readiness is hard; it's a challenging route, especially if you can't find a way to enjoy the journey. The easiest key to unlock the door of lady luck is to find a way to enjoy the journey itself as much as the destination. With studying, I could *never* enjoy the journey. Studying is a nightmare. Endless hours, often staying up until dawn, cramming information in my head almost to the very moment I sat down to take the examination, so that it remained in there just long enough to set down on paper. Yet it has to be done. You really can't be a surgeon without all the technical information at your fingertips. But for me the truly valuable wisdom has come via my apprenticeships with my mentors, which I'd truly enjoyed and which truly prepared me.

Running, on the other hand, had always been a very enjoyable journey for me. Chris gave me a magnificent opportunity and a role model, but I needed to check in with my other running mentor before I could fully commit. I couldn't go running with Keira any more. Since her accident under the wheels of a van, she had been very slow indeed, just pottering around on our walks and happily sniffing the meadow flowers. One evening I came out of surgery after dark and took her for a little walk in the field out the back of the practice, I discussed running the London Marathon with her. I got the sense (strange, I know) that she gave me the full 'paws up' to go for it. I felt like she was telling me that if she couldn't run, then I could, and I could tell her all about my runs when I came back. I was going out of my mind with stress at that time, so once I'd popped her back in the office with Ricochet and Excalibur, I set off into the night. I was on the road and I had a feeling that if I just jumped through the door then Keira would be by my side all the way.

However, soon into my training endeavour, my ankle pain began to flare again and like Bran, I felt that in spite of my opportunity and my enthusiasm, my limbs didn't agree. And yet, like Kasey, I was determined that it was do or die. Kasey and Joey had been desperately holding on for several weeks, waiting for the go-ahead for Bran's operation, feeling terrible that they couldn't do more to get Bran out of pain.

I then consulted with various other surgeons, who ultimately agreed it was right to give Bran a chance, with the caveat that if quality of life was not achieved by six weeks post-operatively, then his family would need to be prepared to put him to sleep.

The irony of ethics adjudication is that it takes time and, during this time, Bran sadly continued to suffer in pain. When finally the panel of veterinary surgeons adjudicated that I could proceed with surgical intervention, the proviso was that if it failed, then there could be no attempt to revise the surgery and euthanasia would be the only recourse. Clearly everyone is trying to do their best, but I do think that we should ready ourselves for a better structure for adjudication of right and wrong in the care of our animal friends. I do not agree that their clinical challenges should have similar finite end points as those applied to animals used as experiments to advance human medicine. Finally, the custom ice-cream scoop implant was manufactured.

Kasey was a bag of nerves and Joey was exhausted, having been working overtime for months to gather enough money for the operation. I reamed out Bran's shallow socket, took marrow bone out of his ilium bone, as had been done for my own surgery, and implanted it behind the new metal liner, within which a new plastic cup socket could be cemented. The angle of the cup needed to be very carefully judged because Bran's only back foot was placed towards the centre of his body like a tripod. A new stem, neck and head were implanted into the femur to complete the new articulation. Bran was out of pain within a week and hasn't looked back since, as he runs around fields and finally got to have a run on the beach and into the sea, as Kasey had promised him. Bran embraced the adventure of every day, full of infinite potential. He was always ready and he barked loudly to tell everyone all about it, his long tongue flapping in the breeze.

By contrast, I was as far from ready for marathon training as one could get in autumn 2021. A month before, the furthest I had run was about twenty kilometres, less than

47

half the distance I'd need to cover on the day. Running in the rain along lonely, dark roads at midnight initially seemed like drudgery, even though I liked running. Forcing up the distance did not feel like practising joyful readiness. But having mentally committed, I was determined not to quit, even if I had to crawl to the end. Over time, I came to look forward to my two or three nights a week running after surgery. I made a conscious decision to detach from the stress and the turmoil of the day as I headed off into solitude and pitch black. Since I broke my neck falling down the stairs, I can't wear a torch on my head, and I think it helped my foot feedback to feel the road without seeing it anyway. Each time, I came back and told Keira what puddles I'd splashed in as we snuggled down for the night. If I was really lucky and got in a daytime run over a weekend, I would bring some grass or a flower that she might have sniffed had she been able to come too. She licked my face and was just happy that I was covered in sweat.

After her injury she was barely able to walk for quite a few weeks and was dragging one back paw due to nerve weakness. Her own 'marathon' recovery constituted the 'pea game', which was a highly complex exercise scenario to get her moving again. It involved tempting her to step forwards by placing a pea in front of her. Then another. And another. Rocket science!

I bought some earbuds and began listening to podcasts as I ran. It became 'me time' – something I hadn't afforded myself for a very long time. I felt free. The ankles were holding up reasonably well. But then other challenges reared their ugly heads. My right hamstring and calf muscles (the same that I tore during my stint in *The Bill*!) were seizing up with cramp, like coiled and painful elastic bands, after fifteen kilometres. This was not good. I rolled them, treated them with a massage gun, hung upside down, stretched them and pummelled them with the rubber ball thing we fill with food for dogs that eat too fast. Regardless, my muscles sucked. I kept hitting the wall somewhere between fifteen and twenty kilometres. I would never be ready for the marathon. Then I discovered running socks, and that changed everything. I had absolutely no idea whatsoever that actual socks existed for running, that had an R for right and an L for left and didn't scrunch up in your shoe. Whether it was a case of 'new gear' psychology, or they actually work as advertised, I've no idea. But the cramps ceased.

One night it was raining hard and I was exhausted, having finished surgery at 11 p.m. I absolutely did not want to run, but I hadn't been out all week because of several late surgery nights and I felt any vague sense of preparation slipping. I couldn't find my earbuds anywhere, so was admonishing Excalibur, because the most likely scenario was that he had found them charging under my desk and made off with them. Maybe he likes the taste of ear wax, because he always chooses to steal and chew my most expensive earplugs too, which I need in order to sleep when dogs overnighting at the practice are barking. That night, however, it was Keira who came to my rescue with a familiar twinkle in her eye as she started pawing a blanket to one side of my desk. Sure enough, the earbuds were hidden in there. She obviously knew how much I needed them for that run. It's truly amazing how about fifteen minutes into a run, tiredness evaporates no matter how exhausted I have been. I did about fifteen kilometres and came back and told Keira all about it. We snuggled for a bit and fell into a happy sleep.

The following day, 7 September, was the day that Keira died.

It was a dark time. I was in emotional turmoil, carrying on consulting and operating, as best I could, just a robot getting through the days. My night runs became my therapy. I welcomed the rain and I welcomed the cold. I welcomed the numbness of feet hitting tarmac one thud at a time. Things were not good at work or in my personal life and I was more insular than I'd been for years. The cleansing balm of the night wrapped me in her arms and welcomed me to a simpler place. Just me and my legs and the road and the darkness. Time was the main problem. I generally only had a couple of hours to run amid the nightly paperwork and reports drudgery, and so my legs grew accustomed to that distance but no more. A fortnight out from the marathon, I thought to myself that if I got halfway, I could walk the rest of it. I'd arranged to be off on the Sunday of the marathon, 3 October, and I was determined to make it happen.

Then misfortune struck and readiness was out of the question. It was around midnight on 24 September, nine days before the marathon. My twenty-kilometre route took me from Eashing to Godalming to Guildford and back again in a loop. On the last leg of that loop I was on my own last legs, under a cloudy, moonless sky, and with no street lights. My head was down, slogging out the final half-mile, and my earphones were in, so I was oblivious to the car that must have come out of a side road. It was certainly going far too fast, so when its beams hit me, all I had time to do was jump up on the roadside bank. The vehicle roared past and didn't stop. I did, as I keeled over on my left ankle, felt and heard a loud cracking noise that by now I knew only too well, and tumbled into a bed of nettles.

My ankle hurt way more than the stinging. I screamed into the deathly silence of the night air as I rolled onto my back, legs stretched out. As far as I was concerned, my marathon dream was over. I could barely move my left ankle without searing pain shooting up my tibia. I didn't know whether it was a break, a tear or a strain, or some combination. After ten minutes or so of feeling sorry for myself, I limped the last few hundred yards back to the practice. Ricochet and Excalibur looked on bemused as I wrapped the ankle in ice.

Fortunately, I was able to have an MRI scan quickly and it was clear that I hadn't fractured the fibula, which was positive. I had, however, twisted the tibia relative to the fibula and torn a fine selection of ligaments too. Fortunately, they were all low-grade tears and, as such, I knew if I strapped up the ankle in an everted position, I should be able to walk and stand at a surgery table. But would I be able to run?

For the following week I carried on with life as normal, hobbling around the practice. Luckily, the ankle didn't hurt too much when I stood still operating and it was strapped up, but it hurt a lot when I took the strapping off at night. Some strong prescription painkillers got me through. But I lay in bed at the practice each night wondering if I was going to be able to push it into a marathon. There'd be a danger of permanent damage if I miscalculated. On the other hand, if I didn't jump through the door I would never know. I had good excuses, but on the Friday night before the race on Sunday, I simply knew that I could not wake up on Monday morning with a niggling doubt that I'd let myself down. I was mentally ready, and that was enough.

Bran's mum Kasey emailed me to say thanks for Bran and to express sympathy for Keira's passing, not knowing I was running the marathon. She wrote, 'Keira's love gave you the strength to build your dream and that dream has given life and love to so many animals and people across the world. She lives on in them all.' She was right, and on the morning of the marathon Keira's love lived on in me. I would run it for both of us.

I'm very lucky that on the rare occasion I can't drive myself, I have a hugely reliable and ever-ready taxi service in driver David. He was of course on time on Sunday morning at 5 a.m. I am definitely not a morning person, but I got up at 4.30 a.m., bandaged the ankle and then locked it in rock solid with tight conforming casting tape. I couldn't flex or extend, but I was also not in significant pain. I tore my special left running sock trying to pull it over the tape, but it would have to do. I tucked a picture of Keira into my pocket, popped on my running top and a waistcoat with tubes of electrolyte stuffed into the compartments, rushed out of the door and fell asleep in the back seat of the taxi, walking only as we arrived at the congregation point. My first sighting of Chris was as I climbed on the bus to the starting line. He threw his arms around me, delighted that I'd made it. We got to the tent beside the starting line, set aside for those runners 'in the public eye', where you can lie low and get a last bite to eat and drink. I wanted some time alone and found a quiet corner to contemplate. When the start time arrived, I gathered myself, took a deep breath and bustled in. Suddenly we were off. I caught sight of Chris about twenty people ahead of me and I caught up with him as soon as the crowd dissipated a little. He kindly asked if I wanted to run beside him for a bit. The pace was fine at that stage.

I soon dropped behind him, feeling my own way through each mile, focusing on his orange heels ahead of me. Running in his tailwind had the added advantage that he absorbed a lot of the crowd's recognition and excitement, while I jogged along anonymously in his wake. Still, I got the odd 'Run, Supervet, run!' Chris was being very patient and even slowed down a bit at the *Cutty Sark* for me. I was okay until we got to Tower Bridge. The ankle was sore but not excruciating and I was coping with running on it in the flexed and eversion-locked position. But as I crossed the bridge, I caught the strapped foot awkwardly on a metal expansion joint in the road and tumbled over. I pulled myself to the side and propped up against the metal railings. Chris didn't realise, and by the time I had fumbled for my painkiller pills, he was long gone. It transpires he did wait for me on the other side of the bridge, but in the thronging masses we lost each other. I'm very grateful for his support because if it wasn't for his belief in my possibility to become 'ready', I'd never have had the opportunity at all. Readiness often needs a mentor and he's been one of my dearest. After all, if he hadn't pitched that Bionic Vet idea to the BBC on my behalf in 2009, I may never have had any career in the media at all and this book may never have existed.

I was feeling anything but bionic as I jogged off the initial pain and continued. But, imagining Keira running down the lane with me in her heyday, I smiled as I put one foot in front of the other. Next came 'The Highway' through Wapping, which is the section of the marathon where competitors are running in both directions, to and fro. I was just past halfway, putting plasters on my blistering toes at mile fourteen, but those already on mile twenty-two were charging towards me on the opposite side of the barrier. One passer-by even had the audacity to shout, 'Eh up, Supervet. Can't you make yourself a bionic leg?!'

Anyone who's challenged themselves on a long run to the limit of their capabilities knows the feeling as small niggles make themselves known – the knots of cramps, the stinging blisters, the painful joints. My right leg started to go dead, so soon I was effectively jog-walking, pulling my right leg with my fist grabbing my running pants in front. I could feel Keira's picture inside my pocket and thinking of her again drove me on. When a thunderstorm arrived on Victoria Embankment, I was delighted. This was more like my training runs in the lanes of Surrey. The water poured down my face and soaked into my pants, somehow easing the pain. By the time I got to St James's Park, running up towards Buckingham Palace, I found another helping hand. The tarmac was slick and I half-skated the last half-mile around the corner and down the Mall, hardly needing to lift my feet at all. I stumbled over the finish line in just over five and a half hours, but I couldn't care less about the time. This one was for Keira and me and for nobody else. We had done it. On our own, just her and me.

The sun came out and glinted down the sparkling Mall, taking in the happy faces of my fellow runners wrapped in foil blankets. I went to the booth with my number on it and collected my medal. I held it up and looked at it in the beautiful October sunshine with an intense sense of achievement and a deep joy rippling through my aching body. By almost any analysis, I hadn't been ready for that marathon, but in the only way that mattered I completely was.

Against the odds, I was ready after all. In that moment I felt in my heart that I was ready for anything.

CHAPTER 3

Humility

It was the mid-2010s. I didn't want to hear the phone. I reached to turn it off. I hadn't been sleeping well and sometimes just lay there for hours worrying. A surgeon on no sleep is no use to anyone. My head was under a blanket of rock bearing down on me. I'd bitten off more than I could chew. I had no time for anyone, not least myself, because I'd been working seven days a week trying to establish my two practices and my girlfriend at the time had found someone with more time for her than I had. I was eating a big chunk of humble pie and it tasted bitter.

The phone beeped again. My in-built reflex was that 'I should look. It might be the practice.' But my barbed wire brain said no. 'I don't want to hear from or speak to anyone ever again.' I lay there in pained silence, my head felt like there were rocks tumbling around in there. I didn't answer. The phone rang again. Then many years of conditioning kicked in. 'Nobody except the practice wants to speak to me that badly,' I thought. I lay there a while longer forcing my brain into some semblance of coherent thought, my head on the now-soggy pillow, staring at the ceiling. I called the practice. 'Puppy with jaw ripped off . . . blood everywhere . . . don't think it can wait . . . don't think we can do much.'

My colleague wondered whether she should advise euthanasia. I wasn't on duty, she just needed my help. The last thing in the world that I wanted to do was get in the car and go to the practice. I didn't want the pain of another living creature on my conscience. I had my own pain to deal with. The sad irony was that it was exactly this situation that had made me addicted to work, insular and emotionally unavailable for another human – endless patients in pain had contributed to my own pain; and now I was asked to save yet another from pain – to be humble in spite of my self-pity, when I had no humility left. I was in bits and I didn't know if I would ever mend. I couldn't pick up anyone else's bits and try to mend them. I just wanted to be selfish and curl up into a ball of knotted wire on my bed and drift into oblivion.

This had all been my choice, all my self-designed destiny. Of course, there are people who save loads of lives and do a magnificent job as a surgeon without wrecking their own lives, but I'm hard work for anyone to deal with. I'm hard work for myself to deal with. I lay on the bed, at rock bottom, and I had no more humility left inside me. But my clinical conscience won over my aching heart. I picked up the car keys.

When I arrived at the practice, years of training and conditioning in the fine art of sublimating everything in my life kicked in – because I am a surgeon, and that's what surgeons do. We compartmentalize feelings with the supreme confidence necessary to save lives. As had happened countless times before, as soon as I met Murphy, a three-month-old golden retriever puppy who had been attacked by another dog, my self-pity evaporated. His lower jaw had been ripped off. Blood was spurting everywhere and his dad Tim was covered in it as he had carried his curled-up body into the practice. I took one look at this bundle of gorgeous vulnerable golden-haired puppy, with my colleagues in the preparation hub now, his fur matted with blood, and decided that his salvation was the only option. Humility was the only currency.

Tim had always wanted a dog as a child, and promised himself he would get one when he grew up. He met his girlfriend Megan as a student and their first date was walking her family chocolate Labrador, Lily. From then on, animals were central to their relationship. Megan was still living and working in Dublin, Ireland and Tim was in London and finally decided to take the plunge, figuring he was probably grown up enough in his mid-twenties. He went to see some puppies and fell in love with the cute ridge of hair on Murphy's nose. He had been enjoying a walk with Murphy in his local park when out of nowhere another dog attacked him viciously, locking onto his face and shaking him violently, ripping off his lower jaw in the process. He arrived at my practice late on a Sunday night.

I sat Tim down to deliver the bad news. Not only had the entire front half of the jaw been ripped off, but some of the bone was crushed and likely not reconstructable, plus there was a very high risk of infection. If the mandible wasn't saveable, then Murphy would either be put to sleep or have the front part of his jaw removed as we do with some cancer cases, and though his tongue would hang out permanently, he may be able to live contentedly without the front part of his lower jaw. Either way, to keep him alive, surgery would be necessary, and the prognosis was by no means clear. Tim was crying and in bits himself. He felt he had let him down in the park and wasn't going to put him through anything that hurt him further for any selfish reasons. In the end, he asked me, like many guardians do, 'What do you think is the kindest thing to do?'

I used to answer this question willingly and give my personal opinion on what was possible. It's reassuring I think when people can trust in such guidance. But sadly, I have become aware that some other vets feel that me expressing my professional opinion may emotionally pressure or 'coerce' families to make a surgical decision, even though clearly they ask in good faith and most vets can still answer the question with the same good faith. But those vets aren't judged like I am, because they are not on the TV. Nowadays, I just give all the options and risks and discuss what I feel are the ethical best interests of a patient. I felt that standard plates and screws had distinct disadvantages for any attempt to reconstruct his jaw because there were pieces missing, poor tissue cover, risk of infection, and puppy bone is soft so there wasn't much for screws to hold on to. Also, the front part of the mandible was just about holding on with the most tenuous blood supply. Many of the blood vessels had been ruptured, and it was essential to preserve those that remained, especially the branches of a big one called the inferior alveolar artery. So I used tiny 1.1 mm wires threaded through the pieces of the mandible like guitar wires in a kind of suspension trampoline which I tensioned on pillars and clamps like the tuning pegs of a guitar mounted on an aluminium U-shaped arch. There were teeth and bits of bone missing and holes with no tissue, so there was still a risk it might not heal or might get infected. I called Tim sometime between 1 a.m. and 2 a.m.

His best friend was happy on sleeping drugs. Humility had saved the day and Tim was the most humble guy you could ever wish to meet. He was intensely grateful.

I crashed into my bed upstairs at the practice. Now that the biological firefighting was done, my mind was on fire again. The irony was that in spite of doing my best and not indulging in my own problems, I still felt like a creep and a weirdo, to echo the band Radiohead, because I wanted someone to notice when I wasn't around rather than just leave. In reality, I couldn't blame anyone except myself though, because everyone needs to feel valued, and to make human relationships work I'd have to learn to say no sometimes to the animals. That would mean training the team up to take on any challenge, even when I wasn't there, so I determined that I'd try to be more patient and humbler to do just that. Sadly, for me, though, because of circumstances in my practice and my profession, which I'll describe, this hasn't yet come to fruition.

Meanwhile, Murphy rapidly became a celebrity in his local neighbourhood, with a massive cone around his neck and scaffolding around his jaw. The great thing about puppies is that they are 'healing machines'. Murphy did get infected, but we cleared it and he grew new bone and gum lining. When his frame was finally removed, with his teddy in his mouth, he had his jaws firmly clamped on the ecstasy in every single moment of his new beginning. He ran for balls that he never wanted to let go of with what seemed like new jaws of steel. He greeted every new dog as if nothing had ever happened. He was a shining beacon of forgiveness and humility. All he wanted was to share love. He held no grudges.

I have certainly been guilty of being overwhelmed by anxiety, fear and depression after difficult traumas in my life, but Murphy has been a very humbling mentor for me in not allowing his post-traumatic stress injury to define him going forward. To forgive and move on requires humility and helping Murphy gave me the strength to try to help myself and to keep going, even through the darkness. Tim and his partner Megan got married with Murphy as the proud ring bearer and groomsman. He would have been best man, but Tim wasn't too confident in Murphy's ability to give a speech with his mouth full of tennis balls. They decided not to have a honeymoon and instead to spend the money on a friend for Murphy – another golden retriever rescued from the meat trade in China. Wilf is even more sociable than Murphy if that were possible – another bundle of effervescent joy. All new beginnings created by the dog who could so easily have come to an end one Sunday night when I wanted everything to end myself.

Where Murphy goes, light and joy follow. I see this time and time again, how caring for an animal when their end seems possible beckons infinite new beginnings. As Tim put it himself when he thanked me for fighting for Murphy's life, 'Even when things look at their bleakest, if you fight like hell, with some help from those around you, then things can turn around.'

Murphy has made him more considerate and appreciative of his other relationships as well – with his sister and mother who helped look after Murphy in recovery, with his wife, because they have been through everything together, and with me too, because Tim is truly a friend of mine, even though I never see him except at dog festivals.

I know that I have made many thousands of friends in my life. I absolutely know that if I picked up the phone to almost any guardian of any animal I have every treated with all of my heart and soul and any academic acumen, talent or skill that I've picked up along the way, they would be there for me in a heartbeat. That's the great honour of being a surgeon – and the privilege of a life well lived. I save their friend and companion and I gain friends and companions, both animal and human, on life's journey forever. That's the greatest blessing of 'being The Supervet'.

In spite of this blessing, and quite contrary to the image of 'super' as a prefix of my TV show, inside myself, I'm forever humbled by the vagaries of biology. I recall few of my successes, but my countless failures haunt me, and each and every day disaster hangs over me like a perpetual sword of Damocles. As such, I have a huge ego and yet no ego at all. I think I can solve any problem if I have a blood and a nerve supply, bending the body of my patient somehow to my will, like the Marvel and DC superheroes I have adored since I was a child. One could even say that I am objectively the absolute best in the world at what I do, because nobody else does it – with the same technology, experience or intractable determination. And yet, I feel inadequate every single day of my life, and I'm plagued by low self-esteem.

I take on clinical cases that nobody else will touch and have saved countless limbs and lives. But I understand all too well the perils of believing your own hype. When I was at the absolute apogee of my ego, which I referred to earlier, I had worked my backside off to get there. Years of late nights studying, writing papers, writing lectures, thousands of surgeries, a hit TV show. I had battled all kinds of adversity to be the best I could be, and whilst I deluded myself that I wasn't particularly egotistical, when I walked up to give the keynote lecture at a major conference in America, subconsciously I thought I was 'the man'. By now I knew that I had performed more surgeries, orchestrated more clinical research, and innovated more new techniques than anyone in my field in the world, and I was about to distil it all into one seminal lecture. I was unintentionally the least humble I have been in my entire life.

As I mentioned, I currently don't get asked to give lectures on advanced surgery in the UK to try to inspire younger members of my profession, since I think, in general, I'm still perceived as somewhat of an upstart who ruffles too many feathers, which 'the establishment' frowns upon. Perception can be shaped by perspective or prejudice, and in my view, ego should never get in the way or progress for the greater good. So, it's pertinent therefore to share a little about my own ego, as it has manifested in my career.

In America, Europe and across the rest of the world, people in my field have generally been very open to listening to what I might have to say. In the thirty-two years that I have been a veterinary surgeon, I've spent nearly all of them trying to be the best 'bone surgeon' I can be. I have travelled all over the world learning from experts in the veterinary and human surgical fields of orthopaedics and neurosurgery, and I have eaten humble pie whenever it has been offered. But when I stepped up to the lectern in the United States, the talk I gave was the distillation of more than two decades of research and development in those fields, and I knew better than anyone what I was talking about. It was well received – a far cry from the mid-nineties in the UK where I was laughed off the stage for suggesting some novel theories I had on developmental elbow disease; theories which I subsequently proved.

As I basked in the applause of the audience, I thought I had finally *arrived*. But there was nobody to phone or rejoice with, since no one I knew would understand what that moment meant to me after the struggles to get there. It's a familiar feeling. All of my failures and successes have been shared with animals – the ones I treat, or the ones I come home to, which was Keira for more than a decade. So, I've become used to internalising any feelings of despair or satisfaction. Perhaps also in the back of my mind were my mammy's warnings about pride coming before a fall. She was right.

In spite of my critics at home, I was rather pleased with myself and my lecture that day. I loosened my tie, undid the buttons on my suit jacket and sauntered off the stage in search of the toilet. In the hallway outside the lecture room, two attendees stopped me, fellow surgeons brimming with fulsome praise about the talk, and expressing gratitude for the insights I'd shared. 'Incredible, just incredible,' said the first man. His friend joined in with similar superlatives, 'Thank you for moving veterinary medicine forward.' *How incredibly kind*, I thought, before I continued my ego-buoyed glide to the men's room. There, while sitting on the toilet in a cubicle, reflecting on my success, I heard two men speaking at the urinals. It took me only a second or two to identify their voices as belonging to the gentlemen with whom I'd just interacted outside the lecture hall. 'Who the hell does he think he is?' one said, with a snarl of disdain. The other cackled, and I listened, mortified, as they laid out their charges against me. That I was patronising, that I am blessed with machinery that others can't afford, that I love myself. One summed up their disdain succinctly: 'What an asshole!'

I sat there, mystified and mortified. Hang on just a second . . . Why did they feel the need to blow smoke up my proverbial one minute earlier, and then eviscerate me the next? It was simply impossible that they had changed their minds in the space of two minutes. I was devastated. I had actually respected these two surgeons. They were my peers. Part of me wanted to interrupt my ablutions and burst out of the cubicle to declare my presence in an attempt to shame them. Instead, I stayed as quiet as a mouse until they'd left. Then I cried my eyes out.

This moment of reversal was the single best thing that has ever happened in my professional career. In the space of five minutes, I learned all one ever needs to know about authenticity, ego, humility and words in the mouths of people – they are what you make of them; they are uttered with whatever agenda people may have and they can be interpreted through one's own perception. Honesty and true fulfilment do not in the ego reside. They were not being honest with themselves – and neither was I. There is too much ego and too little humility in all of us. Unless praise or criticism comes from someone you really admire and implicitly trust, take it with a pinch of salt. I find trust very difficult indeed and clearly I need to be careful whom I admire. I cried and I cried – but in their two-facedness they had done me a painful favour. After one trip to the toilet, I was never properly ego-indulgent again. In the immortal words of Oasis, everyone is going to have a day when 'they're gonna throw it back to you', so it's best, I think, to realise that long before it happens so it stings less.

Over the past decade or so, I have been exploring how I can combine working as a medical specialist with existing as a media personality, whilst not making it all about me. For most highly driven medical specialists, veterinary or human, there is a necessary mixture of striving to be the best one can

be and truly giving one's all to the patient as a compassionate and deeply caring clinician. First and foremost, I want
to contribute to academic and practical advance through education, evidence, efficacy and ethics, the four cornerstones
of any well-founded medical progress. For this, public aware-
ness is key, and I'm uniquely placed to spread a message
far and wide. So in these pages I have sought to be utterly
truthful with you, with humility and respect, whatever may
come of it. If people in my profession get upset because they
may think some of what I say is harsh, I would say that if one
really believes in something, as I do in my profession and our
role as the guardian angels of animals, then one needs to be
prepared to risk it all for the sake of integrity.

I have tried to do my best for all of the animals and all of
the people who cross my path – to leave each minute a little
better by virtue of having passed through it – but I have increasingly been asking myself if it's worth it. I've put myself
in a position where I'm the only person that will operate on
certain cases. Is doing so an indulgence of my ego? Or should
I be more humble and take a step back, even if doing so would
mean some animals would not receive treatment at all? If I
don't take on the costs of developing complex solutions, if I
just chase money and a great work-life balance, and if I choose
not to broadcast better solutions to difficult problems with my
ostensible ego, then there's a price to be paid for that apparent
humility too. I often think back to the days when I was just
on my own in large animal practice, or when I started to take
referral cases in 1997, and I ask myself whether it was any
better. It was simpler, for sure. I was at least in control of my
own actions and reactions, rather than being at the helm of a
very large practice for the past several years. But in other ways,

back then I was unhappy, because I couldn't change anything other than the prospects of the animal right in front of me, and even then with inadequate tools and implants. I couldn't make any difference in the world at large. I couldn't advance the treatment options. I was humble and I was powerless.

Yet, I never forget that for the average vet or vet nurse at the coalface, it doesn't really matter who owns the business or what equipment is available or not. On any day in any moment in time, for them it's not about changing the world for everyone, but rather looking after the world just for that patient. As a result of this dichotomy, it's more difficult to work with me than one may think, because it's extraordinarily difficult for my team to understand how the needs of the many and the few have to be balanced by me each and every day. My ego and my dreams drive me on to try to change my small corner of the world. But the humility of potential success or failure in dealing with one patient in one moment in time is just as important. Writing this book has therefore been difficult for me, because in making time, there are compromises which have been made for the greater good and sacrifices by my colleagues in working around my time availability, for which I am humbly and profoundly grateful.

And so, I search for balance in the middle of these two extremes of humility and ego. This was never more evident to me than during the SARS-CoV-2 pandemic, which forced us all to realise what is important and what isn't. It showed me how humble the world can be in the face of a new and frightening threat, looking out for one's neighbour, clapping for the NHS, doing charity fundraisers for medical research. There is nothing more humbling than thinking you and your loved ones might become seriously ill and die.

By uncanny chance, on each occasion I was offered the vaccine against Covid, I became infected at almost the exact same time. I've now had my shots, but have also been infected with the virus five times (I must have every antibody going). The second infection was by far the worst. It hit me like a train, affecting my ear canals and robbing me of balance so I couldn't stand up. I was having hallucinations at one point, and when I laid down, I felt as though insects were crawling all over my skin, followed by hot flushes and then a raging sweat trickling down my back. My head felt like a giant hand had gripped my skull and was trying to crush it. My limbs just didn't want to receive signals from my spine. The cytokine tornado waged in my muscles and joints and they shut down.

I'd not known crippling pain like it; every joint and every muscle trapped in a vice grip, with barbed wire in my lungs and sandpaper on my skin. To turn even a little in bed, I had to summon significant willpower and, even then, yelped like a puppy with the pain. For me, it was worse than being trapped in my body when I broke my neck, because at least then I could understand what was happening. The symptoms of this disease were ever-changing, and the uncertainty of what was coming next weighed heavily. Soon I began to struggle to breathe. My chest seemed unable to expand properly and there wasn't enough air. I was down to short, sharp gasps. I called an ambulance.

The paramedics were great. I crawled to the door of my house and let them in. I explained that every movement was painful and that I also had profuse diarrhoea in spite of not eating. Eventually after checking my blood gases and other vitals, they concluded that I had a better chance of not dying if I stayed at home: the stats on survival once admitted to a respiratory ward were 50/50, so unless I genuinely couldn't breathe, I should stay at home and try to remain calm. It was my lungs that really mattered; the other symptoms were of secondary importance. It was humbling, indeed, lying there for a couple of days while my immune system staged its counter-attack. Recovery came gradually, and my subsequent infections have been much less severe.

Everyone has had their own struggles with Covid, or the restrictions put in place to meet the threat, and I think it's important to put yourself in others' shoes, and to recognise the pressures others face. I never had a problem with the wearing of masks – I wear one for hours every day in surgery. But in my case there were a couple of downsides. The first was important in that dogs especially are finely attuned to human expression, and my work involves building trust with the animals in my care. When covering the lower half of my face, it's harder to win the trust of a dog. It's like I'm the one being 'muzzled' if they can't see my facial expressions. The second issue was somewhat humorous. I reckon I'm the only person in the UK who is *more* recognisable with a face mask on, because of the TV shows in which I'm routinely masked. Out and about during the pandemic, I couldn't walk down any street without someone shouting out, 'Oi, Supervet, will ya mend my dog?'

One case from that time I won't forget in a hurry is Hugo. His human dad was Billy-Joe, who was a junior charge nurse in an NHS Trust hospital and, like his partner Ben who also worked in the hospital, he was on the front line of battling Covid when he brought Hugo to see me. Hugo, a sixteen-month-old pug, was affected by hip dysplasia, where the muscle and ligaments that should hold the ball-and-socket joint together don't do so and the joint wears away. The head slips out, rubbing on the rim of the socket which becomes progressively shallower. Sadly, Hugo was also affected on the same side by a kind of wasting away of the femoral head, created by a disturbance of blood supply called avascular necrosis. Eventually his femoral head dislocated completely, fracturing off a part in the process. Poor Hugo was in terrible pain. Billy found him in a state when he came home from another long, exhausting shift.

Billy was one of the humblest and best humans I have ever met. He gave selflessly to others all day, every day, and often in extremely distressing circumstances. Sometimes he managed an area within the emergency department, and other times he took charge of the whole thing, including staff allocation and ensuring patients were kept safe. He spent up to twelve hours a day in stifling hot personal protective equipment (PPE), assessing patients while also protecting himself from a disease which we knew relatively little about. Patients would be seen in an ambulance or a cabin pod outside, to decide if their symptoms justified admission, and the resuscitation area inside the hospital wasn't equipped to deal with the number of critically unwell people arriving daily. They had to completely reconfigure the department, with 'hot' and 'cold' zones for suspected Covid and non-Covid patients, but every day the virus changed, and the advice and management configuration were liable to change too. The cleaners could not cope with the demand for deep cleaning every inch of the bays on the ward as patients were moved between emergency care and wards. There was no room for complaint in this arena – humility and teamwork were the order of the day. Even so, as staff began to get ill, the pressures increased, with fewer doctors and nurses to deliver care to more and more patients, many high acuity. Temporary staff were hard to come by as they were scared of falling ill themselves.

At the height of the pandemic, when Billy was the nurse in charge of the department, he told me about one of his patients, a lady in her eighties. She was severely unwell and deteriorating rapidly in the resuscitation area due to her other co-morbidities. The difficult decision was made that she would not be a candidate for the intensive care unit because there was little that could be done to arrest her decline. In short, she was dying and would never leave the hospital. Tragically, because of the risk of cross-contamination and infection transmission, visitation had been all but stopped in most areas of the hospital. It became an almost impossible management decision whether people would die alone, or be permitted to have someone by their side for a very brief time. This particular lady had never spent a day away from her husband in their fifty-plus years of marriage, but being on a ward, the restrictions prohibited visitation, even *in extremis*. Billy couldn't stand the thought that yet another person was going to die alone, so he pleaded with the doctor in charge of the department for a brief family visit in the emergency area. His heartfelt advocacy worked. Billy then spoke to the family, a husband and son, and explained the risks – that they could potentially become unwell and could end up in the same position as their loved one. In spite of all of that, they wanted to be with her in her final moments. They spent a short time, holding her hand, before she died without ever needing to be admitted to the ward.

Billy and his team had a stock of knitted hearts that were

donated to the hospital – two of the same, so the patient and their families could share a connection, even if physically separated. He gave the deceased lady two hearts and her husband and son one each. As they walked through the doors and left the emergency department, Billy and one of the other nurses looked at each other, lips quivering, eyes welling up. They went outside and stood in the cold and cried. The Covid rules were hard for many. In my world, I see goodbyes all the time, as well as the gratitude families have for the opportunity to say farewell. But I'll never forget one elderly gentleman whose cat was brought to us during the pandemic. I had to explain over the phone that euthanasia was the kindest option. Due to the guidance at the time, he could not be with her, to stroke her fur as she passed and whisper goodbye, and he was broken-hearted for the loss of his companion. I sent him a poem, a hair clipping and a paw print. That was all I could do. Every single day of my professional life I see the humility of human beings exposed through the extraordinary and unique love shared with an animal companion, and when our dear friend passes, it's as painful to many as a human friend passing, and sometimes even more. To quote Ricky Wilson from the Kaiser Chiefs, 'there's a hole in my soul, that could only be filled by you'.

Hugo the pug, Billy and Ben's companion, was always there for them when they got home from an arduous shift at the hospital, jumping into their arms, licking their faces and filling their souls. Hugo's pain was Billy and Ben's pain too. It never ceases to impress me the humility imbued upon us by our love of a companion animal. Because they give us unconditional love, we as their guardians feel a profound sense of moral responsibility which subdues our own ego.

We would do whatever it takes to see our friend out of pain, regardless of whatever is happening in our lives. I have seen divorcing couples, at war in my reception area, come into my consulting room and be civil and courteous to each other in a way that would be impossible in a lawyer's office. I have watched people dying of cancer, and all they want to know before they pass is that their dog or cat is going to be okay. I have met people down and out on the brink of total financial ruin, giving up their last vestige of financial means to their animal companion. When it comes to unconditional love, the facades of material possessions and ego fall from us, exposing the true humility of the deep love inside us that is selfless, compassionate, all-giving, all-consuming. It is that humility that can and does change the world, wherever it is allowed to shine.

Billy and Ben were understandably distraught at Hugo's pain. I explained the options, as I always do, which were ongoing medical management, euthanasia, full limb amputation, femoral head and neck excision (FHNE) or total hip replacement (THR). Medicine wasn't working and wasn't going to work. Euthanasia was extreme and unnecessary, as was full limb amputation, but I am morally obliged to mention them in all cases, distressing as it may sound. Femoral head and neck excision involves the removal of the damaged head and neck of the femur, forming a flat surface that then glides on fibrous tissue between the top of the femur and what's left of the socket. The procedure has been around for a couple of hundred years and may result in a very functional limb, but it's never fully weight-bearing and there are potential complications. Bone-on-bone friction can occur or fibrous adhesions may form, leading to nerve pain, and I have published an academic paper on revision surgery of FHNE to total hip replacement, where the initial procedure has failed to address the pain. The gold standard for hip dysplasia and avascular necrosis of the femoral head in cats and dogs is THR, and that's what Billy and Ben elected for. I've performed more than a thousand such procedures, using commercially available off-the-shelf components, and it typically takes less than one hour with an experienced team.

THR involves cutting off the damaged parts of the femoral head and neck, drilling out the acetabulum socket, and replacing them. One has to get the angles of the plastic cup exactly right and one has to match this to the angle of the stem and neck in the femur. Then one applies differing lengths of femoral neck integrated to the head mounted on the stem to create more or less space between the femur and the pelvis (called the 'offset distance'), to keep the gluteal muscles tight. It's a tricky process, sometimes trickier than in humans even, because of how dogs walk, run, sit and lift their legs to urinate.

Everything went well until three weeks after the operation, when Hugo's new head dislocated out of his new socket. Every surgeon meets complications, and if they say they don't, they are lying to themselves and to you. A surgeon can choose to go one of two ways with a mistake or complication – they can take a good hard look in the mirror and come to terms with their own fallibility, or they can blame external factors – their tools, the implants, biological variance, a patient's lack of compliance with post-op instructions, or any manner of other factors. Any or all of these factors may indeed be the case – and I expect, in Hugo's case, that his

73

muscle did get looser, leading to dislocation. However, there is a much deeper lesson to be learned, even if biology has not smiled on you that particular day, and even if the failure was not the fault of the surgeon. That lesson is humility. In my opinion, the only pathway to self-awareness, enlightenment or innovation in cognitive, spiritual or scientific terms, in any walk of life, is to let go of the endless list of excuses – and surrender to humility.

At the time of Hugo's operation, a cup and stem cemented into Hugo's bones was all I had for dogs of his size. Since then and in light of his complication, I've developed a superior system. Hugo was the first step on that road, where the humility of accepting and interrogating failure to fuel progress has helped many other dogs since. For Hugo's revision surgery I used a miniature version of the ice-cream scoop shell that I had used for Bran (now called an 'AceFitz'). This allowed a larger plastic liner cup to be cemented in the shell which pushed further outwards from the pelvis to tighten the muscles and with a more substantial 'ledge' to prevent dislocation. Books can only help so far with judgements like this, so clinical experience and gut feeling go a long way. Nowadays I trust my gut implicitly. If it doesn't 'feel right', regardless of what the book says, I will not do it. And sometimes the literature is wrong – after all, the only information in there is the perceived wisdom from a moment in time, and knowledge expands and changes all the time. Covid provides a suitable comparison. On a daily basis, as the pandemic crisis unfolded, the 'science' changed. Evidence and experience brought new truths to light, and even then they were interpreted, innocently and sometimes cynically, in different ways by medics, politicians and the general public.

Humility is a difficult thing to practise in the face of uncertainty – especially if one has a vested interest in the path to be chosen.

Since then, Hugo has gone from strength to strength and runs around energetically with his new pal, a little Boston Terrier called Hank. But without humility, the innovation would never have happened. Without humility, big questions do not get asked. Without humility, progress is impossible.

During Hugo's treatment and rehabilitation, Billy and I also discussed how Covid had displaced or delayed other urgent medical and surgical interventions, especially the 'Big C' – cancer. Not only were early diagnosis appointments pushed back or ceased, but many patients simply could not get timely treatment with the health services short-staffed and fighting the fire of the pandemic. I was lucky. A couple of weeks after Hugo's revision operation, on my mother's birthday, I also had revision surgery of my own. I had a tumour removed from inside my nose a few years previously, but it wasn't possible to get 'clean margins' on it without taking off a chunk of nose. Thankfully it's not malignant so won't kill me, but it was getting big again and so my lovely and talented surgeon San took it out again.

One secondary benefit of wearing a Covid mask was that nobody noticed the stitches and I went back to operating on my own patients the following day, just as the cats and dogs under my care often get on with their lives with the minimum of fuss. San tells me that if my tumour comes back again and I do want to get clean margins, then he can always chop off part of my nose and replace it with a bit of cartilage from my ear. It's very much the sort of improvisation I practise on my patients, and a reminder to be humble – animal or person we're all the same under the surgeon's knife or on the doctor's table.

There's nothing like a prostate exam to ease home this message. Over the preceding months, I'd had some water-works issues, in that I was having to pee a lot at night. This had already led to me falling down the stairs and breaking my neck – there's a detailed description in my previous book for anyone interested – but I wanted to understand the cause, and my magnificent surgeon Stephen suggested a routine prostate check which showed no abnormalities. However, there were suspicious areas on the MRI scan of my prostate, so Stephen organised to have biopsies taken. Easy enough, or so I thought, until I realised that the biopsy process was a rack of forty or so needles inserted through the perineum, between the testicles and the anus. It sounded like something medieval, or a scene from a particularly nasty horror movie, and it's safe to say I wasn't looking forward to it.

When the day came, I couldn't help reflect on the experience of being a patient by comparing my own treatment with that of the animals who come to my practice. I was led down the corridors of the hospital to my very own 'kennel' that I'd be staying in on the ward, a lovely little room replete with incontinence pads, very fetching paper knickers, a nappy liner and two compression stockings to prevent deep vein thrombosis. The sign on the door read 'Dementia room'. Not a good omen. I settled down to an exhaustive multiple-choice examination. There were pages and pages of the stuff, quizzing me on maladies past and present. Did I, or have I ever, suffered from allergies, liver disease, diabetes, colon issues, back pain, headache, forgetfulness, Creutzfeldt-Jakob disease, or any number of other maladies known to man? I thought to myself how easy dogs and cats have it, with Mum or Dad doing all the paperwork.

Most of the lovely nurses and attendants had seen *The Supervet* on TV, and told me about their dog or cat as they poked and prodded me, jesting that I could probably have performed the operation myself. Their jokes reveal a sad truth. Though it's the case that the similarities between human and animal biology mean the operations performed on both are comparable, there's little communication between the respective fields. This is in spite of the fact that most innovations to treat humans, drug or implant, have evolved from prior animal experimentation, as I've already mentioned. Members of the public are generally surprised that vets and human doctors don't talk more. The fact is that we all live in silos, and rarely does information exchange happen at the clinical coalface. This giant chasm of understanding in medicine has existed for centuries. When I actually meet and talk to medical practitioners, most find it unbelievable that the stuff I do with animals on the television isn't shared freely with my human surgical colleagues and vice-versa, so that we can all learn and move forward together. It seems that my greatest life purpose, which is the reintegration of animal and human medicine through 'One Medicine', is completely obvious to most people, and yet most of the world is completely oblivious to it.

Prostate cancer diagnosis and treatment are similar in man and dog, and yet if I were to suggest that we treat a hundred dogs who really need it with a new treatment that may ultimately benefit humans, most drug companies and doctors would just pass on by. The conventional paradigm of injecting cancer into a completely normal animal is generally the way that drug and surgical trials are conducted for human benefit, and is in fact often required by governing bodies to certify that a treatment is safe for humans. But just because we've always done something one way, doesn't mean that there isn't a better approach, and there's a growing body of evidence that naturally occurring cancer in animals may in fact be a superior model for human cancer than experimentally induced cancer. In my opinion, the governing bodies of human and vet medicine should embrace this, and allow properly constructed clinical trials whereby families can choose treatments that may be superior for their dog, in addition to the range of conventional treatment options. Then the data could be shared with all for the greater good. Of course, this would require regulatory oversight to allow the administration of a drug under an experimental licence, or as an act of 'recognised' veterinary practice (RVP). The key elements are the four Rs – to reduce, refine and replace experimental animal models by reciprocity. These are the four foundation stones of the Humanimal Trust charity which I founded to try to give animals a fair deal, whilst also moving medicine forward for humans too.

The reality is that this isn't likely to happen anytime soon, because most drugs and treatments will make much more money when sold to humans only, and ironically dogs may not have access to the drugs that their species helped to create for many years, until after the drug company has recouped their considerable investment. I don't think this is anyone's fault per se, and nor will it change overnight, as humans need safe and effective treatments. However, I strongly believe that there is a middle ground, where drug companies could actually save money by working in a clinical veterinary environment, helping dogs and cats and shortening the drug development pipeline. Real-world data has other value in the case of cancer treatments specifically, because it has been observed that many drugs that show promise on experimental cancer fail when treating naturally occurring cancer. This is because experimental cancer has a very mono-dimensional (homogenous) cell population, whereas naturally occurring cancer has a stroma and variety of cell types (heterogenous) allowing it to become an 'immortal organ' with cell division proceeding unchecked and so ultimately destroying the organism.

I was telling the nice nurse all about this and desperately hoping that I didn't have such a cancer inside me, as she politely asked me to lie on my left side and hug my knees. Next thing I knew, as I pontificated about the intervention needed for integration of human and animal medicine, I had my own medical intervention. I'll spare you the details but let's just say there's nothing that punctures the potential pride of someone used to being the doctor rather than a patient quite like the thrust of an enema tube. There are few things as humbling as the aftermath of an enema or trying to urinate what feels like scalding barbed wire through one's urethra after a multi-needle prostate biopsy. I understood with clarity those many furtive looks of embarrassment I'd seen in the eyes of dogs who've let rip in front of me. I have, however, observed that cats on the other hand just seem to have a self-satisfied glint in their eyes and a grin on their whiskers when they do.

The battle for humility is a constant one for all of us. Luckily for me I have considerable personal empathy for the ailments of my patients to keep some balance.

CHAPTER 4

Passion

Stevie was passionate about everything. A six-month-old dachshund puppy, she loved to run, lick faces, wrestle with stuffed toys and play her favourite game, 'Where's Stevie?' This elaborate ruse involved Stevie hiding in exactly the same place every time, while her human dads scurried around and pretended to search in the many places they knew she wasn't hiding, just to build the tension before the inevitable giant Stevie snuggle. The snuggle might be giant but Stevie wasn't. She was a four-kilo, brown-and-tan long-haired dachshund.

Her human guardians, Ben and Owen, were a couple who had separated a few weeks previously, and Stevie now had two homes. In November 2021, Stevie was walking with Owen in a park in South London, but a normal afternoon walk turned into carnage when Stevie collided with a bicycle on a path of the park. She flailed in the spokes, trapped and screaming, before being flung off onto the path. Poor Stevie, dazed, confused and undoubtedly terrified, ran away as fast as she could, clawing the ground with her front legs and dragging her back end behind her. She made it out into the road where she was hit by a car. The traffic ground to a halt as people gathered around her tiny, yelping, writhing body. Frantic and shell-shocked, Owen rushed over, scooped up her crumpled body in his arms and got her to the vet as quickly as he could.

When I first met Stevie, she was anaesthetised on a surgical table and my neuro-surgeon colleague, Joana, who had admitted her, called me in for an opinion on how to stabilise her damaged sacrum, the triangular bone that sits at the end of the spine, between the pelvic bones. She was double incontinent and there was real concern that multiple crush fractures of her sacrum had stretched and may have even severed the tiny, thread-like sacral nerves which supply the urinary bladder and anus. If severed, then she would never urinate or defecate normally again, which would obviously have massive repercussions on whether she might have a reasonable life or not and could result in a recommendation for euthanasia, even after going through surgery.

Her pelvis was also fractured into more than twenty pieces – exploded by the multiple impacts she sustained – and her left hind leg was badly fractured with significant nerve and muscle damage. Clearly there was an ethical dilemma whether or not to proceed with surgery at all. I am quite sure that when I graduated as a vet, in 1990, I would have said, 'I'm sorry, there is nothing I can do,' and that would have been the literal truth. But this was 2021. Now there were many things we *could* do, but it was a question of whether those procedures were ethically justified given the seriousness of the injuries. We had to factor in not just potential quantity of life but also quality of life.

This is now a real challenge in veterinary medicine. Just because something is possible to do, doesn't make it the right thing to do. No boastfulness intended, I can now mend the vast majority of skeletal trauma, just like surgeons can in human orthopaedics, as long as we have a nerve and blood supply. Even so, it may be entirely correct to say, 'I'm sorry, I think the kindest thing is to put Stevie to sleep.' Even this last statement needs to be qualified by 'in my opinion', since a different surgeon might have a different view. Herein lies one of the many dilemmas for my governing body, the RCVS. They have to police what is and is not considered ethical, but at the same time they have to embrace advancement in the care level afforded to companion animals in the United Kingdom – a difficult tightrope to tread. Conversely for my human surgeon counterparts, human life is sacred and must be preserved at all costs. Though there are certain circumstances in which the decision is made to stop life-sustaining treatment, we certainly don't euthanise humans for severe trauma, but rather we try our best to preserve limb and life. Of course, ethical challenges are also present in human surgery, for instance where severe vascular and nerve trauma or infection prompt consideration of limb amputation, and so the patient's consent is always sought where possible, with the risks laid out to the best of the surgeon's knowledge.

It is said that we must not anthropomorphise our animal companions. Even now among veterinary surgeons, most consider that an animal is an animal and a human is a human, with different inherent rights. And there are different regulations that govern animal and human medical care, with a finite end point of euthanasia being legally considered a 'treatment' even now in veterinary medicine.

I would be completely ridiculed if I said to any group of veterinary surgeons that I felt that dogs and cats should have the same rights as humans (and I can only imagine how my dear deceased father, with his farming experience, would react to such a suggestion). But I do wonder why we consider ourselves to be a more deserving species, when many of us personally experience the compassionate, unconditional love for our companion animals. Do we really *not* want to have a level of care for them that is comparable to our own?

The clients of vets are paying for this treatment, so should they not have some say in the quality of the product? Given a choice, if a vet were paying, would they opt for mediocre or optimal care? That's a real choice and it does need to be made. Those corporate entities now directing the finances of more than 60 per cent of all primary care veterinary practices in the UK and more than 90 per cent of all referral practices would likely be happy to support any treatment that made adequate profit for their shareholders. So, is it profit-making that will determine the ceiling of care we will offer, or is it some ethical 'boundary' as determined by the loudest voices in the veterinary community? Or is it the views of the people who love the animals and pay the bills?

I could have become a human surgeon. I didn't. I am passionate about providing companion animals a comparable level of medical care to that I expect for myself. It surprises me that some veterinary surgeons are not more passionate about advancing animal care, and are content to work within a system that upholds the status quo, which in reality means suboptimal care: cheaper, less effective drugs, less refined surgical techniques and implants, poorer quality aftercare. Ask a vet why they got into the profession, and a common answer is that they 'love animals'. Therefore, many must be conflicted when they utter the words, 'There is nothing that can be done', because whilst this may be true in the immediate sense, with the resources at their disposal, possibilities *could* exist with a shift of perspective and priorities or with a more open referral environment and more open mindsets. Maybe, though, some vets are conditioned to think that humans are due a level of care that animals are not. If so, I often wonder why some vets didn't become human doctors. They would have had the grades and could have made the choice. I wonder why vets seem happy to be ambassadors for a medical profession considered inferior to human clinicians when it is animals that provide most of the solutions for the medical challenges of human patients? Why are all vets not passionately standing up for the rights of all animals to a fair deal, I wonder? As my countryman Gary Lightbody sings with his band Snow Patrol, maybe we should 'forget what we're told, before we get too old'.

Euthanasia is still a taboo subject for most human societies, but in animal care it's a line that each veterinarian draws for themselves in the sand. I respect that, and appreciate that when most vets recommend euthanasia it's because an animal is suffering without reasonable hope of redemption in a reasonable time frame. However, many of the techniques and procedures we perform at Fitzpatrick Referrals have moved the dial somewhat regarding what is possible. I wish they could see what we are doing day to day with the best intentions and integrity, and how devastated we are when infection or mechanical failure foils our earnest efforts. I am well aware that I am polarising and some of my contemporaries believe that I over-treat animals because they think that I want to show off on television. I am passionate about changing this perspective for the good of the animals. One day I will die, and I feel it's a shame if more patients of future veterinarians die than need to because others in my profession do not open their minds. I wish the people who dislike me could simply see that it's not about me, as I've said before – or indeed them – it's about the animals who are suffering, when we should be providing solutions in my opinion.

I accept that I have greater means and resources at my practice than many other surgeons, but I would ask them not to dismiss or prejudice my efforts because of that. I am able to draw my line differently not because I care about my patients more or less, but because I know what is possible through experience and I have forced solutions into existence through rigorous evaluation of ethics and efficacy for every technique we employ and investing heavily in solutions where we are falling short. I am able to see hope in cases others might view as hopeless. As we'll see later, I know that my TV show may focus on the most dramatic narratives or high-tech solutions, but this neglects to show the hard years of slow incremental progress over which the medical techniques or implants were developed – or the many times I recommend some medication, amputation or euthanasia when anything else is not in the patient's interest. Such cases often do not create enough narrative journey to warrant inclusion in the TV show. I believe that in the scientific papers and lectures I have authored and presented, in the day-to-day operation of what we do, there is much that anyone interested in caring for animals can learn from if they choose to do so. Some vets simply do not believe that there may be something that can be done which might be superior to what they can offer and is still in the ethical best interest of the patient, in spite of me showing such techniques on the TV show. In fact, families come to me all the time, having seen a particular treatment on the TV show, which they have been told by my own profession is not possible, available or 'the right thing to do'.

Many clients are simply not aware that certain care options exist. In the moment of desperation and confusion, one trusts one's vet to make an appropriate recommendation on the 'best' course of action. In such circumstances, I have found that there are various misleading and perpetuated perceptions regarding Fitzpatrick Referrals, such as that it's impossible to get to see my team, that we are too expensive, too far away or only see complex cases. Our pricing is the same as any other referral hospital that we have compared with and we welcome both emergencies and routine surgeries. In my personal experience, the TV show has been a double-edged sword. On one hand it allows people to see what is possible and on the other, many practices decline to recommend our services and may infer that Fitzpatrick Referrals is a TV show practice rather than a day-in, day-out dedicated team of fantastically talented clinicians and nurses who offer all of the options all of the time to everybody. I question whether absence of free choice is in the patient's best interest? It's true to say that passion is not always appreciated.

Thankfully, Stevie's primary care vet was very open-minded and gave his daddy, Ben, all the options. Ben had no idea of the lengths we could go to in order to save the life of a dog. And even his ex-partner Owen, a consultant in human cancer treatment and the oncology lead at a prestigious hospital in London was, by his own admission, completely unaware of the level of specialisms within veterinary medicine that would be needed in helping Stevie, including me and my colleague, Joana. Such is the disconnect between human and animal medicine, that even well-meaning, hugely compassionate people like Owen rarely consider the potential intersection of animal and human medicine, even though animal experimentation (in many cases, using dogs) provided the oncology field with their medicines and his surgical colleagues with all of their implants. Why would he? Human medical practitioners are not required to study animal medicine and surgery in their specialist examinations. Whereas for my specialist exams I was absolutely expected to have a working understanding of all current knowledge and best practice in human surgery. Within human medicine, multidisciplinary teams are the usual practice when caring for a cancer patient or any patient, which affords superior care through combined knowledge and experience. Why would it not be the same for surgery in companion animals?

Joana and I fixed Stevie's sacrum as best we could, pulling the shattered pieces together and stabilising them with pins and cement. But we still had no way of knowing if Stevie would ever urinate, defecate or walk again due to nerve damage. I have often thought that moving the tiny, delicate nerves at the end of the spinal cord (the cauda equina) is the closest I ever came to being a guitarist. One doesn't pluck these nerves, but when one is operating, one does manipulate and move them and they do look very much like strings over the frets of the neck of a guitar as they course over the lumbosacral disc and the three vertebrae forming the sacrum. I have been doggedly passionate about trying to become the best surgeon I can be and fixing this particular anatomical region is an area in which I have developed specific expertise.

After the surgery, I had to sit Ben and Owen down and have a very serious conversation with them. We didn't know whether Stevie would have any quality of life, and we still had to repair all of the other fractures of her pelvis and leg. They had a massive dilemma, one I've seen many times in my consulting room. They were head over heels in love with Stevie, but they didn't want to act selfishly in trying to keep her alive if she might suffer unnecessarily. Equally, they didn't want to feel that they had given up on their best friend and family member prematurely. What I always try to do in the face of such difficult choices is compartmentalise the decision-making into bite-sized chunks and set goals for each stage of treatment. If we don't reach a satisfactory point at a given stage, we should consider euthanasia. Any effort to repair Stevie's fractures would be complex and demanding, and the healing process prolonged.

Owen told me later that he had many sleepless nights thinking about this, and even with the well-honed mind of a specialist human clinician, he struggled. He thought in the end about paediatric human medicine, where young children, like a dog or a cat, cannot make an informed decision about treatment escalation or choices. Trying to act in the best interest of the child is paramount, with discussion and consent of the parents. He wondered whether Stevie's life might be equivalent to that of a child, and if not, what was it that made it different? He reasoned that she was 'a being' with cognition, personality, moods and thoughts, and came to the conclusion that in his mind there was fundamentally no difference. To Owen and Ben, Stevie was, to all intents and purposes, a child in their family.

Many people who come to see me feel exactly like this, and I am always wary of anthropomorphising, shying away from terms like 'fur babies' for that very reason. I have steadfastly not called animals 'children' in my TV show, because I do believe that there is a difference. I grew up on a farm, where a functional attitude to animals was the order of the day. However, emotionally, and from a spiritual perspective, I am 'all in' with the concept of a companion animal being an integral family member, deserving of levels of care and responsibility afforded to human family members.

Owen and I also had important conversations about funding and it was abundantly clear to him and to me how much people take the extreme level of passionate care afforded to NHS patients for granted. When it comes to the care of our animal companions, every aspect of treatment – drugs, implants, disposables like syringes and drapes, surgery or rehabilitation care – is itemised, and it becomes rapidly apparent how expensive a case such as Stevie's actually is. We would all have to compromise practically and financially to get her through, and the ability to do this is one of the many reasons my practice remains staunchly independent.

Stevie had been with Ben every single day working from home through the coronavirus lockdown, as Owen had been out at work in the hospital, battling with the horrendous consequences that the virus was having on his team's ability to treat patients with cancer. Stevie had been a single puppy and had only just survived at birth. She was extremely loving, very independent and infuriatingly stubborn at times. Having her asleep on a cushion on his lap gently snoring for the endless days of lockdown gave Ben great comfort and he couldn't imagine life without her. Owen felt exactly the same and yet they both didn't know whether they should put her through more very major surgery because of the passion of their love for her, or whether they should just acquiesce to circumstance and allow her to pass away peacefully.

As I thought about Owen's understandable lack of knowledge that Stevie could have the same care afforded to a human patient in his own hospital, I remembered giving a lecture to a group of human orthopaedic surgeons at a distinguished London hospital on the subject of trauma management in dogs and cats, including the use of the external skeletal fixation technique I was proposing for Stevie, only to hear comments from one of the registrars afterwards, wondering what the point of such involved procedures was, given that the patient was 'only a dog' and could be put to sleep. In fact, he was missing my point entirely, or failing to see it with compassion.

Veterinary and human medicine absolutely *have* to change. In my opinion it is not until the divide between human and animal patients disappears and both simply become recognised as sentient beings who happen to be 'patients' that we will ever make real progress. As Owen said to me, 'This is actually "just medicine", irrespective of what life it's being acted upon.' I am a pragmatist with regards to moving medicine forward and though there is zero point in being an extremist or an absolute idealist, it's worth pointing out that many of the challenges arise because of money, which is necessary for all drug and implant development. One needs to show drug and implant companies that they can make the same money for their shareholders by doing things better with joined-up thinking in animal and human medicine. Few would argue against decreasing the overuse of antibiotics in animals which can jeopardise human healthcare by propagating bacterial resistance, and many would be interested in cross-pollination research to decrease the number of animals killed in research and promote human well-being in a more expeditious way if one could make this new paradigm profitable.

We could have safe drugs and implants for our children and make enough money in a kinder system if we got passionate about it. One has to try to change the system from within and work with, rather than against, the people in the systems. I am minded of the lyrics of a Biffy Clyro song, 'Victory over the Sun' – 'We can change the world despite all our enemies' – but I would add that change is likely easier to achieve if you show your perceived enemies that you are actually their friend and encourage them to maybe meet you halfway. That's why I founded the Humanimal Trust charity, as a platform to give animals a fair deal and bridge the divide between human and animal medicine. We live on 'one' planet with ever-dwindling resources, where we have a moral obligation to think about the effect of what we are doing on the children and the animals of the future, and in my view there should be 'One Medicine'. The Humanimal Trust raises money to educate, share ideas and investigate diseases that affect both humankind and animals. We aim to fund research in infection and antibiotic resistance, stem cells and regenerative medicine, cancer, diseases of bone and joints and also diseases of the brain and spine. In all of these areas, significant progress could be made through collaboration. We now have many non-invasive tools to study naturally occurring disease and it's recognised that such study can be a superior model to artificially induced disease, where we induce disease in a lab animal and then kill them. There are a number of legal and regulatory challenges with this approach, but I believe these would not be insurmountable if a passionate critical mass of people wanted this change to happen. I believe that we're all on the same side, wanting better care for patients, we just need to find a way to compromise so that everything is better for everyone.

I see the results of these problems every single week of my life when I cut out primary bone tumours, most commonly osteosarcoma, and replace the tumour, which is often about to fracture the bone, with a large metal implant called an endoprosthesis. I have invented endoprostheses for replacement of bone cancer of the pelvis, knee, shoulder, wrist (carpus) and ankle (tibio-tarsal) joints, and these can restore dogs to full or near-full motion. However, the median survival time for each of these dogs affected by this cancer, from the time they are presented to me, is about eleven months – and that's even with four or five sessions of chemotherapy. Simply put, this is just not good enough. The chemotherapy drug we use for dogs has been in use for three decades, in which time human chemotherapy medicine has been transformed. We could have a much better drug to treat these cancers in dogs if we took a joined-up approach to developing new drugs for humans and animals in tandem by carefully studying naturally acquired cancers in dogs that really need help, rather than injecting cancer into dogs that are normal and then killing them just for our benefit.

While Stevie was in wards at Fitzpatrick Referrals, I was also treating a seventy-kilo, eight-year-old Russian black terrier called Dimitri. I had to tell his human guardian Susan that though I could remove the osteosarcoma from his forearm with relative ease and replace it with an endoprosthesis implant, I was limited in what I could do to prevent the cancer spreading to Dimitri's lungs or elsewhere, which would ultimately kill him, most likely in under a year. Dimitri had sat or slept by the bed of Patrick, Susan's husband, throughout his own terminal cancer, placing his head or paw on Patrick's arm to comfort him. Since Patrick's passing, Dimitri had been her only companion. Some days, her only reason to want to get out of bed in the morning was to take him for a walk. When she was sad, Dimitri snuggled his big furry black head into her chest to comfort her too. As I write this, Dimitri has been running around happily more than a year, but sadly by the time of publication of this book, he may be dead. I wish I could give Dimitri and Susan longer together and I also mourn the thousands of animals and humans who could have lived longer, if human and veterinary medicine had worked together. That they don't – that 'One Medicine' does not widely exist – is down to our blindness, our biases and our vested interests. The central passion of my life is to try to make medicine better and fairer for all of us, animal and human.

Being fair to Stevie and giving her the best chance was also foremost in their minds when Ben and Owen kissed her goodbye for a second time, not knowing whether they would ever see her again, as I set up for the complicated procedure to fix all of her pelvic and femoral fractures. The method I would use was in fact developed first in animals, for human benefit, as I had explained to my human surgical colleagues when I shared my lecture with them. Rather than dissecting off all of the traumatised muscle to fix plates and screws to the bone, it involves making smaller incisions and fixing the fractures using pins as anchors in the fragments which are realigned and locked together using clamps and rods on the outside of the body. External fixation is still used in humans as a temporary stabilisation method after someone crashes their motorbike, for instance, and crushes their pelvis.

I have lectured many times on this technique in veterinary orthopaedics, but very few if any specialists apart from me employ the technique, as it largely disappeared from veterinary literature in the 1970s. Yet I have performed it successfully on several hundred dogs and cats. As is by now self-evident, both veterinary and human medicine are somewhat 'set in their ways'. It took me about five hours to fix Stevie's multiple pelvic and femoral fractures and by the end the poor little girl had a massive contraption of rods and clamps over her pelvis. But she recovered well from the anaesthetic and was immensely patient. She needed to be, because the frame holding everything together needed to remain in place for several weeks.

A few days after Stevie's surgery I did not know if she would regain significant mobility or toileting function. There was a chance that everything we had done was in vain and I would end up putting her to sleep anyway. Owen and Ben could barely get through the days and I was struggling myself, laden down with life's problems as I curled up for a few moments with Stevie in the wards when she was waking up, comforting her, but finding no comfort myself. I was experiencing significant management and personnel challenges at the practice, in addition to personal problems. On top of this, a complaint had landed that same day regarding a case I had operated on four years earlier. The patient was now dead, but the family were alleging negligence because the implant system of a commercial manufacturer which I had implanted had failed. Sometimes people do lash out, conflicted by grief, pain and anger that a procedure hasn't been as successful as we all hoped. I take little joy in successfully defending such complaints – time fighting these cases is time I could be spending saving lives. To this day nobody has ever 'won', and I don't expect anyone ever will, because as in this case, I had done my utmost for the patient and the family, as I always do. I'm not a miracle worker, and failures can occur in spite of my best and legitimate efforts.

To escape my own mind I attended a mindfulness evening held by a couple of friends of mine in a church. I was desperately seeking something outside of the emotional turbulence and sometimes overwhelming stress that comes with the territory of my life's passion, perhaps seeking the more spiritual path of a universal passion within. I absolutely know that each and every one of us is connected through love to what's really important in life. I call it the 'universal string of oneness'. At that time, I felt a profound need to reconnect with some kind of love for myself within myself, some kind of peace in the storm of feeling helpless in spite of my passion, some food for the soul so that I could keep going.

By the time I got to the church I was out of my mind with stress and the endless traffic, and was as far from being 'mindful' as one could ever be. The journey did, however, afford me a trip down memory lane, as I passed by the first and second practices where I worked as a vet in the UK in the early nineties. I spotted the village hall where my then boss bopped to 'I'm Too Sexy' by Right Said Fred at a Christmas party, a pub where I asked a girl out and was rejected, and then a stables where I had attended my first horse call-out in the UK and where I was propositioned by a lady whom I politely declined. She didn't get the message, because the following week, on my return, she undressed spontaneously in the stable box. On reflection, the drive had been good for me in reminding me where I had come from and where I hoped I was going to – and what I did and did not want along the way!

Upon arrival, just in time, I ran over a bridge which had been there for hundreds of years, the wind tugging on my coat, to the welcome vestibule of a church that had been there even longer. I crept into a pew but was soon invited to come up to the microphone to share anything I could about mindfulness. I did so, struggling to make sense of the many colliding thoughts in my head. So, I spoke from the heart. I asked the assembled congregation to close their eyes and imagine that they could not see, hear or smell, sensing the world only through the fingers of their hands which I asked them to place on their knees as they sat. Then I asked them to imagine a long-haired dachshund puppy called Stevie. I asked them to feel her breathing and her heartbeat in the silence and then take a leap of faith with me and imagine drilling into her spinal canal, and feeling the guitar strings of her nerves, feeling carefully the difference in sensation between skin, muscle, sinew, bone and nerve.

Thus, I took my audience to what I told them was 'Stevie's space'.

When I operate, I enter a place where every other thought is banished. I am totally and absolutely present. With our eyes closed, I explained to those people in the church how we completed the surgery, talking through each detail, inviting them deeper into my world, to bring their compassion into

Stevie's precarious existence and in symphony with biology, to be mindful of the fragility and preciousness of their own lives in the absolute 'presence' of that moment. I asked them to be grateful for life and love in their own lives and explained quietly that I didn't know if Stevie would ever walk again. Then I asked them to focus all of their passion in the silence of their minds on Stevie's space for a few moments, willing her to get well again. The vicar told me in the days that followed that many people were enquiring about Stevie's well-being, and I truly believe that their spiritual attention, bringing their passion to a single cause, actually did help to change my little corner of the world in that moment. A few days later, Stevie began to stand up and soon after that she could poo and wee voluntarily. I had found the peace I had come looking for and the redemption I yearned for Stevie. The universal string of oneness had linked the random dots of life and made everything okay in the end.

It wasn't all plain sailing though. Stevie suffered an infection which spread to her leg and though we used specific antibiotics based on laboratory culture, I ultimately amputated her limb due to infection and irreversible nerve and muscle damage. Her prognosis remained guarded. Most antibiotics were developed in animals for human use and interestingly due to problems with bacterial resistance, some are necessarily restricted for use in human patients, with their use discouraged in animals, even when the bacterium may be resistant to all other antibiotics. The irony is that the life of dogs like Stevie could be lost even though we have the drugs to treat them, which dogs and other animals helped give to humans in the first place, because the life of a dog is deemed intrinsically less valuable than that of a human for all the obvious reasons. The RCVS code of professional conduct states that 'Veterinary surgeons must be seen to ensure that when using antimicrobials they do so responsibly, and be accountable for the choices made in such use.' This is one of the many areas of medicine that could be improved for both humans and animals if doctors and vets worked together.

It is also very important to me to explain that the concept of One Medicine is very different to One Health. One Health is a good initiative that asks humanity to look at the well-being of global ecosystems of man and animal. It embraces habitat conservation alongside agricultural pursuits as well as huge issues like antibiotic overuse in meat-providing animals which contributes to pervasive antibiotic resistance in humans. However, almost all of the time, though One Health initiatives do study animals and humans, they are set up primarily to benefit humans, whereas One Medicine resolutely helps animals and humans *equally* – everyone wins in a passionately compassionate world if we choose to build it. But sometimes, as I've learnt to my cost, passion alone just isn't enough.

My heart was in my mouth as I held the phone to my ear and listened to the ringtone at the other end. It had been almost exactly fifteen years since I'd last spoken to Mike – would he even remember me? A woman answered – his wife, Angie. 'It's Noel, the vet,' I explained.

I first met Mike with his Labrador, Petra, in 1999 in a primary care practice where I was operating in a wooden hut beside a dwelling house in a small village called Ewhurst in Surrey. My boss at the time had been very kind and supportive, and I had started to take referral surgeries in orthopaedics with the certificate-level non-specialist qualifications I had at the time, alongside my continued work as a general primary care vet. I drilled bones with a Makita DIY drill and performed spinal surgery with a Dremel wood drill wrapped in sterile coverings. Back then, I was still performing Caesarean sections on cows and dogs, delivering piglets and lambs, looking at lame horses, mending the broken bones of a hamster, removing a tumour from the head of a Koi carp or from the dewlap of a male lizard. I had unbridled passion for every new experience and I was single-mindedly passionate about making veterinary medicine better for the animals, who continued to be my best friends.

Mike, who lived locally, came in with one of his dogs from time to time and we chatted as I vaccinated one or other of them or dispensed medication for stiff joints. I shall never forget the first time I met him. He is tall, but to me he was a 'giant' in every sense of the word – one of my all-time musical heroes. Mike Rutherford founded Genesis in 1967, the year I was born. Whilst my guitar playing had begun and ended with twine on a fertiliser-sack-wrapped bale of hay, he played a double-necked guitar – a Shergold Modulator twin-neck in the 1970s and then his legendary Rickenbacker double neck, which had begun as two guitars duct-taped together. I was quaking in awe and trying desperately to hide my reverence.

Mike was gentle, kind, softly spoken and a true gentleman. I was a relatively young man with unbridled passion for my dreams – dreams I shared with him as we chatted. He listened patiently to my stream-of-consciousness ideas about building the greatest orthopaedics and neurosurgery veterinary referral practice in the UK, and then a soft tissue and oncology centre. After that, the possibility of a musical concert to celebrate and promote medicine that helps both animals and humans (back then the concept of 'One Medicine' wasn't a tangible entity). As he was leaving, I plucked up all my courage and rather naively asked if such a concert was something he might help me with, when the time came. His answer was a simple 'sure'. God bless him – Mike, one of the nicest men you could ever meet. I can still see his benevolent smile as he crossed the lawn outside the window to his car, undoubtedly prompted by the eternally optimistic folly of passionate youth. I consoled myself that he would likely have understood because, after all, he had a hand in writing the 'Land of Confusion' Genesis song, and that definitely reflected what I felt about the world.

It would take fifteen years, but I did deliver on all three goals, although I borrowed many millions to do so. At the time the oncology hospital was due to open, after a three-year phase of preparation, I set up VETFest to promote physical, mental and academic wellness for vets, as I mentioned earlier. I also created a concert that would close VETFest, called 'One Live', in honour of all animals and humans being 'one' in medicine and living on 'one' planet together. And so, one Sunday night in September 2014, a not-so-young but still evidently naive me telephoned the house of a rock god, asking for a favour. I was dreading what he might say. I absolutely hate asking people for anything, but I was about to ask him if he would headline my very first music festival for One Medicine. Mike's words still echo in my head when I'm having a bad day, reminding me that there are still beautiful souls in the world: 'Oh, hello, Noel, I've been expecting your call.'

Miraculously, not only did he remember our conversation

fifteen years before – but he said yes! I set up a media company and designed a 'flower power' logo with the message
'One Planet One Love One Medicine'. The wheels were in
motion for the very first One Live music festival in summer
2015. If somehow I could translate what I saw every day
as unconditional love in my consulting room into a music
festival where like-minded people could come together, then
I just might be able to spread love and hope across the world
I thought. I wanted to build a community of compassion
through my two passions and their shared ability to elevate
the soul – medicine and music. My plan was that any money
that we would make from the concert would fund the Humanimal Trust charity. Ultimately, I had my favourite music
festival, Glastonbury, in my head, but I wanted something a
little different – 'Pets, Hugs and Rock 'n' Roll!'

It was really important to me that Mammy could attend
what I knew would be her first and last ever proper festival.
She was becoming frailer than ever in her wheelchair. If I
could pull it off, I knew it would likely be her final trip from
Ireland to the UK as well. She subsequently referred to this
time as 'the most exciting week of her life'. She had a car
driven by a chauffeur 'with an actual peaked cap', as she
later regaled anyone who would listen. She was all glammed
up in a beautiful hat for the opening of the hospital, and
only a couple of days later she was being escorted as one of
the two guests of honour to the very first One Live music
festival. The other guest of honour was Minnie, my 'mammy
in the UK'. Minnie was the mother of my friend Chris Evans
and she was extremely kind to me. We had many chats down
through the years, and she's given me lots of sage advice on
life, girls and money, among other things. She was a great

character and, like my own mother, she always had a laugh and a cup of tea for everyone. Needless to say, she and my Mammy got on really well.

With their bodyguard and chauffeur ushering them regally into the grounds of the One Live festival, they were like two schoolgirls full of excitement. A man called Kev was playing a guitar on the footpath near the entrance to the festival ground and they assumed he was one of the acts, so invited him along with them into the festival compound. He was only too willing, because in fact he was a busker hoping to listen to Mike + The Mechanics from outside the fence. By the time I found them, they were stage-side in their special VIP enclosure singing whilst Kev played the guitar. Mammy proudly exclaimed, 'We have formed a band.' I hired Kev to busk at DogFest and VETFest a few times thereafter. He is a truly lovely man.

Ultimately Rita and Minnie became the beneficiaries of the light and passion they themselves put out into the world. And this was to repeat itself one last time before Minnie died. I visited her regularly in the final months in hospital and at home. Like my own Mammy, she wanted to die in her own house because the hospital was 'full of people complaining'. A few months before Minnie's passing, I rang Kev and asked him if he would come for a little musical reunion. I'd bought identical jelly sweets that I knew both Minnie and Rita loved. I sent one pack to Ballyfin, Laois, in the Republic of Ireland and the other came with me to Cranleigh in Surrey. What I didn't realise was that Kev stayed up late for several nights practising all the requested songs on his guitar and then drove several hours from where he lived to get to Minnie's living room, where he sat on the sofa and played while Rita

102

and Minnie enjoyed an epic band reunion as they fed each other identical coloured jellies on FaceTime, and sang along to their personal playlist.

Kev didn't want to accept any payment and though he had nothing, like my mother used to say, 'he gave me half of it', by gifting me his guitar to remember the evening. He said he had another, but I knew he treasured this one and I treasure it too and will one day learn to play it properly. I forced a few quid on him to help him out, as he said over and over how much of a privilege it had been to meet Rita and Minnie.

Not long afterwards, I had the sad privilege of helping to wrap Minnie's body as she left this world. I delivered Minnie's eulogy and I closed with an Emily Dickinson poem. 'Hope is the thing with feathers, that perches in the soul . . . and . . . never in extremity, it asked a crumb of me.' This refrain has echoed loudly in my mind as my dreams haven't quite gone according to plan. Hope doesn't ask anything from us, it just gives to us if we keep it alive with passion. Even in the midst of failure and adversity, I know that there's opportunity for growth. 'Change is the only constant,' according to the Greek philosopher Heraclitus – and of course it's up to me and to all of us whether we keep our passion alive and grow with hope or wither with despair when change is foisted upon us. As both Mammy and Minnie were wont to say, 'What's meant for ya, won't pass ya by.'

Mike + The Mechanics gave their time and musical munificence free of charge for the very first One Live music festival. They're all really wonderful musicians and fantastic human beings. I paid only the set-up and tech support. It was a proper festival set-up though, and having never attempted such a thing before, I had absolutely no idea how expensive infrastructure could be. From toilets to security, stage rigging to lighting, sound system to tech support, the costs racked up. And bands need to make a living, so all other bands on the bill were paid their fee. I made a loss, but remained passionate about the cause. As Mike says in his song 'The Living Years', 'don't give up, and don't give in . . . [and] you may just be okay'.

I persisted in the belief that I could just work hard and make the money back somehow, because it was a major life purpose for me to make One Medicine a legitimate and respected currency to give animals a fair deal. However, business, and especially the medicine and music businesses, don't work like that, as I rapidly and painfully learned. I lost a pile of my own money again the following year with One Live. And still, I refused to give up, because there were truly glorious, surreal and beautiful moments like when Mark Owen from Take That stood up and read out a letter from his dog to the audience. One could have heard a pin drop in a field of several thousand people. In that moment, as everyone sang along with Mark singing a cappella a stunning version of Take That's hit 'Shine', the world was just perfect and everything I wanted it to be. I was on stage in my support cast after my ankle injury but I could not have been happier . . . until the bills came in.

I thought I'd give it one more go in 2017. I really felt that the event had great potential. The losses of my own money hadn't bothered me as much as the failure of the event to stand on its own two feet and make some money for the charity. What I have since learned of course is that almost nobody puts their own money into big events and certainly not for charity – and almost nobody organises it without access to a

104

massive infrastructure, including marketing and sponsorship deals. I was driven by passion alone, and that wasn't enough. Yes, I know I am hopelessly naive! By June 2017 it was apparent that we wouldn't sell enough tickets for the event, and we had to cancel a few weeks out. I lost hundreds of thousands of pounds, and was distraught. The headline act of the last One Live had been supposed to be The Boomtown Rats, but I had to tell Bob Geldof, whom I'd never met, that the event couldn't go ahead. He replied with a short text that read *'Dnt wry abt it N. Hpns all the time. RocknRoll is a tough game! BG.'* Oh, how right he is.

All I've ever wanted is to change the world for the better. But sometimes passion alone just isn't enough. I have learned the hard way that you can have an ardent passion for many things, but you cannot be master of all of them, and that you might lose a great deal along the way unless you seek guidance and admit that you can't know it all, no matter how passionate you are about something. Now I firmly believe that all passion benefits from a healthy dose of realism – preferably before you lose both your wallet and your mind. I believed passionately in One Live, but stupidly invested my own money without appropriate commercial partners and I felt the full force of how potential is born in dreams, fuelled by passion and realised in effort, but success only comes with a generous sprinkling of good fortune, and the blessing of good guidance.

I have learned in recent years what I'm good at and what I'm not and how to better focus my passion. I didn't get to learn guitar but I did learn how to do a pretty good job with a scalpel blade. Yet, even in my field of ortho-neuro surgery, the severity of injuries, vagaries of biology and potential complications may stymie even the most ardent passion to save limb and life.

Thankfully, in the end, Stevie's passion for life and the passion of more than forty nurses, ward and theatre auxiliaries who looked after her and loved her was duly rewarded. She now runs around as boisterous and joyous as ever on her fixed sacrum and pelvis, peeing and pooing as normal, albeit with only one hind leg. Ben and Owen have difficulty keeping up with her and she's even more snuggly than ever before, passionately gulping down every moment of every day.

I met her recently for a check-up and she gave me one of her inimitable snuggles and face licks. It remains awe-inspiring for me how the universal string of oneness ties us all together in love and in medicine – how the passion of everyone who has cared so deeply about her actually did save her life. That same day, Dimitri was having another cycle of chemotherapy and Susan and I once again chatted, as we did every time we saw each other, about how it was such a shame that human and veterinary medicine do not work more closely together – for the sake of patients like Dimitri and Patrick too. We both yearned for Dimitri to live longer with Susan, and we both wished we had better therapies to stop the spread of her cancer cells. I do not believe we will anytime soon though, unless human and animal medicine allow the universal string of oneness also to tie them more closely together in their efforts for all patients.

That same week, I was treating an identical tumour in the leg of a 92kg mastiff called Frieda. Her dad, Adam, had driven nine hours from Scotland to Surrey, since he had been told, like many are, that limb salvage for her forearm cancer wasn't possible. She was in awful pain. I cut out the cancer, popped in a radius-ulna endoprosthesis, and within five days she was walking well without pain. It was possible. A photographer called Dave Hogan was with me that day, taking pictures of my work. Dave had been an official photographer for Live Aid, the concert organised by Bob Geldof in 1985. Bob saw that thirty million people were starving in Africa and people said it wasn't possible to make a major difference. It was. I had hoped with One Live that somehow a few molecules of the spirit of Live Aid might drop like stardust on all of us to build a lasting 'concert of caring' for the greater good of both man and animal. Alas, that wasn't to be. There just wasn't enough fizz in the bottle, as it were, and not enough people wanted to drink that particular bottle of medicine in my field.

But maybe people just didn't understand how important One Medicine is or how it really could make life so much better for all of us.

As the central passion of my life is to give animals a fair deal through medical advance, improvements in welfare and greater respect for conservation of species, all of my efforts and failures so far have led me to visualise that all of our thoughts are just fluid in the bottles of our brains. Fluids can flow and change over time, and in my imagination, our passions are 'the fizz' in our fluid – the things we pursue in life for better or worse. Sometimes our fizz can be chaotic, making us confused, unfocused and unproductive, and sometimes we have fizzled out, our thoughts as stagnant as used dishwater, leaving us directionless and apathetic. I often see people behave like shaken bottles, their passions fizzing and liable to blow off a lid, spraying everywhere, expending energy on meaningless things, looking for attention, getting nowhere and contributing to nothing – a short burst that can leave a mess in their wake, in their own lives and those of people close to them. And I see others who just let life suck the fizz out of them. I am learning to quell my erratic bubbles and harness the useful fizz, for release when the time is right. This has helped me not to lose direction or feel out of control and actually to become a calmer and better person I think. The most important thing I have learned about passion is that I have fizzed all over the place sometimes and achieved exactly nothing. So am determined henceforth to save my bubbles for release when the time and circumstances are right. The fluid in all of our bottles won't last forever, so what we spend our time thinking about or getting passionate about really does matter.

When everyone's bubbles of passion were aligned for a few moments in the meditation of 'Stevie's space' of unconditional love or when everyone's fizz settled for a moment and Mark Owen sang a song at One Live, the fluid of the conscious mind of everyone present calmed down and the fizz of everyone's bubbles reverberated in harmony. We were together on some kind of higher plane, where a common passionate connection sublimated all the trials and tribulations of our day-to-day existence. That's what love in both medicine and in music can do. Wouldn't it be really great if the bubbles of passion and love deep inside the fluid which makes up each and every one of us could fizz in harmony more often, linked by our universal string of oneness? I am 100 per cent sure that this could not only make medicine better for all living beings, but it would actually change the world. Wouldn't we all like a more passionate, compassionate world?

CHAPTER 5

Thankfulness

I didn't get home in time.

My sister Frances had called me during the night to say Mammy was 'slipping'. The first flight I could catch from London to Dublin was 6.35 a.m., so I spoke to her by video call. I hope that she heard me as Frances held the phone up for her. She was unable to speak, but I told her how much I loved her and thanked her for bringing me into the world. Her eyes were open, though apparently closed soon after. I managed to hold back my tears. Nobody thought she would slip so fast, and she died around one in the morning. I was the last person she opened her eyes for. I was blessed and will be forever thankful.

Frances's husband, Liam, had stayed with her in the house in which I grew up while my brother John picked me up from Dublin airport. The journey home took just over an hour. John and Liam retreated to have a cup of tea in the kitchen, so it was just me and my mammy in the bedroom. When I picked up her hand it was cold. When I kissed her forehead, her beautiful grey hair was still. I knelt by her bed and I whispered, 'I love you so much,' in her ear. My mammy was gone. I cried.

It wasn't a bad death, they told me. A gentle passing into the light, just as she had prayed for. A few short sighs and she let go, Frances and John by her side. I was so glad that I had spoken with her only two days before and got to tell her how grateful I was for her encouragement down through the years and for holding my hand. I wish I could have held her hand too in the end but maybe I wasn't supposed to hear her last breath, rather to hold her in my head and heart eternally vibrant.

For most of the years of my secondary schooling, it was just her and me, and her mother, Granny Annie. My immediately younger sister Josephine and older sister Grace were in boarding school. My older sisters Frances and Mary were mostly away. My older brother John was in England and Daddy was always working. Each day I'd come home from the misery that was school, say the rosary with Mammy and Granny, then do my chores, getting in turf for the fire, feed a lamb or two, or bed a shed with straw for the cattle, before locking myself away to study and write until the early hours, occasionally popping out to Mammy to ask her to help me with a big word for an essay. She always did, although she often professed her worry that I would kill myself over-studying, becoming so exasperated that she once threatened, 'I'll burn those bloody books if you don't go to bed.' She didn't mean it. She was my biggest supporter. Without her I wouldn't be a vet and without her I would not be alive today. She allowed me to dream that anything was possible and she taught me to be thankful for absolutely everything. Daddy did his best but he was always grafting on the farm. I inherited workaholism from him and gratitude from her.

My mammy was the most humble and thankful person I have ever met, and I am so grateful for her light. Throughout my entire life, whatever crisis befell me, or whatever situation I found myself in, hers was always a voice of calm, reason, encouragement, hope and eternal faith, on the end of a phone. I didn't call often enough. Nobody ever does, I suppose. She was my one constant safety net and comfort blanket.

It was dark in the room where she lay. I didn't want her to be in the dark, so I drew back the curtains a bit to let in some morning light. When I phoned her, Mammy had often spoken about the birds she had seen that week from the window. She had been bound to bed and chair for the final few years. She loved it when the swallows came and, like me, she rejoiced in the sighting of the occasional robin. The sun was trying to push the clouds apart with faint fingers of light over the hedgerow out the back of Esker House. And then there was something quite extraordinary. A robin redbreast, head bobbing from side to side, looking up at me from the windowsill. I stared. She stared. We both knew. Her head bobbed one final time and then off to heaven she flew.

The room was silent but for the ticking of the clock that hung beneath a framed painting of an idyllic canal bank walk. I climbed up on a chair and took the battery out. To the left was a photograph of my parents on their wedding day, and next to that the only certificate my mother ever cared about – The Pioneer Total Abstinence Association of The Sacred Heart of Jesus, a badge of honour for never drinking alcohol.

I was lucky. I got a precious hour with her before people

began to visit and pay their respects. Everyone would mean well. Everyone loved Mammy. I knew I should be stronger, meet them and shake their hands, but I wasn't strong at all. Anyway, my sisters knew them all and I didn't. I would try to be of service later in the proceedings, but at that point I regressed to being a scared little boy without his mother. I couldn't speak. I was numb. I went up to my old bedroom, still with the same flowery wallpaper, still with the same dusty window and its same mesh curtain. There was nothing to say to others and nothing that could be said to me. I was terrified of well-meaning, sincere words of condolence and I didn't want to be disrespectful to the lovely people offering those words. Curled up on the bed, I was paralysed with fear. I could hear the people downstairs, expressing sympathy to my sisters, drinking a cup of tea, reminiscing on memories of Mammy. I winced and clenched my knees tighter when I heard the occasional, inadvertent laughter punctuating the gentle tapping of flecks of rain on the window pane. Soon the funeral director would arrive in his dark suit and take Mammy to be embalmed so that she could be laid out in the 'resting robes' that my sister Mary had made. I listened to him come and go. I heard her leave the house, but I remained where I was, alone. As the afternoon wore on, I drifted in and out of a half sleep. I dreamed that I was walking by her side to Barkmills as a child.

Whenever Mammy needed to clear her mind, she walked to Barkmills. As the name suggests, it used to be a watermill, over the River Owenass that runs from the Slieve Bloom Mountains to the west of Ballyfin and through the nearby town of Mountmellick. Mammy loved the birds that come to the water. They would fly away – and with them her troubles would fly away too. She especially loved the kingfisher and sighting one was an absolute highlight, their bright feathers reflecting in the babbling stream. Mammy was so thankful for nature. Barkmills flurried with life – birds of all colours, trout jumping for flies as dusk descended, endless colourful plants growing amidst the rocks and in the shallows. Especially in her later years as her sense of smell and her eyesight faded, Mammy often spoke of the garden of heaven which awaited her and Daddy on the other side with beautiful streams, brightly feathered birds and light blue, pink and especially white flowers (daisies were her favourite), just like Barkmills.

Waking after a grief-filled, restless sleep, I decided I would take a walk there. I pulled on my trousers and coat and headed into the impending dusk. I sneaked out the back door, past the shed where my friend Pirate the sheepdog once lived, out on the lane, sidestepping some visitors in the yard. I walked slowly and deliberately. One foot in front of the other. Feeling the road. Looking down. With the pungent smell of silage drifting from a cattle shed down the lane, I came to the pump – a metal obelisk jutting from a cement slab with a long metal handle dangling from its head. Mammy and I had drunk water from that pump on a hot summer's day, and Mammy always said 'Thank God' for it. I guess we were immune to rust and bacteria back then. I pumped the handle now, but there was no water today. However, something in the hedge behind caught my eye. An old rusty, broken metal pot. Snarled up in some wire in the undergrowth. Mammy and I had planted daisies in that pot some forty years before. It was empty now. I crouched and stared at it for a while.

A few steps further on at the crossroads of the lane was a sign with an arrow directing people to Esker House – the farmhouse where I grew up. It just said 'Funeral' – a generic sign used for hundreds of funerals, I supposed. It seemed so simple, so ordinary and so final – a reminder that we all share the same destination, all equals in the end. In that moment, it made me desperately sad to see it used for a woman as special and as extraordinary as my mother. But perhaps it was fitting. Mammy was a no-frills kind of person. She had led a simple existence, uncluttered by any desire for material things. She was thankful for the smallest and seemingly meaningless action or possession. She hadn't had what anyone could consider an easy life. As a child during the war, she was sent to live with people she didn't know when her family was split up. She had no shoes and barely enough clothes, and she worked hard manual labour from a very young age. I once asked her about this time. She said it was 'best forgotten'.

She had a tough time in school for what little education it afforded her. She went to work for no money at all in a drapery shop and even when she did eventually get paid, it was very little. Then she fell in love with and married a workaholic farmer. They had six children. In the early days she drew water in a bucket from a well, carrying a baby in the other arm, with two small children walking beside her. She expected nothing, and indeed that was often what she received. She was thankful for her health, her family, a roof over her head and for a handful of good friends. She put food on the table for her family and a plethora of workmen who came and went with cattle and sheep, silage and hay. She said a prayer of thanks morning and night every day of her life.

She told me that she had once waited for Daddy at the crossroads where I now stood, on his way back from a cattle market. He would pick her up to go to a dance in a community hall about fifteen miles away. He was late that day, so she walked to the dance herself, figuring he would turn up at some point, whenever he was done with work. She said that she was 'well warmed up' by the time he got there. Dancing and playing a game of cards were her little pleasures. She and my father would go to play the card game 'whist' with a few dozen people from surrounding areas, gathering in a community centre somewhere on a Sunday night, colloquially known as a 'whist drive'. There was tea to be drunk and chats to be had over the feverishly competitive card shuffling for two pence a game. Daddy was often late. The animals always came before Mammy, the dance, the 'whist drive' or the children. I guess that's the blessing and the curse I have inherited too. Mammy was thankful just to get to go anywhere at all and if Daddy turned up it was a bonus. When Mammy was dancing, she was happy and free. She was a good dancer – as was my father apparently, when he tore himself away from the silage, hay, sheep and cattle. It was in stolen moments like these that I suppose their relationship stayed alive. They undoubtedly loved each other. But I saw them hug only once in my life.

Right till the end, Mammy loved a dance. I had known that Christmas 2021 would be Mammy's last. She did too. But she was upbeat as always and hugely thankful that I'd come to be with her. As soon as I came through the door of the living room where she sat, she said, 'There you are now, Noel. Thanks very much for comin' when you have important things to be doing.' I told her not to be silly, and that there was nothing more important than her. Quick as a flash, she replied, 'You're so right Noel, sure I'm your mammy. Now put on that poncho and dance for me!'

While one of her hands still worked, she had crocheted a kind of shoulder cover with a hole for a head. I did as I was told, donning the garment and dancing as best I could. She smiled widely. 'Now relax and leave the problems outside for a while,' she said. 'They'll either still be there just the same or be gone and done with when you get back to them. You're with your mammy now, and we have a lot to be thankful for.' And so we did.

Most of Christmas Day it was just her and me together. She was sitting in her armchair by the fire. She needed a hoist to be moved from the chair to her bed and back again, and she couldn't raise her head to look up because of increased deformity in her upper spine. So, I put the poncho on the floor, lined up a cushion for myself and lay down at her feet where she could see me. She liked it when her feet were rubbed, as they were quite swollen from poor circulation, so I rubbed them for her. We talked about how she rubbed my little feet for me when I was a child and sitting on her knee. She joked that she didn't want to be 'looking down on me', but that it would do me good to 'look at things from a different angle' for a while. Ever the joker, my mammy, but there was often profound wisdom in her words.

Mammy had absolute faith in God and in her destiny. She was looking forward to joining Daddy in heaven, where she said there would be plenty of time for dancing. As she was talking about this imminent joy, I popped out a black box with a nice ribbon on it and wished her 'Happy Christmas'. I opened it for her, since her hands were too frail. Inside was a pearl necklace. Mammy had always wanted one to go dancing with Daddy, but never had the wherewithal to get one, and my father wouldn't even have thought about it. She wasn't able to cry because of her condition, but her eyes grew waxen. She said how beautiful it was and how grateful she was that she would look great at the dance to come.

I couldn't help myself but to explain that they weren't real pearls. She paused for a moment in her own inimitable way and then proffered, 'Don't you worry about that, Noel. Beauty is in the eye of the beholder, and they're real to me because you're my son and they came from you. I'd be thankful no matter if they were marbles.' Then after another pause, because she always had to have the last laugh, she added, 'Though I suppose a string of marbles near a dance floor wouldn't be the best idea.'

I could see that she was ready to go. The cancer had eaten away her breast and into the side of her chest and occasionally it bled, but the lovely community nurses visited daily to dress it. Mammy didn't want a diagnosis or any treatment, having long before said in no uncertain terms that she would not be going back into hospital and that the next time she'd leave the farmhouse would be in a box. And so, it would come to pass.

She was completely at peace, a picture of serenity. I said, 'So I suppose you have your bags all packed then, Mammy?' She simply replied, 'Ah no, Noel, sure where I'm goin', you don't need any baggage . . . In fact the lighter the better . . . There's no need for any possessions the end, Noel . . . You just need to be grateful when you get there.' And so she would be. Thankful to the end.

Less than six weeks later, Mammy would by now be back at the house I supposed, lying in repose in her bed, as I trudged on towards Barkmills, my heart weighing heavily in my chest. I put my hands in the pockets of my coat, pushing them deep; pushing the pain down. Soon, I could hear the waterfall as I rounded the last corner. A heron in a nearby shallow pool looked up for a moment, swishing his beak like a knife through the air. I could hear her voice in my head, 'That's God, Noel. The work of God. Always be thankful for God. He is everywhere.' I ran my fingers through the felt cigar heads of the bull reeds I had once used as drumsticks. A trout jumped like a twirling stone. And then I saw the tree with a hole in it, a tree I remembered exactly from my boyhood. It seemed like a kind of miracle that it was still there, a testament to the power of timeless love. Water still collected in the hole, though the tree branches were lopsided. Mammy and I used to bless ourselves with that water. She'd say, 'Aren't we lucky, Noel?' and 'Thank you for a lovely day.' I blessed myself and slumped against the tree. I put my head on my knees, wrapped my hands around my ears and sobbed, as dusk closed in, grabbing the last wisps of light from the silver waterfall, taking one bobbing branch at a time. Time. It's all we have, and then it's gone.

I made my way back to the house. It was spitting rain as I walked through the yard, my collar pulled up. I don't think the people arriving and parking in the old cattle yard could see tears against the drizzle of the rain. Inside, I dried my face, put on a shirt and crept downstairs, through the kitchen, through the living room, through the huddled friends and cousins, biting hard on my cheeks. I stood to the right of her bed by the window. The rosary was about to commence. Truth be told, regular rosary recitation and Catholic practice had faded for me in adult life, so I was silent. Mammy wouldn't have approved. Others led the prayers, and I couldn't speak anyway. That night, after everyone had left,

I pulled a mattress onto the floor beside Mammy's bed and I talked to her. I said my own little prayers, of profound love and gratitude. I was thankful that I could 'mind her', as she had asked me to that past Christmas, on her last night in her own house.

I twisted and turned on the mattress, filled with thoughts of memories past, troubles present and an uncertain future without her guiding light in my life. To comfort myself, I thought of a gorgeous six-year-old black Labrador retriever called Barney, whom I had been due to operate on that very day, but had to cancel the appointment. His mum, Imogen, was a really wonderful mother who, like mine, encouraged her children, Sean and Mary, to chase their dreams and gave them every support to do so. She was desperately worried about her boy Barney, because he was not bearing any weight at all on his right front leg due to the failure of two previous attempts by another surgeon to repair his elbow fracture (for privacy I have changed their names). He was crippled with pain and also bad osteoarthritis affecting his other elbow and both of his hip joints. In spite of his pain, he was stoical throughout, much like my mammy had been in her last years. However, his hitherto frenetic tail-wag and brilliant smile had recently been subdued by severe pain and disability. From his radiographs and CT scans I knew it was likely that the edges of the broken bones and broken metal implants in his elbow were rubbing on his nerves and I was really anxious to get him out of pain as soon as I could. Initially I felt guilty for thinking of him as I lay there beside my mammy, but reverting to the only thing in my life that I had any control over was the only way that I could feel any hope at all that night. This was one problem that wouldn't have gone away when I came back to it and I knew that Mammy would have approved of me doing my best. She would have been thankful that her son could bring Barney some hope. Finding a solution for him would require a creative thought process and a determined mindset, both of which my mammy encouraged within me in that same house some forty years earlier. She would be pleased that it had been time well spent. In these thoughts, looking after her and her legacy, I finally fell asleep with some sense of peace on that cold and lonely night. When I awoke, I determined that I would call the new device which we'd invented to screw the pieces of the humerus bone in Barney's elbow back together a 'Rita bolt' in her honour.

Next day, we were ready to take Mammy to the church. I had promised I would 'tuck her in' when the time came. The coffin with its blue velvet lining stood in the living room. I folded the bed sheet around her and helped carry her limp body to her final rest. I held her head as we lowered her into the coffin. The men in suits arranged her. I tucked in her sheets, like she did for me so many times in my little squeaky white camper bed. Silently, when the men turned their backs, I popped a heart into the coffin beside her. I'd made it myself from orthopaedic cement a few weeks earlier, while waiting for the cement inside the femur of a hip replacement to set. The simple message 'I love you XX' was stencilled with the sharp point of a periosteal elevator that was close to hand. I had intended to give it to her while she was alive. Technically, the cement was bacterial-resistant antibiotic-impregnated polymethyl methacrylate, which would never corrode. A love that would last forever. People came and people went for a little while longer. A kiss, a touch, a sign of the cross above her body in the coffin, a tear.

I went back up to my bedroom to get ready for Mass that evening, and I sat on the bed in silence. There was a rustling in the window, and I leaned over to pull aside the mesh curtain that was suspended by a wire over the damp-trickled glass. A royal admiral butterfly was flapping there. No doubt he had been awoken from slumber by the unaccustomed heater that I had used to thaw out the room the day before. I was mesmerised. As a child I had believed that when we died, it was that very butterfly who carried the stardust we're all made from up to heaven. I scooped him up gently, opening the window and letting him off, fluttering and dancing on the hazy breeze. Off towards the Slieve Bloom Mountains out the back of our house, with Mammy's stardust on his wings.

Dressed for the Mass, I joined my brother John and others downstairs, and we lifted Mammy's coffin into the waiting hearse. Always feet first, we were told by the men in suits. A slow snake of cars followed to Ballyfin church, where once I had been the longest serving altar boy in the parish, and where my father had been the very first lay reader at Mass, garnering the nickname 'The Bishop'. Mammy told the story that when she got engaged to Daddy, a woman where she worked in the drapery store said to her that she was 'too holy to have a fella'. Mammy replied that this lady clearly didn't know that she was marrying 'The Bishop'.

I got up and gave a reading from the Bible in front of Mammy's coffin. After the service, there was a procession of maybe a couple of hundred people who passed by me and my siblings, shaking our hands and nodding grave condolences. Many wore Covid masks, but I wouldn't have recognised the majority anyway as Ballyfin hadn't been my home in a very long time. After everyone had left the church, it was just me and Mammy. I sat in the front pew, head bowed in front of Jesus on the cross above and Mammy in the coffin below, directly in front of the altar. I had knelt beside that altar innumerable times serving Mass as a child, I had swung the thurible and carried the golden cross around the stations of Jesus's journey depicted on the walls around me. I fancied I could still smell the incense now.

I thought someone would come to close the large double doors at the back of the church, but nobody did. The wind blew through the aisle. I sat down beside Mammy's coffin, clenched my hands on my knees and welcomed the cold. Mammy was cold and I wanted to be cold too. I had lost my faith as a teenager, for myriad reasons, not least the horrors I knew, and those I saw inflicted on the innocent under God's supposedly omniscient gaze. I held significant pain inside me from the bullying I'd been subjected to, as well as other more unspeakable things I had been through with no recourse to God. I also felt some resentment for spending so much time singing hymns and saying the rosary in primary school rather than learning geography, history, maths and languages, so that I was very poorly equipped for the onslaught in secondary school. As I looked around at the Stations of the Cross from where I sat that night, they only emphasised this pain for me. I always struggled with the concept that a loving God could watch his human son being nailed brutally to a cross, a crown of thorns on his head, but I suppose that was exactly the point – to hold a mirror up to man's inhumanity to man and to show that the path to salvation was through unconditional love and forgiveness. As I grew older, I shied away from situations where I might be exposed to the cruelty of humans and have gravitated toward a deep companionship with animals which has simply grown stronger over the years. I am so very grateful for all of the animals I have been blessed to know and who have brought me hope and salvation through the wonder of their love. I've come to see God as a kind of universal consciousness, a 'oneness' that pervades and links together all living things with an invisible thread of unconditional love. I think God is love and love is God, and that we are all part of the universal string of oneness to which I have referred earlier. I've channelled that love and sense of oneness into my life as a veterinarian. I see it everywhere, and it's my salvation.

But nothing could save me that night. I sat by Mammy's coffin in the church until about 10 p.m. when someone finally came to close the doors. I didn't want to leave her alone with the doors open. I kissed her wooden box goodbye and made my way out into the dark country lane. I walked past the house to which I was taken from the hospital as a newborn, carried by Brother Germanus, his loose false teeth chattering as he tickled me. He'd picked Mammy and me up because Daddy was busy cutting horns off cattle.

I walked in complete darkness down the country lane to my sister Frances's house, clenching my fists, pushing the coldness within me out into the chill night air as I strode, trying to comfort myself humming Eric Clapton's song 'Tears in Heaven'. I knew 'I must be strong and carry on' somehow. I arrived as the priest, Father Joe, was with her, organising the funeral Mass for the following morning. I would again read a lesson from the Bible, and I thought I would be writing some kind of eulogy for Mammy. But both the priest and my sister told me that Mammy hadn't wanted a eulogy. She had specifically instructed that she did not want to be celebrated for herself, but would rather we used the time to thank others who helped her in her life and in her death. This presented a dilemma for me, as I later sat up in bed, the Bible to one side and two sheets of paper on my knee. How could I respect her wishes, while still giving thanks to her, for all she had done for me, my siblings and so many others? The paper remained blank for an hour or so. Eventually, I tried to sleep at 2 a.m., but couldn't. So I got up again and finally managed to write until about 4 a.m. The alarm went off at 8.30 a.m. I shave for only two people – my Mammy and the Queen. I'd bought Mammy a hat from the Queen's milliners, after much prompting from Rita herself, soon after I'd met Her Majesty. She loved that mauve broad-brimmed hat. Even though she had nowhere to go in it, she liked to look at it in its beautiful box. It would make an appearance during the celebration of gifts brought up by her grandchildren to the altar during the funeral.

At the Mass, I read *Ecclesiastes 3*: 'There is a season for everything, a time for every occupation under heaven. A time for tears, a time for laughter; a time for mourning, a time for dancing . . .' This particular version of the Bible left out my favourite bit of that lesson: 'For the fate of human and the fate of animal is the same: as the one dies, so the other dies; both have the self-same breath. Human is in no way better off than animal. And I saw that there is nothing better for mortals than to rejoice in their work; for this is their lot.' I agree with all of this. I do rejoice in my work and I am happy with my lot. I was so grateful this was the lesson on the day.

I tried my best with a eulogy which wasn't a eulogy. Two pages of it was thanking others on her behalf, but I couldn't help adding just a little bit about how much she had given to everyone that ever had the good grace to know her.

Mammy Rita was the humblest person one could ever wish to meet and she purposely requested no eulogy – and so we obey Mammy Rita! Mammy made a fuss of everyone, but never herself. She was thankful, but never asked for thanks. Mammy grew up with nothing, and all of her life she never asked for anything – always helping where she could, and making a loaf and a fish feed a dozen people. She was proud of all of us, but warned us frequently that excessive pride would take a fall. Her humility in the face of her greatness is an example to us all – the endless kindness of a wonderful woman, a comfort to all of us, no matter what the troubles. It was never about her, but rather about the light she could share with all of us, for which we are eternally grateful. We now give you back to the light, Mammy – the eternal light.

My brother John and I linked arms and with the other pall-bearers we hoisted Mammy up on our shoulders for the final journey, out of the church, up the hill by the bell with its long rope that I delighted in pulling as a child, in contravention of the Father's instruction. A slow sombre walk followed to the graveyard. The old rusty rotating gate by the entrance to the cemetery which I played on as a child had long since been removed. Within, Father Joe said a few words, and I held my end of the strap and my brother the other as four of us lowered Mammy six feet to lie by Daddy's side. A cover was pulled over the gaping mouth in the ground. The prayers, muted conversations and murmurs of stilted condolence drifted away. I crouched by the grave, finally on my own, clawing clay in a fist from the mound of soil to the side, rocking back and forth.

I stayed there until the gravediggers, Tommy and Joe, arrived. I knew them both from a long time ago and asked for a spade. In silence they handed me one, and I threw in the first shovelful of clay. It made a dull thud against the wood. I shovelled faster and faster, letting the sweat mix with my tears. I was lonely, grief-stricken and determined all at the same time. Mammy had asked me to tuck her in for her final rest and so I did, with blankets of soil. I didn't care about my suit or my shoes. When it was done, Tommy and Joe pulled back to give me a few moments. I stroked the soil with my fingers and wished her 'Nighty night', just as she used to say to me. And then, in remembrance of our walks to Barkmills, I added, 'Tomorrow will be a lovely day . . . because of you.'

It was a very sad trip back to London the following day, but I was thankful that I could look forward to helping Barney. I also knew that Mammy would want me to get on with life as best I could, to be fulfilled and to be happy. She wouldn't want prolonged sadness because she firmly believed that she would be happy after life. In the words of Elton John's 'Song for Guy', she firmly believed that 'life isn't everything'. Barney's mum, Imogen, was really lovely and brought me some scones in a tin with robins on since she knew that Mammy and I loved robins. We had designed customised implants for reconstruction of Barney's fractured elbow joint based on his CT scans, because off-the-shelf implants had already failed. I operated as soon as I got back to the practice.

Sadly, Barney was one of many dogs I have seen recently that have had very poor-quality surgery performed and his complications were absolutely avoidable through better training, better technique and better implants in my opinion. I'll discuss this in more detail a bit later in this book. Amputation of his limb was not a good option due to severe osteoarthritis in multiple other joints. By coincidence I performed his surgery on the first day of filming for series eighteen of *The Supervet*. It was a very challenging surgical revision. As I had anticipated, the nerves were indeed rubbing on the jagged edges of broken bone and implants and were stuck down with scar tissue. In addition, the joint was affected by much more severe cartilage erosion than I had hoped and by significant damage to the ligaments and tissues around the joint. I took out the old implants and achieved the repair with a custom-made plate and screws, a partial joint replacement and the special device which I had named the 'Rita bolt' that night, lying by Mammy's bed – in thankfulness for all the creativeness and tenacity she had gifted me. I have no doubt that I shall save many elbows with the 'Rita bolt' in the future.

Initially, the repair seemed very successful and Barney was doing well, but very strangely, on what would have been Mammy's birthday in May 2022, he suddenly became very lame again. It turned out that the ligaments around his badly damaged and arthritic elbow had given way and the joint dislocated. But just like Mammy never gave up on me, I wasn't going to give up on him – and Imogen wasn't going to either.

I fused Barney's elbow joint solid (an arthrodesis) using a new version of a special plate system that I had developed as a result of observing failure with other implant systems.

I felt that Mammy was looking down on me as I fixed him, and I was thankful. As Mammy taught me, all success stands on the shoulders of failure.

I saw Barney for sign-off of what I hoped was his final repair on 25 August 2022, and he was walking very well indeed, without pain, though his elbow fusion inevitably creates a mechanical limp with a waltz-like gait. He was again wagging his marvellous tail, smiling and bringing joy to everyone he met. We shall treat his other arthritic joints with injections and tablets and hopefully give him much more time in this world. Sean and Mary were thrilled that he could hopefully soon go back to dancing around with them in the garden, as was his wont. Entirely coincidentally, 25 August was the exact date of the passing of my father in 2006. I couldn't help but feel that it was a sign that he and Mammy are indeed dancing in the garden of Mammy's dreams in heaven, with all the time in their world to enjoy their waltz.

Exactly a month later, I was running late after some other surgery. Driver David is used to that. I rushed around my office grabbing a jacket and shirt, trousers, T-shirt, pants, socks and boots, chucking them in a carry-on travel bag before throwing that in the back of the taxi. It's never any different if I get in David's car anywhere. Lie on the seat, breathe deeply and watch the hedgerows of Eashing pass as my heart rate slows down. By the time we get a few miles down the A3 a few minutes later, my eyes are closed and I'm half asleep.

I hurried through check-in and then to the crammed Dublin departure gate in Heathrow Terminal 5. The next gate over was for Warsaw, also busy. I generally try to avoid being recognised when I'm in a crowd and look for somewhere to hide, so I slumped down in a small space in the corner by the wall, beside another man. I accidentally nudged the green rucksack beside him as I squeezed by. He lunged to catch it before it toppled over, and from how he handled it, it looked heavy. I apologised. 'That's okay,' he replied. His accent wasn't

British or Irish. We both had Covid masks on, but there was something about his eyes above the mask that drew me to him. Big eyes – wide, friendly and expressive. I don't know why I felt the urge to speak to him, but I nodded at the bag. 'Well, are you all kitted up then for your trip to Ireland?'

'It's not for me,' he said. 'It's for my friends in Ukraine.' It turned out he was a nurse, travelling with medicines and other vital essentials to Warsaw and then by car to Kyiv. We sat there for about half an hour waiting for our respective flights. He told me about his friends and some family members caught up in the conflict in Ukraine. The atrocities of which he spoke – a cousin blown apart by a shell, a friend raped and her husband killed in front of her – the detail being too painful for me to write.

He asked me why I was going to Dublin. I said it was for the 'month's mind' of my mother. He was unfamiliar with the term, so I explained that it was a Mass in a church to remember her and celebrate her life a month after she died and to thank God for accepting her into heaven. He said that was nice. While in Ukraine, he was going to bury the pieces of his cousin, collected by his aunt. I was speechless for a few seconds. By comparison, my sadness in the normal passage of life seemed almost insignificant by comparison with such pain and distress. I just nodded and murmured that I was very sorry for his loss. Respectfully, he replied, 'I'm sorry for yours.'

My temporary buddy at the airport gate was interested in my work as a vet and we discussed some medical matters. Bizarrely, amid all of his own suffering, he thanked me for what I do for animals. I felt terribly self-conscious about the compliment in the light of the sacrifices he was making, and I asked him, perhaps insensitively, if he wasn't scared that he might not come back from his trip. He simply replied, 'Not really . . . I am thankful to be able to go and try my best.' And with that, my thankful and inspiring friend was called for boarding at the neighbouring gate. We nodded at each other to say goodbye, then I reached out my hand, and he shook it firmly. I watched as a kind and gracious man pulled a heavy bag onto his shoulder and went off to help his friends. In moments like this, I often think of my own life in the context of the Duran Duran song 'Ordinary World', where Simon Le Bon sings that 'beside the news of holy war and holy need' my everyday moans, gripes and concerns are 'just a little sorrowed talk'.

In Dublin, my brother picked me up at the airport and drove me to my sister's house where I collected the three things I needed. I had a job to do. It was a bitterly cold night. My hands were freezing as I gripped the handle of the shovel and walked as quickly as I could along the perpetually dark country lane to the cemetery. At the graveyard, I flicked on the torch that my brother-in-law had lent me and dug down a little way at the side of the grave. I pulled out from my pocket the black velvet box that I'd given to my mother the previous Christmas, unwrapped the ribbon and took out the pearl necklace, laid it carefully in the soil, then covered it over. Cement would be poured on once the ground had settled, and this was my last chance to fulfil Mammy's wishes. When she and Daddy went dancing in heaven, she would be the belle of the ball.

The following morning, I woke in my childhood bedroom, knowing that again I would be delivering the reading at Mass in less than an hour. I was very tired and more than a little irritable as I got dressed, and my mood darkened further when I tried to put my right foot in my boot and it wouldn't fit in.

A wave of horror washed over me as I suddenly realised that, in my rush to make the flight, I'd packed two left boots from the pile of clothes on the floor of my office. I have very few 'civilian' clothes that I wear regularly, donning the same type of trousers, blue shirts and scrubs daily at the practice. This makes filming continuity for *The Supervet* easy. Otherwise, I have two favourite pairs of jeans, two check shirts, two hoodies and two jackets that I mostly wear to gigs, two pairs of trainers, one to run in, one to consult in, and two identical pairs of Doc Marten boots. This makes continuity in my life easy too, or so I thought. Now, I had no option but to squeeze my right foot into a left boot, as I certainly wasn't going to wear trainers to deliver a reading by the altar. And so, with a very self-conscious inward twist of my right leg, I marched from pew to pulpit and back again. Later, my brother-in-law Liam asked me if I was all right, because I had a noticeable limp. I explained that I wasn't actually suffering some new disability as I'd walked up the aisle and we laughed. But not as much as Mammy was laughing in heaven, no doubt. For it was forty-six years earlier, in the same childhood bedroom, that I had been complaining that my new shoes hurt my feet. Most of my wardrobe to that point had consisted of hand-me-downs, but these lovely brown brogue shoes had been bought to match my lovely brown First Communion suit. I was being a brat, insisting that they pinched, but Mammy told me I should be more thankful and then, standing at the door of my room, she glared at me and said, I kid you not, 'Well, you'll miss me when you have two left shoes.'

I did indeed.

As I mentioned earlier, Mammy often told me about the birds she had seen, formerly on her walks and latterly from her window. She would fly with them one day, she said, 'to a place of perpetual peace'. I am quite sure she is there now. Mammy weathered many storms with dignity, ensuring the comfort of others, and never asking for a crumb herself. She never needed anything, she said, because she had everything already. At her funeral Mass, having thanked everyone on her behalf, I read the same poem to the congregation as I had for her friend Minnie when she had passed, in celebration of my Mammy Rita – a magnificent, humble, generous, funny, hard-working and very thankful human being.

'Hope' Is the Thing with Feathers
by Emily Dickinson

'Hope' is the thing with feathers –
That perches in the soul –
And sings the tune without the words –
And never stops – at all –

And sweetest – in the Gale – is heard –
And sore must be the storm –
That could abash the little Bird
That kept so many warm –

I've heard it in the chillest land –
And on the strangest Sea –
Yet, never, in Extremity,
[*She*] asked a crumb – of Me.

Thank you, Mammy. I love you very much.
　　Nighty night xx

CHAPTER 6

Openness

I'm going to talk about something I've never discussed publicly. I know there will be some readers for whom descriptions of sexual abuse in this chapter will be too difficult to read. For those who need to skip this chapter, I understand and my heart goes out to you.

I share this now because I have met some other victims of sexual abuse and all of them have felt alone, lacking self-worth and impaired because of the trauma. I hope to help others not to feel as abandoned and hopeless as I did by sharing my journey towards healing and forgiveness. I couldn't talk of this until after the passing of my mother since I did not want her to feel responsible or feel pain on my behalf. I have asked her permission before she passed away to share my story with you. And also, I am exhausted from running away from the trauma all of my life and burying it deep such that in times of extreme stress it has surfaced for me and has caused significant emotional and psychological challenges. It is now time for me to stop hiding from the ghost.

He will always be with me. The smell of tobacco on his breath, his mouth full of decaying teeth, like tombstones. His cheeks cold like cement, his thinning hair combed over his scalp. His voice that sounded like he chewed gravel. His cracked lips as he grinned. He said he was 'just playing', that it was a game. I was too young to remember much when it first started, but I remember his fingers. Brown, stubby fingers, stained by tobacco, hands calloused by toil. Hands that in his younger years would have held the reins of the plough horse. Hands that had wielded a shovel alongside my father, digging drains into the bogland. And now, that gripped my head and made me do things. Perhaps there had been the heads of other boys too, crushed by these hands. I will never know. Afterwards, I ran away to the cowshed, crying, confused, not understanding what had happened.

Mammy and Daddy didn't leave the house together very often, but he always made sure to see them off attentively. I could hear the reassurances that everything would be fine and he'd 'take care of things'. He smoked innumerable cigarettes daily, holding the butt with a pin he kept in his jacket somewhere so he could suck on the last few drags before he came into the kitchen. Sometimes Daddy was out working and Mammy had to go to town or somewhere else. My four older siblings were generally either in boarding school or out of the house for whatever reason, whilst my younger sister was generally in bed or, later, as the abuse spanned several years, she also was out of the house. Like all predators, he always waited until the coast was clear. He wasn't interested in girls. He'd pretend to send me to bed too, but I knew very well what would happen. He'd say we could both 'do with some company', and would I like to come down for a while from my room and sit with him on the sofa in our living room? Maybe we could even watch some television, unbeknownst to anyone. The first time, this was an easy ploy and I thought I was in for a treat. I wasn't. It was an ageing sofa and I can still remember what it smelt like against my face. It was all 'just messin' around', showing me 'things'. These were things I didn't understand and didn't want to see. I was five years old. I knew nothing. The 'things' he did to me grew worse over time. I remember it in snapshots, but sometimes just blackness. Just the musky smell of the sofa lingering. There were quite a few times over several years. They blurred into a kind of haze and looking back to time and place, I struggle to fix my age. There was innocence before, and then just pain.

There were other places too, always when nobody could hear my muffled protests. A few bales in our hayshed doubled as the sofa for him sometimes. He told me if I made a sound it would be worse for me, and if I ever told anyone, nobody would believe me anyway because it was only a 'game', a game I would get to like in time. I despised him and I was terrified of him. There were other times in fields, in the tractor and even in the cottage that was supposed to be haunted in the glebe. It is certainly haunted now.

The last time he had his way with me I must have been ten years old, because I had on the Timex watch that my daddy gave to me for my tenth birthday. It had a round face and a brown strap. After he had satisfied himself, in the cowshed, about a hundred yards from the back door of our house, I huddled against the wall, shivering and crying. Pirate was chained up. There was nothing either of us could do about our shackles, except to bear them and have a cuddle. The minutes ticking by, as I prayed for my parents to come home soon, even though I knew Mammy would chide me for being there with 'that dog' again if she found me in the shed. As soon as I heard their car coming down the road, that meant the house was safe once more, and I ran through the back door and scurried up the stairs to my bedroom. From there I could hear him laughing with my parents in the kitchen. Nothing abnormal here at all. All is well. Mammy and Daddy only went out five or six times a year – to play cards or go dancing in the community centre of a nearby town. But that was enough for him to leave me scarred, petrified and stricken with shame forever. I closed the door of my room quietly and tightly and I pulled the blankets around my ears to block out the noise. I was scared of the dark, but I would keep the blackest darkness locked deep inside my mind, behind a door I was determined to never open again.

He worked on our farm. He was trusted. Mammy and Daddy didn't know about what this man did to me as far as I'm aware. But I sometimes wondered, looking back, whether they questioned why they found me one too many times crying in the cowshed. Maybe they just thought I was a bit of a loner and wanted to 'play' in the cowshed or hayshed rather than indoors, or after Pirate arrived on the scene, whether I preferred his company. Maybe I hid my tears too well. One occasion which stuck in my mind was my mother and father having some kind of heated discussion in the yard out the back of our house. I could hear them from my small bedroom window. They were talking about the man. Mammy seemed upset. I remember to this day, Daddy just said, 'Sure, he's a good worker,' and walked away. I would never know what this conversation was really about. On a few occasions during my life, I considered going home to Ballyfin and telling Mammy everything that had happened to me. But I was afraid. Afraid she wouldn't believe me; afraid she would say that I was making it all up; afraid that I would hurt her. It was easier to keep it hidden, to keep my pain to myself. If that conversation went wrong somehow, I wasn't sure how I could live with myself thereafter.

In my eleventh year, it stopped, and I dared to hope that my ordeal was over. But school was about to plunge me back into purgatory. On Monday, 1 September 1980, I attended my first day of secondary school and soon realised I was a complete idiot. I could not read and write properly, because my primary school, run by the Church, had prioritised the rosary and hymns over functional learning. In secondary school, when I tried to better myself through study, it brought a campaign of bullying from the other boys. Cruel words were the least of it. The torments were comprehensive. Most days they kicked the shit out of me one way or another, either pummelling me with fists, ripping my clothes, or throwing me in the slurry pit in the quarry behind school. They poured milk on the copybooks I had worked so hard on and trampled my reading books in the mud. They broke my bike in a cattle grid, wrenching the wheels. If I could, I ran away and hid. And I have been running and hiding ever since – from the past and the pain, from people who tried to get close to me with the very best intentions, from talking openly about what happened. For years the pain churned like barbed wire inside me, eating up everything that was good or that brought me joy. I ran to Dublin, and then to America, and then to England as soon as I could. Working as hard and long as I do is, I suppose, another form of running and hiding. I have always been too busy to spend any time alone with my thoughts and I avoided them like the plague. Every bandage I put on an animal in my care is another sticking plaster on my own wounds. Every smile I bring to a worried human's face is a vicarious flicker of joy in my own heart. Every plan I make for a new surgical method is a way of keeping my eyes on the brighter future. All of my life I have sought to help innocence because I lost my own and sought to save lives because I wasn't sure I could save my own. There's a deep cave inside me, where that little boy still lives, and where no light ever shines. And I knew if I looked back, and if I ventured inside, the darkness might swallow me up. To paraphrase U2, I gave everything of myself away all the time to the animals and to those who love them because I couldn't live either 'with or without' myself. I had 'nothing to win' and now I have 'nothing left to lose'.

I cannot keep running. And that's why I'm writing about this now. I've hated myself for too long. I have hidden away, first in the endless nights of study and examinations and then work, books, academic publications and more long nights in hotel rooms across the world writing lectures until dawn. Then I founded all kinds of events, helped to found a veterinary school, became a professor and even pushed hard to get a television show. All the while, I was never good enough for myself and I never would be. There was no amount of tiredness or hard work that could even come close to filling the inner emptiness that drove me onwards. I could try to save everyone except myself and as long as I could keep running and looking ahead, I'd never have to look back. Each morning as I washed my face, I shut my darkness inside as I put on my blue consulting shirt or my black operating scrubs with the Fitzpatrick Referrals logo on them. Inside, over time, I had such poor self-esteem that when I was spent at the end of yet another sixteen-hour day, sometimes in the blackness, I could not sleep, and if I did, I never wanted to wake up again. The nightmares got worse. I felt worthless and I felt like a fraud, because I couldn't even be honest with my own feelings about what had happened. I took no joy in any achievement or any operation when I succeeded, rather just sank into vast despair when I failed.

I've seen too many people hate themselves for lots of different reasons and waste their time in this world. I've seen too many people take their own lives. I have had nightmares all my life. Flashbacks. I've fallen into deep chasms of despair from which there seemed no way out. This has been particularly so if I have ever been accused of doing the wrong thing for animals, which is anathema to me and attacks my very soul, or whenever the practice has been threatened, despite my best efforts. This is not just a job to me. As I've said, I could never sell the practice where I help animals, because it is my home; it's not a business but it is rather my heart and my soul. So when that has been threatened, my very existence has been threatened. It's not bricks and mortar and work colleagues, it's the bionic bunker of the superhero Vetman whom I had dreamed up as my saviour to escape the bullying and abuse; it's my family, it's all my hope, redemption and dreams for doing my best for the innocents. It's hardly surprising, on reflection, that when I have been overtired and very sad, the demons seek to consume me.

I have felt worthless sometimes, and very angry other times, because my innocence was stolen from me. Lucky for me, though, I have been blessed with a vocation to protect the innocents that can't speak for themselves – the animals I serve. Yet still, sometimes in spite of the light they share with me, I have from time to time spiralled into the darkness. I have sat on bridges, railway tracks and by rivers and seen the enticing possibilities of ending my pain right there – anything to take away the self-hatred and the shame. As a vet, it doesn't escape me that I have access to drugs that could end my life in seconds. Some vets take this path – it's horrendous, but true. Yet, in my darkest moments, I always thought of my mammy, and she always saved me. I don't for one second use the words 'suicidal thoughts' lightly, because I know only too well the pain and heartache left in the wake of suicide. And I want to be clear: self-harm and suicidal thoughts are not normal or just 'part of life'. We all get down, but if that tips into something more severe, please seek help wherever you can find it. I have been incredibly lucky to have had the constant, comforting presence of animals and their unconditional love in my life. They have helped me to see a world bigger than myself and they've given me a reason to keep going. Friends, both human and animal, can lighten the burden, if you let them. I have found it incredibly hard to let people in, because as Oli Sykes says in a song by his band, Bring Me the Horizon, 'The emptiness is heavier than you think,' and I have actually felt guilty about burdening others with my heaviness. But one has to fight hard to let the light in. It is there, though, if you choose to seek it. I have been shown this light in the most powerful way possible by a girl called Olive and her dog, Tess (names changed).

Tess came into Olive's life as a rumbustious black Labrador puppy in December 2015. I didn't know that Olive was battling similar demons to me until she and her mother, Heidi, confided in me when explaining how important Tess was in Olive's life. They have given me permission to share their story in the hope that, like mine, ultimately it brings light to others and to us as well, such that the rawness of the sharing will hopefully ultimately be cleansing. Olive was fourteen years old in 2015, and an inpatient in a psychiatric unit where she had been for a year. After going through the same horrible things as a child that I had, she had been struggling with her mental health for a couple of years, which eventually reached crisis point and she became suicidal. It was unsafe for her to be at home and so she was hospitalised. She felt worthless and deeply unhappy, tortured by her memories. She thought that the only way to make the pain stop was to make everything stop. She didn't want to be alive and I empathised with every fibre of my being. Even after spending months receiving a high level of care, she didn't make a great deal of progress. She had been diagnosed as autistic, with post-traumatic stress disorder, but nothing was improving for her, and the people around her, including Heidi, were at a loss as to what to do.

Olive had always loved animals. When she was younger, she'd had cats, hamsters, rabbits and chickens. At the time she went into hospital she had a horse on loan. He meant everything to her, but she couldn't keep him while she was away. She was heartbroken when he had to go and she felt as though her world had been decimated. So, in preparation for Olive coming out of hospital, she and her mum decided they would get a puppy. Tess was a source of comfort, love and distraction for Olive as she was making the adjustment to living at home again. Puppy training classes followed, where mum did the practical work during the sessions and Olive continued the training at home. She absolutely loved learning about dog training, and Tess was such a good girl, the best in her class. Olive began to suffer from anorexia in addition to her other emotional and mental challenges, but throughout, Tess has continued to be an amazing support. After teaching Tess all of the basic training, Olive also taught her how to interrupt her panic attacks and help calm her down when she became distressed. Tess slept on her bed and was constantly by her side when she woke from her frequent nightmares. She had given Olive a reason to get up in the mornings and was a companion for her if she was alone at home. Olive has told me that she honestly did not think she would still be here if it wasn't for Tess. Having been through similar experiences with both Pirate and Keira by my side at different times of my life, I knew exactly how she felt.

In early 2020, Olive noticed changes to Tess's front paws which deteriorated considerably over time. Her toes were effectively falling off her knuckles, which is to say that severe inflammatory and degenerative joint disease had resulted in total destruction of the metacarpophalangeal joints of both front paws. The cause of this is unknown ('immune-mediated polyarthritis', but the effect is that the metacarpal bones – which are the bones of the palm in you or me – were bearing down like hammers onto her pads, splitting the skin open and resulting in bleeding and really bad infection. She could not walk much because her front paws were so painful.

Tess had attended her local primary care vets many times, had radiographs, painkillers and antibiotics. They were referred to a specialist centre and were told that nothing could be done. Olive and Heidi tried many different boots

Over the last few years, Ricochet and Excalibur have looked after me. Excalibur is mischievous, hides things in secret places, including my bed, and also hides away himself in secret places that only he knows. Ricochet is my guardian angel, snuggling in my bed or jumping on my knee and throwing his arms around me when he knows I need a hug. In the background is the saw

that my daddy handed me to cut horns off bullocks when I asked him for a guitar – and the very important message on my Batman sign.

(Far left) I love Ricochet and Excalibur beyond words.

(Left) I released the blood from Ricochet's aural haematoma and fixed the thin skin back down to the cartilage with a very fashionable button sandwich.

Initially Ricochet was not best pleased at my handiwork – but soon all was forgiven and we had a little nap.

Baby Noel.

Treating cattle in a crush chute with my daddy.

Me in 1987 at the University of Pennsylvania in Philadelphia. I figured if 'Rocky' could achieve his dreams there, I could, if I worked hard. Here I am working with one of the very first MRI scanners for dogs – which I could evidently do with my eyes closed!

Taking the American dream and my love of music a bit too far! Aged nineteen.

(Right) Me, aged three or four years old, getting to know a new animal friend – I think this absolutely counted for the 'keen horse rider' entry on my actor's CV!

(Left) My Heathcliff years! One of the pictures from my acting days – I always played the 'bad boy'.
Credit: Barney James

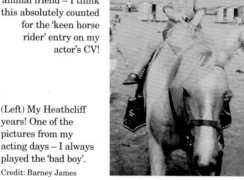

(Far left) The very last picture of all of my family together. Two days later, my little girl Keira was dead.

(Below) My little girl in a critical state, having been hit by a van, from which she recovered. She died almost exactly a year later.

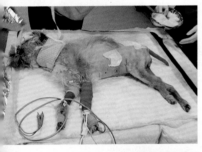

Keira's memorial –
To our beautiful baby girl.
May you run in the stars forever.
Your light remains inside us
And you are always by our side.

I ran the London Marathon in 2021 for Keira and me.

The shrine of Keira pictures donated by viewers of *The Supervet* which I walk by en route to my consultations – it gives me hope every day.

(Left) Stevie and me – my little comfort blanket in 'Stevie's Space'.
(Below) Stevie had an uncountable number of fractures. Repair was achieved with pins and cement in the sacrum and an external skeletal fixator for the pelvis.

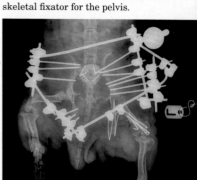

Little kitten Pretzel was born with dramatically deformed back legs.

I straightened Pretzel's legs using specialised external frames. Here she is on Nicole's knee.

Finally, Pretzel's legs were straight – now with customised internal plates – and she could walk properly again.

Tess was affected by severe osteoarthritis and infection of all of the knuckles of both front feet. Her toes fell off and I rebuilt them with customised external skeletal fixators which are called PAWS (pedal arch wire scaffold) – an idea I got from the superhero Wolverine, with the metal claws coming out of his knuckles.

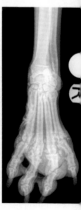

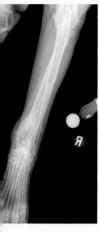

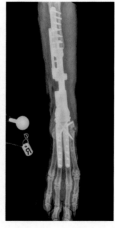

A radiograph showing the osteosarcoma tumour in Dimitri's front leg above the wrist.

Dimitri five days post-op.

A radiograph showing the radius-ulna modular endoprosthesis (RU Fitz) replacing the tumour.

Betsy's necrotic infected foot was replaced by a PerFiTS device – which is attached to the bones of her forearm, and an external foot is then attached to the outside – giving her a bionic leg.

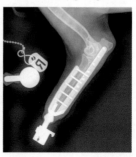

Puppy Murphy after I repaired his terrible jaw fracture with a specialised external skeletal fixator. Soon Murphy, who was the best friend of Tim (right), was healed, running around and greeting everyone with an excited tail-wag again.

(Left) Bumblebee (with her bionic foot), Heather, Vicky and me – the very best of friends.

(Right) Mammy and Minnie playing the guitar in their 'band' at the One Live music festival.

(Left and right) My last two visits with Mammy – when I went home to have my very important chat with her and my very last Christmas with her. She said 'Put on that poncho, Noel, and dance for me.'

(Centre) The royal admiral butterfly that was in the window of my childhood bedroom and who carried Mammy's stardust off to heaven on his wings.

(Left) Outside Buckingham Palace with my cast and John Travolta flared trouser leg, about to meet the Queen for lunch.

(Above) The cement star I fashioned for the Queen – which turned out more like a very strange gingerbread man.

Ollie on his trolley.

Angus survived losing one of his front legs and fusion of his remaining wrist, having accidentally fallen over a cliff edge.

When I visited South Africa I felt like I was 'coming home'. The veterinary professionals I worked with reminded me of those who mentored me when I'd started the journey to be a vet in the first place. I felt a deep inner peace and an extraordinary connected 'oneness' with all of creation. (I've purposely not shown pictures of any animals – because of a 'surprise' I have for you at a later date).

Even in the savannah, I found bones to put together. Once an orthopaedic surgeon, always an orthopaedic surgeon.

Down the valley in the distance I saw 'the source'. The animals melted out of the darkness at dusk to drink at the waterhole. In that moment I knew I had to go back to my source too, to find what I'd been looking for all along.

Rici the lion roared out across this valley to his friends on the other side – and gifted me a little bit of his huge lion's heart to make me stronger and braver than ever before.

to protect her feet but none helped, and by the time I saw her she had permanent open sores. With so many avenues explored, all leading to dead ends, they felt that they were running out of road. Hopeless, Olive and Heidi were considering putting Tess to sleep. This is always a heart-wrenching decision for any family and especially so in this case. After all Tess had done to support Olive, she blamed herself endlessly and felt that she was letting Tess down when she needed her most. Heidi and Olive had seen *The Supervet* on TV and, as a last resort, asked for a referral to Fitzpatrick Referrals. I examined Tess and obtained radiographs and also CT scans. I explained that in my experience, the only reliable solution was a procedure I'd invented more than a decade earlier, called PAWS – pedal arch wire scaffold.

The PAWS procedure involves fusing the knuckle (metacarpophalangeal) joints solid (which is called an arthrodesis). Because in Tess this would be for four toes in each front foot, there was no room for internal metal plates and screws. I realise this next bit is difficult to visualise, so I've included a photograph of the radiograph in the picture section of this book. The plan would be identical for each front paw. I would drill out any remaining cartilage from the bottom ends of each metacarpal bone and from the top ends of the first phalanx bones, which are the uppermost bones of each toe. Then bone marrow harvested from the top of each humerus bone would be implanted with the goal of fusing these two bones, which would be 'skewered' together on wires like a kebab pin.

The problem is that one can't just stick pins (or, in this case, wires) into the knuckles like Wolverine, who inspired this invention from my childhood comic books, and leave it at that. How would Tess be supposed to walk? And in any case, a simple wire would bend and certainly wouldn't be strong enough to support healing. Therefore, I would build a frame around the paws. I conceived of a way to apply more wires crossways at right angles to the four Wolverine pins, through the metacarpal bones in pairs, like support struts for a trampoline. These two groups of transverse and longitudinal wires would each be attached to an aluminium arch using bolts, and these two arches in turn would be attached to another arch like a horseshoe, subtended beneath the foot itself. By attaching all three arches together, the toes would be held on the metacarpal bones and have a chance to heal with the graft, whilst the foot pads would not touch the ground at all because the horseshoe arch would take the full weight of the limb. However, the wrists (carpi) would then be floppy, so I extended a large aluminium rod up the side of each forearm and anchored the aggregate of arches and wires in the paws to pins screwed into the side of the radius and ulna bones using clamps on the rod. This would temporarily immobilise the carpi and would allow Tess to walk on what was effectively metal scaffolding.

However, we would still have to contend with active infection, the risk that the bones might not fuse, and all manner of other potential mechanical and biological complications. Plus, even though I would be recouping costs only and trying my best to help, the price of such a procedure – a long hospital stay on antibiotics and painkillers, plus significant aftercare – was going to be very challenging for Olive and Heidi. I wish I could carry out all my surgeries free of charge, but as I hope is self-evident, Fitzpatrick Referrals has a large wage bill, as well as significant overheads. If the practice makes no money, it ceases to function or to give hope to any animal at all. We are reasonable in all of our charging relative to our costs, and in fact less expensive like for like than many referral practices but even then, the costs for major surgery like this can be prohibitive. We have strict rules around charity fundraising, in that families cannot use *The Supervet* TV show, me or Fitzpatrick Referrals to raise money on public-funding websites. As one can imagine, there are literally thousands of deserving cases. Olive abided by these rules and raised what she could from public donations plus loans from friends, money from her mum, and contributed all of her own savings. They would do whatever it took to give Tess a chance, and so would I.

It was Olive who cemented my view that I should tell my mammy about the trauma of my boyhood, not least because seeing what Tess meant to her reminded me so much of the relationship I'd had with Pirate in my darkest days. Like me, she wanted the best for all of the animals, who were her friends. I had to try to help Tess for her, but I also had to try somehow to be honest with myself and my world – to try to help the little innocent boy that I once was too. I couldn't carry the burden any more. I couldn't keep running from the ghosts inside me. As in the Iron Maiden song 'Fear of the Dark', I had a phobia that someone was always there, even when I was desperately searching for the light.

By that time, my mammy was dying and knew her next Christmas would be her last. In autumn 2021, I determined to go home and spend a little time with her. In the months preceding, my mind was in constant turmoil. I had wanted for many years to tell her about my sexual abuse as a child and how it had affected me all of my life. I worried that this may be a selfish thing to do and too much of a burden for her to carry to the grave, but I also wanted to make peace with the demons and to find some kind of catharsis in the sharing of my pain with her, which I couldn't do as a child. Most of all, I just wanted Mammy to put her arms around me and tell me that everything was going to be okay.

I got home to Esker, Ballyfin, and walked into Mammy's bedroom. She was propped up on pillows in her bed, unable to raise her head because of her progressive disability. 'Ah, hello, Noel, sure there you are! I can't believe my eyes – even if I could see right,' she said with a smile. 'How are you?' And so the banter started as it always did. We drank a cup of tea. She ate a chocolate biscuit which I'd brought and said it was very good. As I looked at her and held her small, frail hand, my heart faltered. How could I do it to her? Might I add to her suffering?

Now I was finally sitting by Mammy's bed, I started to cry. Her eyes had become cloudy over the years and indeed she couldn't see very well, but her hand squeezed mine a little. 'What's wrong, Noel?' she asked. I paused, holding back the sobs, heart and mind still in turmoil.

'I have something I need to tell you, Mammy . . . and I don't know if I should or not . . . because I don't want you to be upset.'

'Ah, sure, what would upset me now, Noel?' she said. 'Isn't there awful things going on in the world, and sure, I'll soon be out of it all anyway, looking after you all from beyond.'

'Mammy, something really bad happened when I was a child.'

'What did you do, Noel? You can tell me . . .'

'It's not what I did, Mammy; it was someone else.'

And so, through tears, I confessed all.

Afterwards, I put my head on the protective rail of the bed beside her, still holding her hand. She was silent for the longest time. I was terrified what might come next. Her lower lip quivered. She wasn't able to shed any tears with her condition, but her eyes took on a deep sadness.

'My little boy, Noel. You poor little boy. I'm so sorry.'

The silence stretched again. I just held her hand and sobbed, rocking back and forth, and I told her I'd been afraid to tell her because I didn't want to hurt her. I told her what happened in the barest details. She asked how many times. I said, 'A good few, Mammy . . . for a few years.'

I told her that I went to confession when I was making my First Holy Communion, and that I told the priest about it. I was an altar boy for that same priest for years and helped him in his house on occasion, but opening up to Mammy now was still the hardest thing I'd done. I told her that his response was that God would punish me and send me to hell, and that I was a bad person bringing these words into God's house. His parting instruction was to say penance prayers and never speak of it again.

I had always wondered why Mammy suddenly started going to a different Mass on a Sunday; not in Ballyfin, but in nearby Mountmellick. I'd wondered whether there had been some falling out between her and the local priest. I asked her if something had happened between the priest and her.

Mammy simply said, 'I knew there was something about him. I never liked him. Always a frown on 'im. That's why I changed to Mass in Mountmellick instead.'

I asked outright, 'Did you know about him, Mammy?' referring to 'the man'. I told her I'd overheard her 'words' with

Daddy in the yard, which I'd surmised were about him. She said she didn't know anything, but that she 'had a feeling there was something not right about him'.

So, there it was. My suspicion that Mammy didn't want to be around the priest and had suspicions that the man wasn't all that he appeared to be had been true. She believed me and supported me, even if the priest had not. She said she didn't want to know any more details and I didn't offer them. After another long pause, she said, 'Noel, you must put all of that behind you now. You must bury it in the past and open a new book in the future.'

I told her I couldn't; that I felt heavy with a 'terrible secret' hidden deep inside me, eating me up from the inside out like some kind of parasite; that the thoughts were with me every day; that his shadow followed me every night, feeding on me when I was stressed or down. It wasn't as simple as turning a page or having any real openness at all in my life. She reiterated that I had to move on. And so, I asked her for permission to write about it, openly and honestly, to let the light in before the darkness tore me apart.

'I can't keep running. I'm tired, Mammy. I'm very tired.'

I lay my head back down on the rail, holding her hand as tight as I dared, and we talked on. Mammy asked me if I could just say that 'the bad things' happened to someone else in this book and not talk about myself, because she didn't want shame on me or trouble for me. I said to her that I felt being open was the only way forward, because living with the pain of what had happened was destroying me. Its poison was spreading into other aspects of my life, turning them toxic too. All of my relationships had failed, in no small part because of my inability to trust others. She said that those relationships may not have worked out anyway, because I'm a workaholic like my father before me – 'hard to put up with'. I smiled and agreed, but added that I thought there was probably more to it than just genetics.

I poured out my heart to her, about the challenges of my profession, and the loneliness I felt when my colleagues left. She said, quite rightly, that everyone should be able to spread their wings, just as I had done, and I of course again agreed, explaining that I was in pain because I had loved them and really missed them, as they were the family I had made for myself. I guess those in-built responses to being 'abandoned' just stayed with me throughout my life. She said there was nothing I could do about the changes in my profession and if the worst came to the worst, I could always go and live in the small house in the middle of the Glebe bog that I had reclaimed with Daddy during my youth. I felt I had to tell her that 'the man' had taken me there once too, when we had been alone and working on the bog draining the land. I also said to her that I did not think I could keep silent about what I felt were transgressions and a lack of openness in my profession, and if I was going to be honest in my personal and professional life from now on, I had to face all of the demons at once. I said that I did think there was something I could do and that even if there wasn't, that I needed to try my best. Most of all, I told her that there were lots of other people out there like me who had been harmed as children, and if I spoke out, they might not feel as alone as I had felt all my life.

'But I have always been with you, Noel,' she said.

'But you couldn't always be with me, Mammy . . . and that's when he did those things.'

I regretted saying that, and I told her it wasn't her fault,

149

and that I know she always did her best, for me and all my siblings. She sighed and squeezed my hand a little, with what strength was left.

'I will always hold your hand,' she said.

'Like we used to do at Barkmills, Mammy,' I said.

As a boy, when I insisted on getting close to the danger of the waterfall, skipping on the mossy stones by the river's edge . . . 'Don't let me slip, Mammy,' I said back then, and I needed her support more than ever now.

'I can't stop you slipping, Noel,' came her reply in Barkmills . . . 'But I will catch you if you fall.' And so she did, many times in my life, as she did just then. Now as I held her fragile hand, she whispered, 'I'll hold your hand tighter, Noel, even tighter. I won't let you fall . . . If this is how you need to do it, then that's the way it'll be . . . I won't be around by then, Noel . . . But I'll hold your hand . . . and sure, by then, I can really be with you all of the time . . . yes, all of the time.' She trailed off.

Then after a long pause, she added, 'That priest, Noel (she never said his name once) . . . He wasn't talking with God the way I know God. You should try to talk to God again. It'll be all right. I'll hold your hand.'

She drifted into a kind of sleep as I cried quietly by her side, still holding her scrunched up little fingers in mine. And when she woke after a while, she suggested we say a little prayer together. It went like this:

Take my hand O Blessed Mother, hold me firmly lest I
fall.
I am frightened when I'm walking and on you I humbly
call.

Take me to my destination safely, and help me in all my
    undertakings,
And when evening comes upon me and I fear to be
    alone,
Take my hand O Precious Mother,
Protect me in my home.

Keira died in early September 2021, which delayed the operation I had planned that same week for Tess. I was too upset to function – the operation was high risk, would take several hours, and I was the only person in the UK who had ever applied a PAWS frame or was prepared to perform the procedure and give Tess a chance. That's not my ego talking, but rather my sadness that this remains the case a decade after I presented the technique at a scientific meeting. When I finally performed the procedure on both front legs, it went well, with no complications. Tess stayed at the practice for a prolonged period, during which she did indeed have a major issue with infection, as we'd anticipated she might, but which was eventually and thankfully resolved using culture-directed antibacterials. When she went home, Olive sat in Tess's crate with her a lot, cuddling her and reading her stories. She had her frames off just before I went home to see my mammy for her last Christmas. This was the best Christmas present Olive could ever have wished for. She has since sent me a video of her training Tess to dance. I may have performed the surgical procedure, but I'm in no doubt that it was Olive's love that saved Tess, just as Tess's love had saved Olive.

Just as my mother's love, always there when I needed it, has saved me.

I have struggled all my life to be open, because I did not trust anybody. Closing myself off was the only way I could survive. I have decided to open this vault of pain because Mammy is dead, Keira is dead and the man who abused me is long since dead. I couldn't bear hating myself and carrying the burden of shame any more, and I can't bear to see countless lives ruined by childhood traumas. I have been emotionally crippled for too long, running away from the scared little boy inside me. So, if my story helps one person to cope with their trauma, then it's worth the pain in the admission. *Beyond Supervet* for me isn't about what's coming next in my media or professional career or my personal life, but rather about learning to deal with what had come before. Could I learn to cope with what happened? Could I not feel worthless? Could I somehow forgive and could I somehow heal? Was there another way to sublimate my pain other than with endless work?

Could I be brave enough to sit by Mammy's bed and ask her, 'Did you know, Mammy?'

Yes, it transpires that I could.

The night before Mammy's funeral I asked the priest, Father Joe, for a private word in my sister's house. I confided in him about the abuse and I asked him how I might deal with the feelings of profound worthlessness I had going back into that same church to say goodbye to my mother. He offered some comfort and expressed sincere sadness about what had happened, and especially about what had been said to me in the confessional. A month later, when I returned to Ireland to make sure Mammy had her pearl necklace in the grave with her, to go dancing with Daddy in heaven, the same priest asked me to visit him at home.

He had some thoughts to share with me. He said that we can hold on to pain and it can fuel us, but if we can be open to forgiveness for the pain and through it discover love, we can in fact transform into a powerhouse of endless possibility. Then he said something that I shall take with me to the grave. He said that he believed 'the *gift* is *in* the wound'.

These are truths which I'm only beginning to understand. My gifts have indeed arisen from my wounds and my pain, but I've ignored that pain at great cost. I've neglected my own healing for too long. In talking about this, to my mammy, to the priest and to you, I'm not running away any longer. I'm opening the wound and dealing with the infection as best I can. It is my deepest hope that this openness might bring healing and maybe even forgiveness.

CHAPTER 7

Kindness

Betsy was an adorable cockapoo who, when she was six months old, was chasing a bird when she was hit by a vehicle, suffering multiple spinal fractures. Fortunately, these did not damage the spinal cord itself, but there was severe damage to the brachial plexus, which is a network of nerves that carries signals to and from her right front leg. Using electromyography (EMG), a type of special nerve conduction testing, we could see that the nerves down as far as her elbow had recovered after intensive physiotherapy, but the nerves below her elbow were permanently damaged and she would never be able to move her right front foot again. It was dragging and had to be repeatedly bandaged. She was also suffering from dysaesthesia, which is an unpleasant sensation of 'pins and needles' when tissue has suffered nerve damage. She was trying to chew off her own foot as a result. Inside the bandage, some tissue had sloughed due to disturbed nerve and blood supply and then that necrotic tissue became infected. That's when I was asked for an opinion on the possible 'kindest' next steps.

It was 2020 and Sophie and Dan, her incredibly kind human family, were about to have a baby and at the same time had to choose whether they wanted Betsy to have a life on three legs or four. Euthanasia was also an option, but not for them. This is a difficult ethical decision, since many would argue that the 'kindest thing' in such circumstances would be to amputate the limb entirely. Betsy was a small dog and should therefore manage well on three legs. Equally it could be argued that if anything were to happen to her other front leg during a likely long life, then there may be valid justification to try to save the injured limb. Many vets would argue against this option being offered at all because full limb amputation has been the gold standard for so long. However, I strongly believe that the technology has now reached such a proven level of efficacy that to not offer it as a treatment option to guardians of animals is no longer the right thing to do. Of course, there are risks, as there are with any surgery. The kindest thing to do is not always obvious, especially when opinions vary, even among people who are intrinsically kind. Sometimes the kindest thing, in the case of an animal in pain, is to end the life of the animal rather than seeking to prolong it. I am obliged to mention euthanasia as an actual 'treatment' in most cases, as I did for Betsy, even if it was anathema to me in her case. However, from the point of view of animal guardians, because they generally implicitly trust in the kindness of vets, it is an odd fact that I have been thanked many more times following an act of euthanasia than I ever have been for my surgical successes. People simply assume that all vets make the kindest decision. There is no measurement scale for kindness in this context and for me this raises many fundamental ethical questions.

A decade before I had faced a similar dilemma with

Bumblebee, a three-month-old basset hound when she came to the practice. Bumblebee was the best friend of Vicky's daughter, Heather, and Vicky was unsure how any procedure that affected Bumblebee might also affect Heather. Heather had been born prematurely, needing resuscitation, and had spent six weeks in intensive care. At three years old Heather could not stand, walk or talk. Diagnosed with ataxic cerebral palsy, she had daily physiotherapy and speech therapy. Throughout her life, plagued by constant ill health associated with her disabilities, she had become withdrawn and depressed. Her suffering increased when she was hit on the head by a swinging boom on a school boating trip. Her dogs at the time were a miniature poodle called Katy and a basset hound called Clueless. They lay by her room or on her bed all night comforting and protecting her. She had delirium for months and needed to be fed, bathed and cared for around the clock. Vicky had five other children to care for, so it was a very tough time for them all. As the years went by, Heather's memory began to deteriorate. Heather would eventually lose Clueless through old age at the same time as being diagnosed with frontotemporal dementia (FTD) when she was twenty-nine years of age.

A few months later, Vicky brought another basset hound, Daisy, into Heather's life and she had a soulmate once more. Daisy had puppies by Caesarean section and one of them had a deformed foot. Vicky didn't want to put this little girl to sleep and Heather called her Bumblebee, after her favourite comic book character. Out of all the puppies in the whelping box, Heather was instinctively drawn to Bumblebee. Her antics made Heather laugh and when she was calm, she often sat on Heather's lap and kept her calm too.

A search of the entire UK genetic database had not revealed anyone else with Heather's particular genetic disorder. The doctors told Vicky that this would be a life-limiting disease for her daughter, and this news came just days before I met Heather and Bumblebee for the first time.

Animals were her refuge, her confidants and her closest friends. She did not understand most humans, and humans did not understand her, but she was a magnet for animals, with whom she could always relate. Animals understood her aura; she was gentle with them and they with her. I felt a great affinity with Heather in this regard, as in my own mind I am often still a small boy sitting in a darkened cowshed talking to our farm dog Pirate and hiding away from the rest of humanity. I was also one of six children and she and I laughed over our shared interest in comic book superheroes.

Bumblebee had been born without a proper socket of her shoulder blade (glenoid) and with a forearm where the radius and ulna bones did not align together properly and were split apart, so her wrist (carpus) was deformed and hanging off. She was missing most of her toes and the two that remained were separated like a lobster claw. This is a congenital condition called ectrodactyly. No good treatment had ever been invented for this in dogs.

The quickest route would have been to perform full limb amputation, since Bumblebee was in discomfort and, though trying, she was not using the deformed leg well. This dysfunction would only grow worse over time. From Bumblebee's point of view a full limb amputation would be challenging because her breed has such a huge deep chest, and it would only be more difficult to get around on three legs as she got heavier and older. Not impossible with an appropriate harness sling perhaps, but Vicky was worried about managing such a situation whilst also caring for Heather and her five other children. One could even argue that the kindest thing was euthanasia which would be a single sharp pain for every-one and then it would be done. All kindness is relative to the perspective of those on the giving and receiving ends.

In our everyday lives, 'kindness' is an oft-used word, but it can sometimes sound insipid and insufficient, unfit to deal with the problems we face. Can kindness really make such a big change in difficult societal issues like homelessness, violent crime or drug addiction? Or for larger humanitarian tragedies such as war-zone suffering, the plight of refugees or children starving in a famine. That's before we even approach global crises like the destruction of our habitats through climate change, or the extinction of other species. Even for normal, everyday difficulties like a friend going through a divorce, or a child affected by bullying, or a cancer diagnosis . . . can kindness meet the challenge and make much of a difference? I believe it can – that the act of 'being kind' is absolutely essen-tial in the world, and that repeated acts are the building blocks of society at all levels. Kindness is, in my opinion, essential for humanity to thrive. It's the only way forward. I have learned this time and again from the animals and their families that I have been blessed to have known. To cite the popular Ameri-can singer Halsey, I can absolutely always 'confide in the one' and 'be kind to the one' that I love, be that the animal or their family. In the kindness department, I'm a very lucky man, because I am bathed in its glow daily.

Kindness always pays you back, as I have found down the years (though my bank manager might take issue with that). I get immense satisfaction from seeing investment in a colleague lead them to flourish, to go off and do good in the world, of hoping that the extra effort of mentorship or expense of training scholarships is reflected in the future of animal care and welfare. I think it's fair to say you won't get far trying to pay an actual bill out of your kindness account, but it pays you back with interest in terms of fulfilment for the soul over the years. I always keep that in mind when thinking about any interaction with a professional colleague or potential treatment for an animal.

With both Bumblebee and Betsy, counter-intuitively, if I was thinking purely financially, the most profitable treatment for both would have been full limb amputation – a relatively routine procedure requiring little specialist equipment or technology. That's not to say that the limb salvage route wouldn't leave both clients having hefty bills – only that my profit margin would be considerably smaller and for a lot more effort, because of the time required to prepare custom implants, plus the extensive aftercare. Simply using a stump-socket prosthesis (SSP) which fits on a stump, like we are accustomed to in human amputees, was not a good option for either Betsy or Bumblebee because the amputation was too high and they would fall off. So, I had a dilemma too. To help both animals, truly to the best of my ability, with utmost kindness, would mean huge commitment from both my team and the families practically and financially. I would be 'married' to these clinical cases for their life dur-ation, since no other vet in the UK knows enough about maintenance and servicing of the sort of custom prostheses anchored to the skeleton which I was considering for them.

To innovate ways to relieve animals of their pain, and to provide optimal quality of life, has been my personal choice throughout my career and I'm not looking for a medal. I am rather trying to understand how one can best deploy this currency of kindness within an economy where money rules. There are kindnesses that are not practically or financially possible, and I'm always trying to find the balance. As I've alluded to, if a specialist practice like Fitzpatrick Referrals can't pay the bills with routine cases, then the well of kindness in trying to help complex challenging cases through expensive innovation is in serious danger of drying up. Animals have given me so much in terms of love and fulfilment. Their gifts far outweigh what I have given to them. And I always wish I could give more.

Fitzpatrick Referrals is the largest orthopaedics and neurosurgery specialist referral centre which offers in-house bespoke solutions and that remains independent in the UK. As I have also mentioned, most families have no idea that they have a choice, they just trust that their vet will do the kindest thing for their animal friend.

The reality in 2022, though, is that most easy, routine cases are operated in primary care vets, by peripatetic surgeons or in specialist centres owned by the same business group that owns the primary care vets, so that the lifetime care of the patient is a 'value centre' in their business model. As a result, many of the cases I operate in my practice are, like Betsy and Bumblebee, very complex and they come from all over the UK and abroad, whereas what we really need to stay alive as a financially viable service is a steady flow of routine orthopaedics and neurosurgery alongside, to make a reasonable margin and pay the bills, as I've alluded to earlier. Betsy's and Bumblebee's CT scans would be imported into computer software. Myself and the engineers would make and perfect a design, manufacture the implants and create special features for bone and skin on-growth.

Surgery would be followed by a period of rehabilitation and recovery, and then longer-term follow-up using pressure walkway analysis, clinical examination, radiography and

CT scans to provide evidence for efficacy in an ethical way. Though such follow-up is necessary to check the long-term welfare of the patient and for academic publications, my detractors have accused me of unnecessarily inconveniencing the animal by performing follow-up whilst simultaneously accusing that some of my techniques are not indicated because they haven't seen the follow-up. In such an environment, one cannot win in terms of the unkind things people say, one can only win in the kindness one tries to garner for all future patients. That's enough for me, because nothing ruins one's perception of success like thorough follow-up! Just because the client didn't come back to see you, doesn't mean that the operation actually worked.

There's far more to bespoke surgery than an implant arriving in a sterilised plastic bag, and if one were to monetise this process properly, charging by the hour like a lawyer, for example, and seeking to recoup investment in factory facilities, one can easily see that even prior to any *treatment*, a client would be liable for significant expense. Put simply, customised bespoke surgery costs more to perform and earns less profit than routine surgery but such effort makes a tangible difference when animals have no other good options. People confuse the magnitude of an invoice with the profit made from that invoice all the time. To approach this process with the mindset of an accountant fixated on profit-margin alone would make no rational sense, but for me, to be 'kind' in this 'kind of medicine' demands compromise on many levels.

It is my personal belief that most financial models of companion animal veterinary practice in 2022 are not prepared to make that compromise. The harsh truth in the real world is that an open heart is not as valuable as an open cheque book when it comes to being kind with all of the treatment options. And importantly, it's not only the total price of a treatment, but rather more the profit made from a treatment that may have the greatest influence on options offered to animal patients going forward.

Kindness begins when a family trusts me to do the right thing for their animal friend and when I agree to treat the patient in the first place. If nobody else wants to treat the dog or cat, either because they don't have the technology, experience or desire to do so, then it falls to me to say 'yes' or 'no'. But I can't say yes to every case. Sometimes that's because I do not feel it's ethically right to proceed with surgery, even if the surgery is technically possible. I may feel that the client's perspective on functional outcome cannot be delivered, or it may not be practical or affordable for the family. Sometimes families disagree with my adjudication, and occasionally I receive abuse and unkindness through their frustration.

An interesting phenomenon in recent years is that the more complex cases I treat, the more the clients who are referred my way come to expect. As the possibilities of technology and surgical advances evolve, sometimes people only see what may appear to be 'miracle' cures, which make an appropriate narrative arc in a television show. The clients who reach our doors have often exhausted every other option, leaving them mentally and emotionally drained and we are all hugely sympathetic. But we are not miracle workers. As the expectations have grown of what I may be able to achieve, so has the disappointment if I decline to treat on ethical grounds or if I try my best but still fail to achieve a happy outcome.

Surgery is full of uncertainty, and I never make promises I cannot fulfil, because I know that I am always ultimately at the mercy of biology and good fortune. Clients are very well briefed pre-operatively about the intrinsic risks of failure.

But, hope can be a distorting lens through which to wish for a possible outcome versus a probable outcome. And hope can quickly turn to disappointment, anger and difficult conversations about money spent on surgery which didn't work out. As my daddy once observed, 'You can take your friend to work in your car for years as a favour, but the day you can't pick them up and drop them home again, you may suddenly become their enemy.' People who can start out on the treatment journey seeming very kind and compassionate can, unfortunately, become aggressive, accusatory and most unkind if I fail.

To use an analogy, if a human heart surgeon operates only on patients who have a very high risk of dying without the procedure, we accept that their operations will likely have a higher mortality rate than those of other surgeons who are performing routine procedures. When I perform routine procedures, my failure rate is very low, but because I often operate on near-impossible cases, many of which have been rejected by other surgeons because they don't have access to the technology or techniques, my failure rate in such cases can be above the average for routine surgeries. Is it kinder just to say 'no', or is it kinder to say 'yes' to such surgery?

In some very rare cases, clients will launch litigation after failure. I can understand their grief and sadness when things don't work out, and though I try not to take this personally, it's hard. In all cases, my team and I will have done our very best, acting with transparency, fairness and integrity at all times. Of course, no surgeon is above criticism, and all surgeons should be expected to perform to a reasonable standard. In such situations, as I have mentioned, people often forget that my time spent defending such cases (in every case successfully so far) takes from time spent trying to heal animals who were in the same state that their friend was when they originally came to see me. Letting people and their animal friends down – seeing any animal reach a point where we cannot help them – is the worst part of my job. When that comes with anger from the client, it's heartbreaking. Some days the pressure really gets to me and I feel like my ten-year-old self, still not clever enough, not strong enough and not brave enough, no matter how hard I try.

Another phenomenon in recent years, as *The Supervet* TV show continues to be broadcast, is the unkindness of certain members of my own profession on social media, in lectures and public forums, or through complaints to RCVS. Some clinical cases shown on television have been cited as examples of over-treatment or even cruelty. This criticism has always struck me as somewhat bizarre, in a profession which is supposed to be motivated by kindness, compassion, care, responding appropriately and being collegiate. I try hard, in the words of Taylor Swift, to 'shake it off', but sometimes their unkindness hurts me deeply. One day there may be no 'Beyond Supervet' for me, just because it's really hard for me to maintain a consistent level of mental health to function as a good surgeon amid the near-constant barrage of painful criticism by some clients and some vets, even if they are a very small minority.

I have twice been accused of malpractice, of 'experimenting' on animals and bringing the veterinary profession into disrepute. The first time was for using an arthroscope to 'second-look' at cartilage grafts post-operatively in dogs with osteochondritis dissecans, a joint condition where lack of blood flow causes large holes in their joints. This is a common and accepted technique in human and equine patients, and is commonly cited in academic papers and textbooks in the USA, but the complainant felt this was an unnecessary surgical procedure, in spite of the fact that it's just a needle with a camera inside, with full volitional client consent and full transparency that we were trying to do our best for each dog to check joint integrity before off-lead activity resumed. The second, which I have mentioned previously, was for applying three bionic limbs to a tortoise who had his legs chewed off by rats in hibernation, which prompted complaints from vets and a direct request for me to lose my licence to practise. There was no evidence in either case of malicious wrongdoing or provable malpractice by me and no further action was taken. Both cases will have cost my governing body, RCVS, tens of thousands of pounds to investigate, which all vets pay for in their annual dues.

I'm only human and though I know the golden rule of the internet, I do sometimes read the comments, especially when it's in a veterinary publication. I am often astonished by the level of vitriol there seems to be out there. A particularly abhorrent recent example was that the commenter would rather use burdizzos on themselves than watch my shows. (Burdizzos, for those intrigued, are large steel clamps for crushing the base of a farm animal's testicles during castration.) All of the comments I have read which have been written by veterinary surgeons strike me as particularly strange, because these are highly intelligent people who passed examinations based on 'fact' rather than 'opinion', and yet are being unkind to a colleague, who they have never actually met, with submissions of conjecture. Sadly though, as Dave Gahan from Depeche Mode once put it, 'people are people', and it is a shame in a caring profession that some of us 'get along so awfully'.

The RCVS code of professional conduct 5.2 states that 'Veterinary surgeons and veterinary nurses should not speak or write disparagingly about another veterinary surgeon or veterinary nurse. Colleagues should be treated fairly, without discrimination and with respect, in all situations and in all forms of communication.'

Though I am always up for having a robust conversation about the ethics of the sort of procedures I carry out, I have to hope that some of the people who criticise me in such hyperbolic and unkind ways would baulk from doing so if they met me in person. There's a perception of me, I realise from some of these messages and comments, that I have a messiah complex, and that I drive my work colleagues too hard to further my own fame, making them work all hours to match my surgical timetable. Nothing could be further from the truth. While it is the case that some very complex operations don't finish until late in the evening, I'm acutely aware of the wellbeing of those who work with me, their shift patterns and need to recuperate from their hard work. I am, for better or worse, the figurehead of Fitzpatrick Referrals, and the television show focuses on me for much of the time, and the most advanced surgeries that I carry out. This sometimes misses the fact that I work closely with many other hugely talented surgeons, nurses and other colleagues. When one criticises me, one also criticises scores of other well-meaning and deeply caring veterinary professionals, accusing them too of hypocrisy, which is both untrue and unkind.

Another somewhat misleading notion is that we will always elect to pursue some high-tech solution to an animal's suffering. In fact, we often choose *not* to carry out complex procedures in favour of routine limb amputation or euthanasia. Sometimes these really are the kindest options for patient and client. Clearly most of these cases do not make the edit, partly because the narratives aren't conducive, but also because in cases where euthanasia is the kindest option, clients are understandably often reticent to share their private grief on television as they hold their beloved for the last time. Giving tablets, performing amputations and putting dogs and cats to sleep does not good television make for a TV channel. I am profoundly grateful to those wonderful people who have allowed us to show failure on my TV show, because I feel that giving a balanced view is very important. I wish some of my critics would come and spend time at the practice to see how suffused with kindness and care our actions are at every stage, whether the cameras are there or not.

A great irony is that when I have offered to lecture on subjects like Betsy and Bumblebee's surgery to vets in the UK in recent years, as I've tried to 'take on the world', in the words of the band You Me At Six, for whatever reasons, my offers have been declined by 'the establishment. Yet, companies are allowed to sell limb-salvage and other advanced or customised implants to vets in the UK without any training whatsoever. It still hurts when peers in my own profession do not accept my best efforts, but I'm beginning to realise that searching for any sense of worth in the eyes of others who ostensibly lack kindness will always leave me feeling worthless, so I'll continue to just do my best for my patients. That will be worth and kindness enough.

The families of both Betsy and Bumblebee chose surgical limb salvage, with skeletally anchored limb amputation prostheses (SALAP) – the most difficult and expensive procedure but with the best potential outcome in these two specific cases, in my view. Whether this is kind or unkind in your view, or in the opinion of other veterinary surgeons, is somewhat moot. It was a choice for my human clients, on behalf of their animal companions. This choice was made with love and kindness and I personally do not feel that my profession have the right to take that choice away.

My trust in the kindness of my client is critical, because if I perform surgery with a SALAP, I am, as I have previously said, married to the care of that patient for the rest of their days, since I'm the only person in the UK who knows what the short- and long-term care entails. This is not a quick-fix, quick-money, 'goodbye and good luck' operation. This is a commitment to that family for the rest of that animal's life, so we'd better get along emotionally and be on the same page.

Betsy had to wait a little for her bionic leg – until her human brother Hugo came into the world in August 2020. In the meantime, I operated to remove her foot and to let the stump heal, in order to minimise the risk of infection when the bionic limb implant was fitted later. The implant itself was designed nine years after Bumblebee's and, during that time, the technology had evolved considerably and we had created a new implant which performed better. The original implant was called an intraosseous transcutaneous amputation prosthesis (ITAP). However, I experienced problems with infection, implant integration and fracture over time, which prompted evolution of a new implant which has performed better in my patients, called PerFiTS (percutaneous fixation to the skeleton). My hope was to license the intellectual property for this implant to a company that could make them for human amputee patients and that royalties from any sales could go to the Humanimal Trust charity. By doing so, the sales of implants for human patients would in some small way help both animals and humans simultaneously, but so far this aspiration has not materialised.

The normal practice for any human implant, as I've mentioned earlier, is to first test it on animals. So animal subjects are implanted, then the animals are subsequently killed to analyse the implant properties. I'd very much like business to be done differently where possible. Nowadays with high resolution CT scans, one doesn't actually need to end the life of an experimental dog to see the results of implant surgery. Plus, there's a wealth of clinical comparative lessons to be learned and shared if we studied dogs that actually benefited from the implant. These include how the muscle and nerves are prepared, how the skin interfaces with either the bone edge or the metal edge at the base of the stump, how to prevent infections and, critically, how implants perform over several years and not just the duration of a short experiment. I live in hope that we can more openly discuss failure so that we can better succeed for the benefit of both human and animal patients. To paraphrase Winston Churchill, if you have never made a mistake, you have never made anything.

In spite of all of my precautions, after I implanted Betsy's PerFiTS device, the infection that had been in her foot returned further up in the leg. The implant itself was becoming infected and I had a very narrow window of time to deal with it. Again, I discussed the ethical implications of trying to treat, versus full limb amputation, with the family. They elected to try, so I opened the skin of the implant again and flushed out the infection followed by application of an antiseptic solution and antibiotics. Then we waited with bated breath for two weeks for the healing of the skin onto the mesh of the implant, the dermal integration module (DIM).

Now, two years later, Betsy has healed very well and is running around happily. She has an 'endoprosthesis' implant inside the skin linked to the bones of her forearm (radius and ulna), and a spigot of metal through the skin which links to an 'exoprosthesis' or external foot. Together the endo- and exo-prostheses constitute a bionic limb. At first, the foot was made of aluminium coated with hard-wearing rubber from a bicycle tyre, but Betsy was so boisterous that she wore out all forms of rubber. So now she dashes about on an aluminium blade bonded to a skateboard wheel. It works a treat. I defy anyone to watch her running with her family and not say it was the kindest option.

I also feel that we chose the kindest option for Bumble-bee back in 2011. For both her and Betsy, the familes were very much aware that if I failed, full limb amputation or euthanasia were the only remaining options. I will always re-member how Heather and I held hands during Bumblebee's initial consultation and I explained that we had a big job to do together for her friend Bumblebee, and that we would have to go through a lot side by side. I explained that I had never performed this type of shoulder operation which we had proposed before, that it was a brand-new implant we'd developed, and that the bionic limb operation was also com-plicated. I told her it was possible that Bumblebee could lose her leg or her life. Heather barely spoke to anybody at the time, but she spoke to me. This was a lot for her to take in and I felt very privileged that she let me into her confidence and shared her feelings with me. She was fighting for her own health and for Bumblebee's at the same time. Vicky told me afterwards that 'it was like a door opened'. I certainly know for sure that every time I opened my consulting room door to Heather, a door opened in my heart that shall never be closed. That's what kindness shared does in real life.

Bumblebee waited for her operation until after her first Christmas in 2011, since she needed to be skeletally mature. First, I operated on her shoulder with what was back then the world's first half joint replacement (hemiarthroplasty) of its kind, since I needed to replace the socket of the shoulder blade (glenoid) with a high-density plastic. When that had healed, I removed her foot and implanted her SALAP, attaching it to her radius and ulna bones and stitching the skin around the DIM, leaving a spigot protruding onto which her external foot was attached. In her case an aluminum blade coated in rubber worked a treat.

After recovering well from both of her surgeries, the first day that Heather saw Bumblebee with her new bionic foot was truly magical. She was sitting on the floor of my consulting room and she could hear the staccato thumps of Bumblebee's bionic foot striding jubilantly down the corridor, long before she could see her. When I brought her into the room, the joy in Heather's face for me was the greatest ever physical embodiment of the sacredness of the human–animal bond. Pure joy. Pure kindness. And that's the reason I do what I do. Bumblebee was ecstatic too, jumping all over Heather and bashing her with her new fancy foot made from metal and rubber. Vicky cried and Heather and I laughed our heads off. Then we had a big group hug with Bumblebee and all was well in the world. Heather and Vicky had trusted my kindness, and that's all I have ever wanted from anyone who comes to see me with their animal friend.

Heather and Vicky once came with me on to a TV chat show to talk about the human–animal bond and how important advanced surgery is. Heather loved having her make-up done. I absolutely hate it and always have since my modelling and acting days. I hate people touching my head – it's a deep childhood fear from the dark days. Heather laughed at me sitting in the chair beside her, as she lapped up the attention.

Bumblebee went on to live a fantastic four years with full pain-free function before she was afflicted by intervertebral disc extrusion. A dried-out disc in her back, which is a common problem in the breed, exploded its pulpy centre (nucleus pulposus) and caused significant compression of and damage to her spinal cord. She had been running around as normal, but suddenly became withdrawn and wobbly on her hind legs. By the time I saw her she was nearly completely paralysed on her hind legs and could barely feel her toes even if I squeezed really hard. We performed an MRI scan to identify the site of the problem, and once again I held Heather's hand and told her that she could lose her friend. Vicky decided that she wanted to give Bumblebee a chance. I operated straight away to remove the compressive material, but the spinal cord took a long time to recover, with many hours of physiotherapy. She did regain most of her function and continued a happy life, helping Heather when she went through major abdominal surgery, horrendous infections and yet more depression. Both Heather and Vicky had many more huge flappy-eared cuddles.

Sadly, a year later, Bumblebee blew another disc. We could have continued invasive treatment, but at this stage we all felt that it was kindest to allow her to pass away peacefully. Heather and Vicky were understandably devastated. But the six years that they did have together were a blessing. Vicky has shared with me that our consultations had done as much for Heather as for Bumblebee in many ways because they had shone a light into her life which kept her company in the darker times. If a life is well spent in kindness and happiness, then the joy of love lives forever. Sometimes I hold a hand and a paw in hope of salvation, and at other times in letting go. Kindness comes in many forms.

I saw Heather again after Bumblebee's passing, with her cat Siam, who was hit by a van which happened to be delivering birthday presents for Heather herself. Vicky and

I both had to tell her that it might be the end for Siam. I repaired his many pelvic fractures and amputated one hind leg because of permanent nerve damage. He ran around happily for another two years and was an amazing friend for Heather, snuggling on her chest when she was afraid and needed comfort. He also kept Vicky company when she found herself bedridden with nerve pain due to spinal stenosis and fibromyalgia. Sadly, Siam was killed by a car just before Heather's forty-second birthday.

Before Siam's surgery, Heather said to Vicky, 'It will be fine. Noel will try to fix him, but if he can't, we have tried.' This was the most lucid sentence she had uttered for a long time before and never since. Dementia has gradually robbed her of her memories and diction – but this one sentence was, in my view, more rational than many made by those who have their full mental faculties.

Heather had never been given much of a chance. Vicky was told she'd be dead by ten, then twenty, then thirty, then forty. She is currently forty-four years old and continues to smile and share love and kindness with everyone who meets her. I send her a birthday video each year, because now that Bumblebee and Siam are gone, we don't see each other any more. She smiles when she hears my voice on TV or radio and says to Vicky, 'That's my friend, Noel.' She never forgets me, nor I her, though we live many hours apart. The love and trust we share has never been lost or broken. If Vicky has a bad headache, she has told me that Heather rubs her head and even now, with all her frailty, the pain goes away. Heather has healing and profound kindness within her.

Heather and I were talking once, as we sat out in the field at the back of my practice on a rug with Bumblebee. A royal admiral butterfly alighted on the rug and I told her that when I was a child, I believed that when we left this body, the stardust from which we're all made would be carried on the wings of such a butterfly to heaven, so I wasn't afraid of passing through and that she'd be okay too, no matter what. Heather never said much because of her medical condition. She just listened and every now and then blurted out, 'You're my friend. You will always be my friend.' That's all she needed to say. That's all anyone needs to say. That's kindness shared.

Nobody knows if this year will be Heather's last birthday. In spite of her dementia, she always has a kind smile for me. When she is in a lot of pain physically and mentally, she listens to the audio of my last book through her headphones, and Vicky tells me that it helps her to sleep. That alone is reason enough to stay up all night at weekends and in between operating to get this book written. Heather will listen and she will smile. Vicky said to me recently, 'I hope this friendship has not been a big burden for you to carry.' I was momentarily taken aback, because it's been one of the greatest honours of my career and life to share kindness with Bumblebee, Siam, Heather and Vicky.

Kindness is never a burden and always an honour.

CHAPTER 8

Commitment

I sat bolt upright in my hospital bed and screamed inside.

The Queen! How could I forget the Queen?

It was Saturday. Lunch with Her Majesty was actually scheduled for the following Wednesday, but out of my mind on opioids I wasn't thinking clearly. I suddenly felt a massive urge to pee and so dragged myself out of bed. As I peeled off my hospital pyjama bottoms, I looked down and noticed the plaster cast on my leg. My brain involuntarily spasmed in panic again.

I called Ciara, who organises everything in my life. She answered as she always does, with a voice of calm and reason, as I blurted out, 'The Queen!' Ciara told me it wasn't a problem and that she'd organised everything with driver David, but that wasn't the cause of my anxiety. To meet the Queen, I'd need to be wearing trousers, and my current predicament meant I didn't have any that would fit over my plaster cast. Neither of us – not even the unflappable Ciara – had foreseen this particular crisis. The following day, Sunday, I was going home, and the day after that was a Bank Holiday Monday. Time was running out to find a solution.

Off the phone, I searched the web for tailors in my home-town of Guildford and called a few with no success. Finally one answered. I told myself not to overcomplicate things. All I needed was someone to make a flared leg. How hard could that be? 'Hello,' I said. 'I'm going to see the Queen and I have a cast on my leg, so I can't get my trousers on. Can you please "let out" a leg for me?' There was a stunned silence for a few moments and a man with a rather posh voice curtly responded that he was sorry, but it would be simply impossible to carry out alterations over the Bank Holiday. 'But it's for the Queen!' I implored. He apologised again and hung up.

I lay in bed staring at the tiles of the hospital ceiling, flicking the switch on my opioid pump every now and then. I'd just had bone marrow drilled out of my pelvis and trans-planted to my ankle to fill bone cysts for the second time. The first operation had failed and the hastily rescheduled pro-cedure had thrown my own operating schedule, and indeed my mental state, into disarray. I hadn't taken more than a few days off since 2000 and I don't take holidays at all. Dis-appointing animals and clients is always distressing, but I'd had to rearrange many surgeries and consultations around my unanticipated hospital visit and recuperation. In the last-minute panic to deal with my operating commitments, my date with the Queen had slipped my mind.

Monday morning at 10 a.m., I was determined to sort out my outfit for Wednesday's special occasion and I wasn't taking no for an answer. I got a wheelchair-accessible cab and headed into Guildford to the tailors I'd spoken to on the phone. I was wearing my scrub trousers with a slit cut up the side so I could pull them over the cast on my right ankle. I left the wheelchair outside the non-wheelchair-accessible tailor's shop and hobbled through the door on my crutches. The man inside nodded and smiled, somewhat bemused at my waddling entrance. Out of a bag I pulled a pair of blue suit trousers and laid them up on the counter in front of him. I explained the problem, ascertaining that this wasn't the same gentleman to whom I'd spoken on the phone. To my relief he said he could carry out the adjustments needed, even adding a zip to the side of the flare. I could, he said, pick the trousers up the following weekend.

My foot was throbbing. I started to sweat. I needed them for Wednesday, I explained. For a lunch with the monarch herself. He looked distinctly unconvinced. In an effort to persuade him this was not a bluff, I scrolled through the images on my phone where I'd taken a snap of the invitation. I thrust the screen towards his face to show him the crisp, marbled, cream-coloured card with embossed calligraphy:

The Master of the Household
has received Her Majesty's command
to invite Professor Noel Fitzpatrick to Luncheon
to be given at Buckingham Palace
by The Queen and The Duke of Edinburgh

Instantaneously, his sceptical smile disappeared and his attitude changed to one of obsequious service. He told me my trousers would be ready by the end of the following day, and even shook my hand before helping me back to my wheelchair outside. It was truly amazing how absolute recalcitrance turned to total commitment in an instant due to a change in belief!

The following afternoon, I went back to pick up the adjusted garment – now with one leg befitting John Travolta in *Saturday Night Fever*. My helpful new friend proudly showed me how he'd added material and a well-concealed zipper which would open and close the trouser leg around my cast. Then he neatly folded the trousers with professional finesse and placed them carefully in a bag with the kind of reverence an artist bestows on his work, before handing it to me with a reverential nod.

I returned to my house and lay on my bed, still doped up with medication and satisfied that I had succeeded against the odds. There was a knock on the door. I went down and there stood Pode, a lovely man and a great carpenter. I had decided I couldn't show up to the palace at the time of the Queen's birthday without a gift, even if I was just one guest among many, but what does one give to the woman who has everything? I'd forgotten that I'd asked Pode ages before and now he handed me a pink paper bag. I thanked him profusely and he departed with a broad grin on his chiselled features. I smiled too as I hobbled up the stairs and sat at my kitchen table to admire the contents of the delivery. Wrapped in pink crepe paper was Pode's creation – a beautiful wooden box made out of bog oak, with an inscribed gold plate mounted on the front. Looking at it reminded me first and foremost of my daddy, and the bog oak we'd pulled out from our land.

Draining the marshland alongside my father is one of my clearest memories from my youth, probably because it had occupied a considerable amount of our time. Together, we dug 'shores' in the boggy ground and laid clay pipes every eighteen inches, surrounded by gravel in the underground channel to drain water away. Dried out, the land could be used for planting grass for grazing or crops for feed. Daddy was 100 per cent committed to the land and the animals upon it; everything else was secondary, except God. Sometimes I'd complain that the ground would never be dry, but Daddy would remind me of his 'Pioneer pin', a source of great pride for him. In the Irish Catholic faith, the Pioneers (*Réadóirí* in Gaelic) glorify God through abstinence from alcohol. My daddy reminded me, 'If any man can be dried out, a bog can be dried out. It's all a matter of commitment.' I became a workaholic like my father, and I think it's likely that committing to work saved me from any number of other vices.

The ground that we were reclaiming was Daddy's favourite bit of land, 'The Glebe', which I've mentioned earlier. Glebe, from the Latin *gleba*, which means 'land' or 'soil', is a patch of ground owned by the Church and assigned to support the local priest. It was to that soil that my father was truly committed. He told me I was to care for it too, after he died, and that I was to never sell it. Though I was only twelve years old, I promised, and committed myself to The Glebe for life. In the same way, I have committed to never willingly selling the veterinary practice I have created. There is no price that can overturn true commitment to doing my best for all of the animals we see and offering them all of the options all of the time. My vet practice in Eashing in Surrey is my very own Glebe, and its soil runs through my veins, much as the bogland did for my daddy.

As we drained the land, Daddy and I had pulled up hundreds of lumps of bog oak. These trees had fallen thousands of years ago and were partly preserved and petrified by the acidic peat. As the ground shrank and dried, the roots and branches occasionally appeared, thrusting upwards like the wreck of some ancient ship from the depths. For me, they were a source of significant trouble. As I drove along 'topping' (cutting the tops off) the thistles so that they wouldn't go to seed and multiply, the cutting bar of the mower periodically snagged on a piece of protruding wood, jamming the teeth and thence breaking the wooden connecting rod between the motor and the blade. It was the job of the connecting rod to snap when such things happened, so as not to thrash the motor, or at least that's what I tried to say to my daddy on the many times I broke it. He insisted that I should be able to see that bit of bog oak hidden in the grass and nettles before I hit it.

As I sat at my table and ran my hands over the polished wood Pode had brought to my door, I felt I was touching the past, that I was connected to the ancestors who lived and worked the land long ago. I felt my father's hands in the smooth grain of knots and sinews in the wood. Prone to making connections at the best of times, I wondered in my opioid drunkenness whether it was this predilection that may have somehow drawn me to the knots and sinews of tissue. Pode's box was made out of 5300-year-old wood, preserved in silt when the sea levels rose about 7000 years ago and the East Anglian fenland basin was flooded, drowning the standing trees. Those trees were preserved in anaerobic conditions, exactly like those under the surface of The Glebe, and that's what had given me the idea for the gift in the first place. Ireland and the United Kingdom shared a similar natural heritage and I wanted to give the Queen a present to reflect our commonality in shared natural history. The shared and often troubled political history between our countries has left its mark on both lands, in the hearts and minds of its people. Northern Ireland in particular bears the deep scars of division, each side understandably committed to their heritage, with generational pain potentially tugging towards conflict, while hope and commitment to peace make us strive towards reconciliation. As Adele says in her song 'Someone like You', 'sometimes it lasts in love' and 'sometimes it hurts instead'. I think it's important to be respectful that everyone alive today has inherited feelings of responsibility for the thoughts and actions of our ancestors, which may remain very poignant arbiters of present perspectives. However, we are not our ancestors and we are not our history. Personally, I have never held anyone alive today responsible for the actions of those who went before them. I am deeply conscious of my own heritage in Ireland and also very grateful to have been allowed to strive for my dreams in England. I am also lucky that my canine and feline patients don't mind where in the world they live as long as there's commitment to respect and love.

The inscription on the box read 'Happy Birthday, Your Majesty. Celebrating 90 years of service in 5000 years of heritage'. On a piece of parchment inside, I wrote a longer message, explaining the significance of the bog oak to me personally, and by comparison to Her Majesty's lasting legacy. I felt that on such an auspicious occasion as her birthday, it was appropriate to thank the Queen for her commitment to stewardship and drawing people together as best she could.

I had written this message a couple of months before when I asked Pode for the box, and now that I read it back, I was riven by doubt. What had I been thinking? It was too *long*, and it was highly unlikely the Queen would even read it. But as I sat there looking at the majestic felt-lined box, perhaps contributed to by my heavy-duty painkillers, an even worse idea occurred. *I must put a jewel in this magnificent jewellery box for the Queen*, I thought.

So, in the delusion of the moment, I phoned my practice and asked for the nurse looking after the total hip replacement equipment. She came to the phone, whereupon I asked if she could supply me with a packet of hip cement. She laughed and asked if I was going to operate on a dog in my 'spare time' on my kitchen table. I laughed back and then, in a deadly serious way, told her simply that I needed to make something. I suppose it's one of the benefits of having my name on the building, that she asked no more questions. The cement was on my doorstep in less than an hour.

I had it in my head that I would make a star for the Queen, because in my drug-fuelled state, I thought that this would be an obvious reference to how she was an empowering star in the firmament, shining out across the world. I was pretty sure it was unlikely that a star made out of orthopaedic cement had been bestowed on her before by either family member or foreign dignitary. It would be a genuine gift, fashioned with a personal touch, that she might appreciate. It was also bacteria-resistant, pretty much indestructible and would last forever. *She'll love it*, I thought. *What could possibly go wrong?*

Well . . . almost everything as it turned out.

Considering my lifetime commitment to perfecting my surgical skills, I hadn't planned the 'star surgery' very well at all. First, I hadn't really thought about how many prongs I wanted on my star. Second, I hadn't thought how much

182

cement should be in each prong as I fashioned it. Third, I hadn't quite appreciated that I am protected during surgery when using such cement by double rubber gloves. I knew that when the white powder gets mixed with the solvent liquid, it's an exothermic reaction, which releases enormous heat, but I had never felt that heat with bare hands before. As I poured it from a bowl onto a breadboard on my kitchen table, my fingers began to tingle. I was trying to shape a five-pronged star with my hands and a kitchen knife, as it set from liquid to dough to rock hard, which took only a couple of minutes. And in that precarious time window, I had committed mentally to engraving the Queen's birthday – *HRH 21-4-1926* – on the front. However, I rushed, working the cement too soon, before it became doughy, resulting in it sticking to and burning my fingers. I tried to use the knife to cut the hot cement away from the board and my fingers, but the stress of arts and crafts was getting to me far more than the stress of any life-saving operation.

Unlike in my surgical career, I had no Plan B of a second cement batch, and by now the nurses would all have gone home. I panicked further and continued in my delusional race of unsticking and engraving against the clock with a blunt knife. Ultimately, the bottom two prongs looked like little fat legs whilst the top prong got a bit elongated as I tried to put a hanging hole in it with a nail I'd found in a kitchen drawer. In my head, at the time, it was entirely plausible that Queen Elizabeth II would take a misshapen star, made of orthopaedic cement by an idiot with zero craftwork skills, and want to hang it up somewhere in a royal residence. The remaining two prongs ended up looking like small stumpy arms. And thus, my intended gift, now setting quickly and inevitably before my eyes, looked less like a glistening star of resilience and commitment, and more like a gingerbread man.

I wrote a very small additional card saying, 'Thank you for being a beautiful bright star committed to shining light for all', and I tied my card to the hole in the star with a bit of parcel twine that I also found in a drawer. I wrapped my creation in crepe paper which I had left over from Christmas, placing it in Pode's box and back into his pink bag lovingly. The Queen would certainly love it, I assured myself, as I went off to bed.

When David duly arrived in the morning, I piled into the van with my crutches and precious pink bag, flared trousers zipped up for my suit and tie combo, and off we went to meet one of the most unquestionably committed people this country has ever known. For the many decades she was on the throne, Queen Elizabeth reigned over her realm with dignity, poise and strength of character. She was a constant in inconstant times. Whatever one's nationality, whatever one's perspective is on past history and whatever one's opinion is of the British monarchy, one undeniable truth is that Queen Elizabeth II tried her best to be a figurehead for goodness. She was also famously a keen horsewoman and the companion of many corgis over the years. I knew of the Queen's keen interest in animals from our first meeting, when she came to open the veterinary school at the University of Surrey in Guildford, which I helped to found. I hoped it would inspire a generation of young people to care deeply about animals and the planet we live on.

The Queen had arrived with her entourage of cars and minders, and came into the room as if gliding on velvet. I instinctively knelt down in front of her, beside a dog called

Scruffy who had a bionic limb amputation prosthesis, to invite her to see how it worked. I had brought an equivalent model to demonstrate how bone and skin grow onto the endoprosthesis implant inside the body, which in turn was attached to an exoprosthesis, which forms a new foot. The Queen was ostensibly very interested in my explanation of how this could help man and animal through One Medicine, and she leaned towards me as I extended the bionic limb model upwards, much like a large biomechanical sword, ending up not far from Her Majesty's shoulder. The implant had a plate not dissimilar to a blade, and the personal protection officer gave me a warning look. Given I didn't want to end up in the Tower of London, I hastily backed away from my unintentional 'reverse-knighting' posture.

On the day of our second meeting, David drove the car through the big gates of Buckingham Palace, where the vehicle was swiped to check for explosives, our IDs were checked, and soon I was standing on a red carpet in the porte-cochère at the front of the palace. I looked around, thinking there would be more cars and more people for a big luncheon. My heart was thumping more than my painful ankle as I limped up the carpeted steps under a magnificent columned portico. 'Good afternoon, Professor Fitzpatrick, and welcome to Buckingham Palace,' said an elegant gentleman as he beckoned towards the door with the grace of a perfectly poised dancer. His starched collar served as the perfect sartorial conduit for his mellifluous voice. I hobbled forward and his white-gloved hand reached out to stop me. 'May I ask what is in the bag, sir?'

I glanced at the pink bag in my hand, balanced precariously on my crutch handle, and explained that it was a present for the Queen – a wooden box, with a star inside! My inquisitor gave me a curious raised eyebrow and then a brief nod to another well-dressed man who spoke into a microphone on his lapel. As the seconds passed, I stood wincing with potential embarrassment that they would want to look inside. Instead, undoubtedly very much quicker than it felt at the time, the package was scanned for explosives and then relieved from my grip to be placed in Her Majesty's private chambers, for review at her discretion, I was informed. I nodded gratitude and continued through the door, which opened into a resplendent reception area decked with vast chandeliers and paintings of who I assumed were *very important* people. I was further embarrassed by of the loud clunk of my plaster of Paris foot with every self-conscious step, whereupon I was again beckoned by a white glove towards an upright wooden board of some kind. The gentleman smiled broadly for the first time, in what I assumed was jest as he announced, 'Professor Fitzpatrick, allow me to introduce you to your fate!' As I looked up, with some trepidation, it must be said, I almost fell over my cast. I'd been expecting a couple of hundred guests but there, on what was clearly a sign board, was a piece of pristine white paper where the lunch seatings were depicted. There were only eight guests, and I, Sean and Rita's son from the middle of bogland in Ireland, was seated on the right hand of Her Majesty. As my immaculately attired guide took me up a marble staircase, that same innocent farmer's son raised his little voice and asked aloud, 'Excuse me, sir, have you any idea why I am here?'

It's a question many of us ask ourselves, and to which there are many answers. But in truth I genuinely wasn't sure why I'd been invited at all. There was no answer as another door opened and I was escorted into an anteroom. It seemed for once that I was early. A server held a tray of beautiful glasses full of something bubbly, which no doubt would have gone down really well, but I abstained, conscious that it might not mix well with my pain medication. Sipping and slipping wouldn't bode well. I stood there admiring the pictures on the walls, the magnificently adorned ceiling, the carpets, the wallpaper and the chairs. My mundane plastered foot and flared trouser leg seemed quite out of place amid such splendour.

A lady came in to check if I was all right. I said, 'I'm great, thank you.' And then plucked up the courage to again ask, 'Why am I here?' She simply touched her nose gently and said with a wink and a smile, 'It's all a wonderful mystery; you're here because you're supposed to be here.' I had found the meaning of life after all!

One by one, all seven other guests arrived. I politely said hello to one gentleman and it turned out he was an eminent figure in wildlife conservation. Another was a professor of chemistry, and another a professor of medicine. I wondered if perhaps Her Majesty had in fact listened to what I had said about One Medicine during our first meeting, because it appeared that she had brought several people together to chat about science, animals, medicine and the environment. I later learned from a guest that occasionally she just invited some people to lunch that she thought might be interesting company.

A tiny bell rang and the doors opened. The Queen strolled in, with the Duke of Edinburgh in her wake, perfectly mirroring her pace and posture. In what seemed like an expertly and effortlessly choreographed manoeuvre, Her Majesty talked to four of us and the Duke to the other four for a few minutes. Then the bell tinkled again and we all processioned into lunch. Here were ten high-backed wooden chairs with embroidered inlays, five on each side of a rectangular table, all set out with elegant china and silverware. Smartly dressed attendants directed each of us to stand in front of our intended seat. The Queen and Duke faced each other on either side of the table with two of us lucky few on either side of each of them. They stood in front of their chairs. Then with a nod, two of the attendants pushed the chairs in behind the Queen and the Duke in perfect synchronicity. Eight further attendants then lined up one behind each of the guests.

As my attendant went to push my chair, I panicked. I was holding crutches and tried to pass them to him rather than risk them touching Her Majesty, but this meant that he was momentarily distracted from nudging forward my chair. As I began to sit down, the chair wasn't in far enough and I missed the edge with my already fully committed bottom. What happened next was the most embarrassing moment of my entire life. As if in slow motion, I bowed forward towards the table – and to save myself from falling directly into the Queen's lap, my reflex response was to kick my foot out to break my fall and push my buttocks backwards to perch on the edge of the chair. Sadly, for me, the foot I kicked out had a giant cast on it. And, horrifically, as I lunged forward, I kicked Her Majesty's handbag underneath the table, from whence she had placed it beside her chair. It all happened so fast, I hoped she hadn't noticed, and so counter-balancing with my right hand on the edge of the advancing seat, I reached down with my left to retrieve the handbag from under the table. At that exact same instant, Her Majesty had the same idea, for she had indeed noticed. Our hands touched under the tabletop, fumbling for the bag, and our tilted heads turned to face each other over the table settings. Our eyes met perhaps a foot or so above the pristine and perfectly laid-out cutlery, our faces possibly a couple of feet from each other. Eye to eye.

I froze in abject terror. What had I done?

'Oh . . . Ah . . . I'm terribly sorry, Your Majesty.'

I should have stopped there, but my panicking mind betrayed me, so for no explicable reason, I just blurted out, 'It could have been worse, Your Majesty – I might have turned up with no trousers on!'

The Queen understandably didn't have any clue what to say next. She clasped her handbag swiftly and elegantly sat back up into her chair, whilst I most inelegantly shuffled my bottom back on mine. I saw no option but to break the momentary silence with a hurried, no doubt somewhat garbled, explanation and apology, trying to explain the predicament I'd faced over the last few days with my cast and trousers while not sounding like a madman.

The Queen smiled the smile seen a million times, but this time it was just for me. It was quite astounding up close – a quixotic cocktail of mild amusement, forgiveness, warmth and just a dash of mischief. I felt very stupid, yet somehow privileged, and a wave of relief flowed through me. I gestured towards my flare and showed her the beautifully sewn side zipper. 'Oh, my goodness,' she said. 'Very fashionable, very fashionable. Could be the next trend.' Then she chuckled like my Granny Keegan used to chuckle. I immediately relaxed and we settled right into a good old natter. I thanked her for inviting me to lunch and she said I was most welcome. She said that she liked my TV show with the 'clever inventions to help the animals' and she remembered our first meeting at the university when I showed her a bionic leg. She also remembered that I had talked about doctors and vets working together. I explained, yes, that was my dream – One Medicine. I was incredibly impressed by her extraordinary memory for detail and her grasp of quite complex concepts.

One isn't allowed to take any photographs at all inside the perimeter of Buckingham Palace for obvious reasons. At the end of the meal the Master of the Household gave each of us lucky guests an envelope with a copy of the seating plan and the menu – so I can forever reflect on a fabulous day. I will not relate the finer details of our conversation, but I will say that over a starter of *Salade de Homard, Avocat et Tomates Mi-Cuites*, we spoke about many topics: respect between human and animal medicine and how that required humility and commitment from both sides, her experience of the war, and that my dear mother was a great fan of her hats. We talked about legacy, being a role model and her frustrations with politics. To my surprise, she felt that she hadn't achieved as much as I felt she had looking from the outside into her life. She was remarkably humble in the face of ever-changing politicians and politics, remarking how challenging it was to 'get things done'. We talked a little about how people in positions of authority should make a commitment to service and to try to leave things better than one finds them. We both agreed that hope was a headline not often appearing in the newspapers. She liked good conversation and I was overwhelmed with how fortunate I was to hear her insights and vision. The main course, I see, was *Poussin Poche aux Truffes, Choux de Printemps au Beurre, Panaché de Legumes, Jersey Royal Potatoes and Salade*. I'm sure it was amazing – but, as a non-meat-eater, I sipped on my Volnay 1er cru Fremiet, Domaine Marquis d'Angerville 2002, and all I could do anyway was savour her every utterance. I knew full well that this opportunity would never happen again in my lifetime and I was determined to relish every moment.

We talked a bit about *The Supervet* TV show and how I wished that it might act as a beacon of light for people and animals, showing redemption in the face of tragedy, and hope in the face of despair. I also shared how I'd like to imbue a greater sense of respect for non-domestic animals and for their environment. Her Majesty had huge appreciation for the love between a human and their animal friend, and soon we moved on to her corgis, and specifically the hip dysplasia in one of her most treasured, who was then sadly ageing and becoming stiff. She asked my advice on whether it was better to give the arthritis medicine in the morning or the evening, archly suggesting that it was unfortunate one of her corgis must have mated with a 'rogue' at some point, thus introducing some bad genes. We discussed the various medicines and options nowadays for treating arthritis and she was particularly interested in stem cells, I remember, and joked that they might be good for herself. The moment that struck me the most, however, was when she said that I seemed very committed to my particular vocation. I was taken aback and touched, because if there was ever someone who lived and breathed commitment to their role, it was the lady to my left.

The Queen was a firm advocate of collective social responsibility – that you can have whatever you desire, so long as you look after those around you and don't expect instant gratification for yourself without a firm commitment to build something that benefits others. She and I both shared a heartfelt desire to see an education system that spoke more to what we could do for others as a conduit for dreaming big for ourselves, rather than just making achievement all about oneself. We discussed how there seemed to be a growing fascination with just observing things from outside rather than committing to becoming actively involved in trying to make a difference. To paraphrase, we agreed that more commitment to talking through and solving problems rather than talking about and observing problems would be a good thing.

As dessert arrived, I told her that I had left a birthday present for her with the Master of the Household. Still worried about how it might be received, I ruined the surprise by explaining a little of the context of the gift, and the struggles I'd had constructing the star, ending up with a somewhat suboptimal shape. She smiled her inimitable smile again, said she was 'most pleased' to receive it, then chortled and paused, spoon of apple crumble mid-air, and suggested I could have used a pastry cutter! Then she left me to ponder my shortcomings as a 'star surgeon', turned and had another little chat with the guest to her left. Her immutable intelligence and deeply perceptive charm was quite amazing and I felt beyond grateful she had taken such an interest in our conversation. After five courses of lunch, very little of which I ate in my childlike excitement, the little bell rang and we were ushered into the adjacent room where I properly met all of the other lovely people who'd been invited. I was introduced again to the Duke by the Master of the Household, who was now chatting to the other four guests that he hadn't spoken to earlier. It was all a finely tuned dream for me. I held out my hand and said, 'Hello, very pleased to meet you.' This incredibly witty and insightful ninety-four-year-old man paused and looked back at me quizzically, a glint in his eyes, before responding, 'I met you before . . . earlier. Don't you remember? I thought I was the one who was supposed to be growing senile.' I smiled and couldn't think of what to say, but from the vacuum of my mind, a voice piped up, 'So, what do you do for fun?' Like that's a completely normal question to ask the ninety-four-year-old prince consort. I really am not very good at this etiquette thing. Anyway, quick as a flash, he replied, 'None of your business!' And of course, I couldn't help myself. 'That exciting, eh?' I said.

We then talked of his love of horses and especially carting in his beloved Balmoral Dog Cart – and how he was the only person ever to have won with both ponies and horses driving at Sandringham, a feat never to be emulated after, since ponies are no longer driven. There was evident pride in this achievement as he glanced over lovingly at the Queen. It suddenly struck me how much love, commitment and respect there was between them, and how much of a rock he had been for the Queen down the years. At precisely 3 p.m., the two of them said their farewells and left, side by side, as if floating out on the same velvet carpet they had come in on, in perfect synchrony. There was a palpable sense of 'wow' in the room, as we eight lucky luncheon guests beamed at one another. We were collectively speechless. Her Majesty and her husband must have partaken in thousands of events like this during her long reign, and yet they were consummate hosts, welcoming us with enthusiasm and generosity. I hope I can show my patients the same commitment for as long as I'm able to hold a scalpel and operate a surgical drill.

Of course, the last word must rest with my own mammy, who was *never* speechless. For me of course, Mammy has been the earthly embodiment of commitment to motherhood, as the Queen has been for so many. Mammy's insights have been a great leveller in all situations of life, big or small. Although she was by the time of my royal visit confined to her home, and increasingly frail, there was absolutely nothing wrong with her tongue. I hadn't told her about the lunch beforehand, and nor did she know about my ankle operation because I didn't want her to worry. After the event, however, I regaled her with the whole story, from start to finish, on the phone. She listened intently, taking it all in, before reflecting, 'Oh, sure now, Noel, she's a great woman. Look at the age of her, and she's getting on grand and doing all the visits to hospitals and everything. Sure, she was over here in Ireland too, ya know. I couldn't get over the lovely hats she wore – a different one for every occasion.' Then there was a long pause before she said, 'That's all grand now, Noel, but I'm very disappointed.'

I was confused. How could my own mother be 'disappointed' when her little boy had just had lunch in Buckingham Palace? She carried on and I could hear the coy smile in her voice. 'Could you not have asked her if I could have borrowed just one of them hats? She surely could have spared one, just to see what it might look like with my brooch – maybe a blue or a mauvey kind of colour. That would be very nice for yer mammy, now, wouldn't it?'

I explained to her that I had in fact imparted to Her Majesty Mammy's admiration of her hats, but added, 'Mammy, you can't ask the Queen stuff like that. That's just silly now, isn't it? Not possible.'

194

She replied, 'Noel, Noel, Noel. If you're humble and committed in the asking, there's a first time for everything – and everything is possible!'

She was absolutely right, of course. As I look back at the moments that have shaped me, I see that commitment has been one of my most important guiding lights. If you find something utterly authentic to you, a passion that drives you onwards and that you are willing to give your everything to, then committing to it feels as natural as breathing. It's a true marriage of purpose. I am a lucky man that I found my vocation when I decided to do whatever it took to be the best vet I could be, and try to make the world better for animals. No night of study, writing or work has ever been too much sacrifice to make because I have been 'all in', to quote a song from the American band Lifehouse, which I often listen to for that specific reason. Thus has it been for anyone who wants to be really great at anything – music artist, sportsperson, scientist – one has to pay the price for commitment, mentally, emotionally and physically, 'whatever it takes' (also the title of a Lifehouse song). For those who are truly committed, every day is a school day. It was abundantly clear to me that Her Majesty understood this from day one – she has been 'all in'. True greatness requires a truly great hunger for learning and truly great commitment. She was without doubt the epitome of these virtues.

There have been so many points where I've felt lost and alone, unsure whether I'm making the best decision. I've discovered these are universal feelings for anyone who is single-mindedly determined. But I've committed to what I absolutely believe in and that conviction has always shown me the right path. Ever since I looked up at the brightest star in heaven as a child and wished I was better, I have realised that it's not about me being 'the one', but rather about being a channel for the 'oneness' in all of us, from which we come and to which we shall return, like my mammy. Seeking meaning in material things, fame or praise as a measure of my self-worth hasn't ever been my bag. Witnessing the Queen's sincere humility first-hand, listening to her talk about her commitment to and love for her dogs and horses, how they had always been such an immense blessing amid the vagaries and vicissitudes of the world, I felt grateful to have this profound shared connection with her.

If you had come and found me that night in the field, as I cried my heart out over the dead lamb, and told me that one day my commitment to animals would take me to a conversation about deeply common interests with the Queen, I would not have believed you. And now, as I put the finishing touches to this book, Her Majesty has just passed away and I am struck by a quite overwhelming feeling of gratitude for our marvellous and unforgettable chat. I met a mother of a nation, a mother of a family who she dearly loved, a mother who truly shone light like a star out into the world for millions of people as a magnificent beacon of dedication and commitment to service and duty. Most of all, I shall forever remember her great and unexpected humility with me and her great and obvious love for Philip. Now, like Rita and Sean, Elizabeth and Philip are side by side, no doubt being their witty and insightful selves, looking down on all of us and still sharing the hope and light of their commitment to each other.

On the day of her final farewell, I took a trip to Windsor to pay my respects to a human being who I greatly admired.

I crept silently and unnoticed, a cap pulled down on my head, along the back of the crowds who had gathered between the vast trees of the Long Walk at Windsor Castle. As I slowly made my way, I overheard dozens of broken conversations about 'oneness' in their respect, honour and shared grief – and I heard the word 'commitment', more than a few times. Finally, I got quite near to the black railings with the gold-coloured points on their posts, either side of the gates leading up to the castle. There were large green hoardings for what I think were television cameras, and I hoisted my foot up on one of them to try to get a look over the railings whilst the Queen's coffin passed by. The funeral procession passed to some bowed heads, some tears and some rippling applause, through the gates and up the hill . . . and then . . . the most marvellous sight.

In the distance, standing motionless with a man beside her on the edge of a carpet of flowers was Emma, the Queen's Fell pony. She'd mentioned Emma to me when we chatted about the animals she loved – and there she was, saying goodbye to her mum, standing just as her mammy had always been: calm, dignified, full of eternal love and deeply inspiring – a vision of absolute commitment.

CHAPTER 9

Authenticity

I grew up on a farm with a necessarily functional attitude to animals. My mammy was never one for anthropomorphising animals. She looked after her family and Daddy looked after the land and the animals. He was devoid of emotion when it came to the cattle and sheep and the only animal I know he had a true 'fondness' for was Pirate. They were both genuine, authentic people of course, and I have since been very fortunate to have been exposed to the transformative power of the actual love of animals, to which I have dedicated my life. I am always my true authentic self, and regardless of what others may think about my ego or my motives, which is entirely their prerogative, I have sat in that ethereal space with hundreds of animals and it's no exaggeration to say that I would not be alive today if I had not found that truthful space of oneness. Our animal friends are *always* authentic. As Marcus Aurelius put it, 'Everything is interwoven, and the web is holy; none of its parts are unconnected. One world, made of all things. One divinity, present in them all.

And one truth.' Or as a more modern philosopher, and fellow self-confessed cat lover, Ed Sheeran, says in his song 'Lego House', no matter what we've been through or done, it is possible to 'pick up the pieces' of whatever has gone before and 'love you better' if you're open to this kind of authenticity – whether that 'you' is yourself or someone else. For me, the love of an animal can allow you to both love yourself and others better and more authentically, if you let them.

I never thought that my own mammy would be open to letting this kind of love in, and yet when I brought Keira over to meet her, she was transformed in a moment and gave her a cuddle. In a FaceTime call I had with her before Keira passed away, I picked her and Ricochet up to 'speak' to Mammy, and she thanked them 'for looking after my little boy'. This was a seismic shift for my mammy, and I felt like she finally truly understood their sentience and their importance in my life, which was a far cry from the pragmatic utilitarian doctrine of my youth.

I have struggled with my mental health in recent years due to a number of factors: the increasingly challenging economic climate for an independent practice, the loss of many of my family of colleagues, the ever more complicated surgery and associated demands of the families of these sorts of cases, and the criticism of my TV show by some of my profession, which has all led me to question the fundamental authenticity of veterinary medicine as it currently exists.

Throughout it all, Ricochet and Excalibur have looked after me.

Excalibur is a mischievous elf with a sensitive soul who hides away behind curtains, under duvets and in secret places that only he knows, whilst Ricochet is the more extrovert, but always knows when I am sad and comes to give me love, pawing my knee. He jumps up, leans back on my right arm like a baby, throws his arms up onto my chest and neck and tickles my face with his glorious furry ears and maned chin, which is usually slobbery from the water bowl, or he gifts me a nice big whiff of tasty crayfish or haddock. Excalibur is naughty, leaves his voluminous hair absolutely everywhere, so that I pull on a sweater and have a mouthful of fur when my head pops out where he has somehow crept inside, and he steals stuff and hides it, as I mentioned for my earplugs. He used to pull bits of implants off the model skeletons in my office, which I found from time to time when I went to bed, as they spiked me in the bum. So, in the end I built perspex cases for them. Reclining on the end of the bed, he simply looked up with innocent eyes as if to say, 'It wasn't me, Daddy.' I couldn't resist but pick him up for a big 'smoosch' of scrunching my nose against him. Whilst he is a shy cuddler, Ricochet is the opposite.

One night recently when I was particularly anxious and couldn't sleep, Ricochet lay on my chest, my fingers gently resting on his ribs as he snuggled his chin into my neck. He breathed gently and I could feel his heartbeat slowly ripple into my body, as if he was sucking me into his body and his thoughts, his calm and his unique authenticity. He reached out and touched my cheek with his paw, soft, without his claws out. Velvet soft pads stroking my bristly chin. I closed my eyes and slowly calmed down. In my mind's eye I saw a huge field stretching out in front of us, with him running on ahead and me following, scampering through the under-growth, my fingertips caressing the fronds of grass as I ran. I was a small child in this reverie. He and I were free. Rico-chet came to the end of the field where there was a wooded copse. He shot off down the path and I followed into a tunnel of bushes on either side of an earthen valley carved out by years of rain and the footprints of animals. The bushes grew into trees and enclosed the tunnel like a womb. I giggled as I followed him out of sight and I was thrown back in time to an innocent and unburdened place, before the abuse of my innocence. In those few moments I was my innocent, uncorrupted authentic self and I fell asleep.

I was grateful for this dream, since the day after would be the beginning of an absolute nightmare. I had a long and sleepless flight to Los Angeles, sitting beside a very lovely and well-meaning lady who spent several hours taking me through every detail of a seemingly unending series of photographs of her cats. It was all very wonderful, but eventually I had to feign sleep. Such is the nature of being The Supervet.

I have been deeply fortunate that I gravitated towards animals early in life, and when I got offered both human medical and veterinary school in 1980, I am very glad I chose animals, since throughout my life, though I have indeed met wonderful genuine people, like the lady on the flight, on balance, I have found the animals I've cared about much more authentic than some of the people I have had the misfortune to cross paths with.

Just as I was about to take a seat in the wood-panelled courtroom of Los Angeles Superior Court, a spasm of pain tore through my butt cheek. A couple of days previously, I had lunged to catch a dog and bulged the already chronically protruded disc in my lower back a little more, squashing the nerve root origin of my sciatic nerve. Or at least that was my self-diagnosis, in the absence of an MRI scan. The irony of the situation wasn't lost on me, because I had been a severe pain in the arse for my legal team, Bam, Maria, Steve and Alastair, for months. Thankfully they all love dogs, though that was little comfort to any of us as Bam and Steve, sat beside me and I squirmed in discomfort. They had all been wonderful supports for me over the painful period following Keira's accident and death, but the reason we sat in court together now was very much a problem of my own making.

I couldn't sleep at all after Keira's accident when she was hit by a van in the practice car park. Night after night I went to see her in the wards to cuddle her and tell her I loved her, then crept upstairs to my bed beside my office, tossing and turning for yet another night, not knowing whether she would be alive in the morning. I couldn't bear it. In my mind I reverted to hiding under the blanket as I had when I was a child, listening to Led Zeppelin's 'Stairway to Heaven' on my scrapheap Sony radio and trying to escape into my own little world. I remembered how I climbed that stairway in my head, away from the pain of abuse and the screams I was silently holding inside me. Now, as Keira lay in intensive care, I was screaming again, with fear of losing the greatest love of my life. I tried not to let my loneliness and terror show. Everyone and everything at the practice depended on me. If the captain of the ship was a mess, how could my crew sail the vessel I had created? Each morning I washed my face, took a deep breath and put on a brave face, walking with my mug of coffee down the stairs to my first consultation of the day.

This isn't a plea for sympathy, but rather a warning to all. I was stupid, naive and emotionally vulnerable, and I wouldn't want anyone else to make the same mistakes that I did. Trust is extraordinarily difficult for me, so how I ended up being taken in by a confidence fraudster, I will never know. I am a reasonably intelligent man, who has for the most part led a low-key existence, preferring the company of animals to humans, and I very willingly spent the money I earned on the dream of the practices I was building, studentships, research and the like, largely eschewing material possessions for much of my life. I'd had a posh car once and sold it. I've had the same house since the mid-nineties. I hadn't gone on holiday for more than a few days since the end of the last millennium. Apart from buying the odd record here and there, my only outlays to that point had been the occasional gig, an escape into music for a few hours on a Friday or Saturday night.

I made the mistake of thinking that I could dull my pain with music now, as I had done as a boy. Thus I found myself, late one night, searching online for original Led Zeppelin vinyl since they'd got me through difficult periods before. It wasn't about the material possession; it was about closeness to my heroes – Robert Plant, Jimmy Page, John Paul Jones and the singular genius of John Bonham, one of the greatest rock drummers of all time. I yearned so much for the stairway to heaven that I made the very mistake referred to in the song itself of being sure that all that glitters is gold.

I came across an auction website and bought an original Led Zeppelin album signed by all four members of the band, feeling the surge of joy of a little boy within touching distance of his idols. It was intoxicating, and I went back for more, buying up several other vintage signed records, like that same little boy left alone in a candy shop. The guy who was selling them called me up directly, and our conversation naturally drifted to dogs. He loved them too, and listened patiently and compassionately as I told him all about Keira's accident. He seemed very nice and kind, and I thought nothing. I wasn't thinking at all, because my defences were down. I was looking for connection and someone to talk to. I spent a load of money on the records he offered me.

Keira gradually got better by Christmas 2019, but I was working harder than ever. As the vinyl shipments arrived from the USA, I didn't open them for a while, promising myself the light at the end of the tunnel once the stressful period was over. Finally, one Sunday afternoon, I sat down and excitedly unwrapped one of the boxes that had arrived. All my Christmases were coming at once.

The first record cover I saw was U2's *The Unforgettable Fire*, which had kept me company every Saturday night through the bullying at secondary school. But it looked weird. By then I'd seen the signatures of Bono and The Edge on other websites. These, however, did not look right. The second record was AC/DC's *Back in Black*, the second-best selling album in music history. But the signatures of Angus and Malcolm Young and Brian Johnson, even to the amateur observer like me, were too symmetrical and all signed with the same pen. My doubts intensified. Then The Rolling Stones – they didn't pass muster either. My heart was sinking as I continued to unpack the contents of the other parcels. Def Leppard, Pink Floyd, John Lennon, Bruce Springsteen, Elton John, Guns N' Roses, Foo Fighters, Iron Maiden, Duran Duran . . . None of them looked right. Not a single one. All fake.

I sat by the boxes on the floor of my office, suffering a mixture of emotions. Stunned, confused, ashamed, guilty, embarrassed, distraught. I was supposed to be ecstatic, actually touching the signatures of my musical heroes. In my own way, holding their hands and finding light and hope. Instead what I was looking at was a complete violation of my dreams. That same week, I sent pictures of the records to some other rare vinyl collectors I'd found online. Their first impressions confirmed my worst fears. I soon tracked down two expert authenticators, and yes, they told me, in polite terms, that I had been an absolute idiot – I had trusted a stranger for no good reason at all, which stung all the more, because I have difficulty trusting anyone at all. The auction website said it wasn't their responsibility to authenticate the items sold through them, so I was on my own. I looked into taking legal action in the UK, but the court decided it didn't have jurisdiction. And so, a year and a half later, I found myself sitting in a US courtroom, face to face for the first time with the people who had duped me.

Ultimately, even with the help of my legal team, I got little recompense, because I chose a meagre settlement rather than go through the further pain of unknown periods of time away from my practice and my patients and the enormous costs which would be associated with a jury trial. No adjudication was made either way since it was simply a without prejudice settlement hearing. I was completely gutted, but I learned a valuable lesson – never to take the appearance of authenticity for granted. This is a lesson I urge others to follow. One must 'vet' everybody for fear they have 'doctored' the truth.

The most shocking thing about the whole affair was how gullible I had been, in my vulnerable emotional state. It brought home to me in no small way how vulnerable people are when their dog or cat are poorly, and how great is the responsibility of veterinarians in whom they place their trust, and on whose authenticity a client's hopes rest. I am sincerely worried that a lack of authenticity in our profession, driven chiefly by financial interests, could set us on the wrong path if we are not careful. There was no question in my mind that the people who had faked the signatures of my musical heroes had no morals or qualms about their deceit.

They were thinking only of short-term profit, and they didn't care if someone else's trust was abused. As I left LA, I felt bad for my lovely legal team who had been very willing to fight it all the way, but back at home I had massive challenges in my practice and I just couldn't deal with the added distress of endless paperwork and time away, so the whole debacle left me humiliated and confused. For someone like me, who strives to live his life authentically, without varnish, treating others with openness and honesty, to see so clearly that others do not have the same ethos pains me deeply.

I'm aware that my authenticity can ruffle feathers. Especially in the veterinary profession I know what I do and how I do it is polarising. I make no apologies for who I am, and I am unlikely to change now, at fifty-four years of age. My objectives have never changed since I decided to be a vet – to do my best for all animals, to give them a fair deal and to make the world better for animals and humans, through compassion and respect. I know most other vets want that too. But the landscape of veterinary medicine has been transformed over the last twenty years, as I mentioned earlier. In 1999, The Veterinary Surgeons Act was amended to allow non-vets to own veterinary practices. This ushered in corporate ownership fuelled by venture capitalists (VCs), keen to make money for their shareholders. It was claimed that this would translate into better care for companion animals and farm animals across the UK. Both primary care and referral practices (the equivalent of human GP and specialist practices) were sold for premium prices as consolidation snowballed smaller groups into ever-larger corporate entities. Corporates now own more than 90 per cent of referral centres where specialists are employed.

Over the past few years, I've sadly lost several colleagues, usually to corporate veterinary companies, as I've mentioned. These are dedicated, compassionate and talented vets, as are all others I know of in specialist referral centres across the land. All have my respect and those that were part of my chosen family are still loved and I am honoured to have worked with them. They will always be authentically great surgeons and human beings, whatever system they are working within. As my dear mother counselled, when I was despairing about the exodus of my colleagues, 'They need to find their way, as you have found yours.' Of course they do.

My issue isn't with the individuals within the system, but rather with the system itself. The vets and nurses may all be authentically trying to do their best on their own personal journeys, but I feel strongly that corporate entities should also be authentic in total integrity and transparency about which primary care and specialist referral centres they own, whether there may be a financial vested interest in keeping patients within their groups and how much of their profits they are tangibly reinvesting for the benefit of animals. I believe that there should be complete clarity and transparency for the public, so that it's also an authentic journey for them and the animal they love.

It's very important for me to emphasise that I truly believe the individual vets in my profession are generally fantastic, and that my governing body, RCVS, are doing their very best in a challenging world. Rather, it's the new financial order that I have an issue with, because I have personally not seen direct evidence that this recent era of veterinary practice ownership best serves the patient in all cases. However, because I am always open to change in medicine for the greater good, if such irrefutable evidence is presented, then I would be delighted to see that my profession is authentically, and in all cases, trying to do the right thing for every animal all of the time without financial vested interest.

From what I have seen, there are pockets of progress with investment for animal benefit, but I have observed that in general the profits generated from corporate veterinary medicine are weighted towards the benefit of human investors rather than for the animal patients they purportedly serve. I wholeheartedly believe that everyone has the right to earn as much money as they wish, and be hugely successful if they work hard. It's not 'making money' that I question, but rather the way in which this money is made. I am simply asking the profession that I deeply love if they can hand-on-heart always be 100 per cent authentic with the families of animals in explaining whether there is any financial vested interest in any action taken or decision made regarding their animal companion. Whether this constitutes a paid-for phone consultation, re-check appointment, laboratory test, radiograph, CT or MRI scan or a referral to another vet, if I were the guardian of the animal, I would want to know that all decisions and recommendations were authentically in the best interests of my friend, without any intrinsic vested interest in financial gain. The public don't realise that they may be paying top-end prices for low-end CT or MRI scans to generate 'in-house' revenue for which reports are outsourced and then charged with significant mark-up. I have no issue with good quality scans and outsourced reporting charged fairly in any practice but I do not feel that the opposite is authentic practice.

It's also important to acknowledge that Fitzpatrick Referrals is a business too, that needs to make money to survive, and it is most certainly not just me. Far from it. So many have contributed to what it is today, just as my practice has contributed to their careers; it's been a fair deal. But as my surgeon and nurse colleague numbers dwindled, and considering the difficulties of recruitment, many people have asked me why I don't sell up myself. I understand their concerns, as I've alluded to earlier. They know the hours I put in. They see the weariness in my face. It's ironic that as I repair the bodies of my patients, my own is falling to pieces. All I can say is that I could not stop what I'm doing as this would betray *my* sense of authenticity. I live and die to be the advocate for the animal in my care, to give them all of the options and not just some of them, and to be a guardian of unconditional love. I can't and won't sign up to anything less than that. There's an idea that 'everyone has a price', but in the case of my vocation, I can honestly say I do not.

I perform a few dozen procedures that nobody else in the UK performs. My engineering colleagues and I have developed solutions for recalcitrant problems which animals really need, and I would find it impossible to stay being a veterinary surgeon at this stage of my career and skill set and be asked to stop offering those options. One example might be the skeletally anchored limb amputation prostheses (SALAPs) I used on Betsy, Bumblebee and Scruffy, otherwise known as bionic legs. Over nearly twenty years, my colleagues and I have evolved this technique to be as reliable as possible, but even then complications with infection or breakage can occur. I'm in the *Guinness World Records* for implanting the first in a cat called Oscar, whom I operated on at two years old. He is still alive and now fifteen years old. He has had complications, which have been managed, but would certainly have been dead if it wasn't for this innovation.

It was exactly the same situation for Rodney, a West Highland terrier who was born without back feet. It's possible his mum had chewed them off. This can happen either by accident, through over-cleaning or in an attempt to sever the umbilical cord, but also as a stress reaction. Rodney was incredibly energetic and like all puppies wanted to run about, but this left him with sores on his stumps, in pain and at high risk of infection.

The charity responsible for Rodney's care wanted to explore options rather than putting Rodney to sleep, but they simply couldn't find a treatment option within a corporate-owned practice. I have treated more than a thousand animals with customised implant solutions, many of whom have also found themselves in a similar situation. I have used scores of different implant systems, from custom joint replacements for horrendously damaged joints, to customised plates for terrible fractures or complex limb deformities, to endoprostheses which replace parts of the skeleton. As I've alluded to earlier, I can understand the business decision for reticence to invest in such solutions. It costs significant money to perform scans, design and fabricate implants, provide hospitalisation and aftercare following surgery, and to then be available for provision of exchange bionic feet (exoprostheses) and monitoring for the lifetime of that patient, such that no one makes significant money on a case like this. From that perspective it is easier to euthanise the Rodneys and Oscars of this world in order to end their suffering rather than trying to provide quality of life with bionic limbs. If your motivation as a business is to make money, then you're staying true to your authentic self by making that decision. If, however, your motivation is to increase the amount of time in which families and animals can share the joy of each other's lives, then you may make a different decision. Authenticity is different for everyone and there may be no right or wrong, but the only thing I care about in this context is that families are told the truth of the situation rather than a bunch of excuses.

The charity went to great lengths to raise the money for the provision of two bionic limbs and Rodney went on to be adopted by Gerry and Sue. Like Rodney, Gerry had lost the use of his own legs and was confined to a wheelchair. Gerry and Sue were committed to do what they could for Rodney, who brought such joy to their lives. The operations were a success and within a few days Rodney was walking well on two new bionic back paws. I know that we were the only place in the UK who could make this happen for Rodney, but I believe this is about more than individual cases. I believe that this is about a battle for what being a vet, and specifically a surgeon, fundamentally means in society today. Vets have enjoyed respect in society for a very long time, and I am very concerned that we may lose this respect if the companies that own our professional output are not completely authentic and honest with the animal-loving public.

One of the ways that being an independent specialist referral centre is difficult is that we provide our own out-of-hours rota, and while my specialist colleagues are paid commensurate with corporate practices, sometimes they may need to work an extra day per week, for example, and work some weekends. Mostly out-of-hours is covered by junior vets in internship or residency training and a senior clinician only called in when needed. I don't know of many specialists nowadays who work five days a week, because the norm is either a three- or four-day week. Of course, I agree wholeheartedly that mental health and work–life balance are extremely important. I wouldn't dream of recommending that anyone works like I do, because it would be absurd. There have to be, therefore, other benefits to attract the best people. I've tried to figure out this equation as I strive to remain independent. But in reality, it's a challenging proposition. Those who choose to join me, and strive for greatness on the path less trodden, are a special breed and I value their kindred spirits greatly.

One of the points of difference at Fitzpatrick Referrals, and one of the reasons we can attract specialists, is our ethos of innovating to provide all of the options and of helping desperate cases as cost-effectively and as compassionately as we can. As I've mentioned, the financial restrictions of corporatised veterinary medicine mean that sometimes the technology required to advance treatments is not available without significant investment of time and human resources. I have invested a few million pounds in such advances over fifteen or so years, but that's hard to justify if routine operations can readily be performed and make more money. There is no National Health Service for dogs and cats, and in private practice many businesses are focused on 'profit per patient'; and implant companies, which are entirely separate businesses, are generally focused on high-volume sales of less advanced products to be commercially viable. Even implant companies who have invested in making customised implants need to sell volume to survive, and for most of the implants I use, the numbers don't stack up in this model. In my practice I have taken a more holistic view: in an effort to advance the field as a whole, and to help individual animals, I have invested in custom implant design and operate at low profit margins, often with great uncertainty about the costs we will incur for long-term aftercare. A cursory glance at our statutory accounts at Companies House will show an average pre-tax profit margin of less than 7 per cent for the past few years, while in corporate veterinary practices the aim is for it to be closer to 20–25 per cent. In simple terms, as I've previously explained, but it's worth re-emphasising, less complex products and services that can be mass-produced make more money than bespoke surgeries that require intensive planning, complex delivery and prolonged aftercare.

Back when I was in my former practice, a humble wooden hut, I was making considerably higher profit margins than I am now, because overheads were low and I was performing multiple relatively simple surgeries daily, often sending patients home the same or the following day. Nowadays, many of my surgeries take several hours with longer patient stays, and much of my work is revising complications of others. The reason there are so many of these complications I think warrants interrogation. My personal opinion is that there are incentives to keep what are perceived as simpler surgeries 'in-house', and to have them performed by less experienced (and thus less expensive) surgeons. In my experience, most clients do not know this and are not always being offered a full range of options, due to financial imperatives. And sometimes they're being pushed towards particular surgeries that will yield maximum profit, whether or not those surgeries are the right option, performed by the right people, in my opinion. This may seem like a damning and uncalled for indictment of lack of authenticity in my profession, but if an investigation of fact is warranted, I have spreadsheets of cases to demonstrate that this is my factually evidenced personal experience in scores of patients. It seems to me that the client should be informed what their choices of surgeon, experience, technique, cost structure and success rate might be. I have no desire to draw the veterinary profession into disrepute, but rather to ask some questions of my profession and animal guardians across the UK about what the best route may be to ensure the well-being of companion animals. This is also the stated goal of my profession and so one should therefore expect no push-back to such questions being asked in the patients' best interests. One specific example is the upsurge in both primary care clinics and referral clinics performing surgery for rupture of the front of the two ligaments inside the knee (the cranial cruciate ligament). There are many possible techniques for repairing this pathology, which in dogs isn't generally a traumatic rupture as in humans, but rather a chronic degenerative rupture with associated osteoarthritis. I have performed a few thousand of these procedures and it was routine operations of the knee (stifle), elbow and spine, each with good profit margins, that gave my banks the confidence to allow me to borrow enough money to build my referral practices in Eashing and Guildford.

If I had just stayed in my hut in the woods practice and played it safe, focusing on routine procedures, I could have retired by the age of forty-five a wealthy man. But that wasn't an authentic goal for me. It's little wonder therefore that both general practitioners and orthopaedic specialists are happy performing these sorts of routine surgeries. However, such surgeries are far from 'simple', the skill level of the surgeon varies enormously and this has consequences for the patient. One does not need to be a surgical specialist to perform this surgery (as I wasn't for many years) and many non-specialists do a great job. In fact, there are so many cases, they simply could not all be operated on by specialists. But it's an unavoidable truth that there are far fewer disastrous outcomes following complex surgeries executed by specialists than there are routine surgeries performed badly. In the past year alone, my colleagues and I have seen more than twenty devastating complications after poorly performed surgeries of this kind in general practice. I have chosen three patients to illustrate this, though I could have chosen many more from my ongoing audit spreadsheet; their names have been changed to respect their privacy.

I am sincerely and profoundly concerned that my profession is ignoring shoddy surgical technique performed by inexperienced vets without appropriate in-depth training and with suboptimal implants because there may be a vested interest in monetary gain. I want to emphasise that every junior surgeon has to start somewhere, as I did, and I am wholly supportive of such personal advancement and fulfilment. The issue I have is not with people who are taking a course for a day and then performing these surgeries, having been totally honest with the client that this is among the first of these one has performed, but rather with the recalcitrance of my profession as a whole to look in the mirror and recognise that hundreds of dogs across the UK every year have suboptimal knee surgery, the complications of which are avoidable with better training and technique. All three dogs, Nora, Treacle and Custard were completely avoidable surgical disasters, all were operated on with poor technique, all had revision attempted and failed by the original surgeon with further suboptimal technique, all were in pain for a very long period, all were charged significant amounts of money, all were offered amputation as a solution and all were vehemently discouraged from attending my practice but insisted, and finally the primary care clinician acquiesced.

All three dogs were significantly lame when I saw them, in significant pain and very deformed. All had been operated on using two of the common procedures employed to treat a rupture of the cranial cruciate ligament inside the knee (stifle) joint of dogs. These are called TPLO and TTA – tibial plateau levelling osteotomy and tibial tuberosity advancement. In TPLO, a curved cut is made in the top of the shin bone (tibia) and the top segment is rotated to take the slope away, so that the knee is stable even without the ligament. In TTA, the big tendon attaching the kneecap (patella) to the tibia is moved forwards to stabilise the knee without the ligament. There are many excellent courses and mentors that one can learn from and I encourage all young surgeons to do so. The best training is through internship and residency, but if you're like me and not deemed good enough to achieve either of these positions, or circumstances don't allow, then one can still train to be a surgeon in incremental steps by choosing courses and mentorship carefully. The fact remains, however, that any vet can take a one-day course for either of these techniques and perform them straight away by buying the necessary tools and implants. In all three cases the outcome was disastrous due to poor expertise, and in my opinion this was fuelled by a desire to keep the revenue generation 'in-house'. To reiterate, I am not insinuating that vets do anything other than their best when operating on patients, nor that corporate veterinary medicine which mandates that patients stay in the practice group is intrinsically unethical. It makes business sense for that veterinary group and is fine as long as the care level is optimal and clients are fully informed of their rights and choices, so that they can make their own decisions regarding what they feel is best to do for their dog. Only consultation between the public and RCVS can determine if the current structure is authentically in the best interest of the patient, in my opinion. To reference the Def Leppard son 'Truth?', 'should I soak up the wave of compromise,' when I 'see the scars' and 'I hear the lies'. Would that be the truth?

I spent five hours realigning Treacle's dramatically deformed hind leg. The story from her human companions has been a common one, which I have heard time and again these past few years. They never actually got to meet the surgeon who carried out the original procedure, just the primary care clinician who belonged to the same corporate group. Treacle's leg had been operated on badly three times after the initial procedure at a total cost of £14,500, including what I estimate was a healthy profit of a few thousand pounds. Any operation can go wrong, as do my own, but it behoves all surgeons at that point to do their best with authenticity, integrity and transparency. The primary care clinician still insisted, with each operation, that the surgeon carrying out the work was the best in the UK, but failed to mention that they were strongly encouraged by their head office to refer to that surgeon alone. When the poor client, and the long-suffering Treacle, were finally told 'no more could be done', they directly asked to be referred to Fitzpatrick Referrals but were told that I was only interested in money and being on TV. Treacle's family were distraught, and as is often the case, were going through other traumas in their life that all distilled into the pain of Treacle's crisis. The same was true for both Nora's and Custard's families as well, including near-death experiences with Covid and cancer and actual loss of a loved one. Their dogs had comforted them through their pain and they were all desperate to find a solution for their dogs' pain in return.

For Treacle, Nora and Custard, I invented a new kind of plate which allowed me to cut (osteotomy) and repair the shin bone which had badly collapsed in all cases, correct the deformity and rotate the joint surface all at the same time, so that the knee was stable without the ligament. I called it the FROG plate – Fitz rotation osteotomy guide plate. Innovation was necessary because conventional plates had failed and, in my opinion, they would fail again. In all three cases, the planning was done inside the computer (in silico) based on a CT scan of the limb, cutting guides were 3D-printed and the highly customised plates were designed and manufactured by my colleagues at Fitzbionics. This required weeks of planning long before picking up a scalpel blade, several hours of surgery in each case and then a few months of aftercare, drugs, physio and hydrotherapy. Fitzpatrick Referrals made a few hundred pounds rather than a few thousand pounds profit from weeks of painstaking work. Happily, the outcome for all three cases has been great and all are running around without pain at the time of writing, albeit there was osteoarthritis affecting all of the knees at the time of my surgery, which will be progressive over time.

It seems *wrong* to me, from a perspective of consumer choice and patient well-being, that a client should only have access to a very limited number of referral centres that are owned by the same company that owns your local vets. Most people don't know their choice is restricted and don't question, because they trust that their local vet is making the most appropriate recommendation of surgeon and that surgeon is making the most appropriate recommendation of technique. In my personal experience, they may or they may not be.

I hear, on a weekly basis, all of the excuses why a cat or dog in a primary care practice should not attend Fitzpatrick Referrals, and these tend to generalise as claims about excessive costs, excessive waits or excessive treatment. Some primary care vets have directly said to clients that where they are referred is *not* their choice to make. As for avoidable surgical failures, I keep a factual list of all of these excuses should anyone ever care to investigate the veracity of my claims. Many actually use *The Supervet* TV show as evidence for these assertions, but all are erroneous. At any practice, we generally see all emergencies quickly, our charges are very much in line with the average in corporate practice, as I've mentioned before, and my colleagues and I always do whatever we feel is in the patient's best interest – medical or surgical. We do ask for a deposit in advance of surgery, because we have had a significant amount of bad debt which cannot be absorbed without inhibiting our ability to pay wages, but equally we sometimes give clients discounts on longer-term care. If making money was our primary goal, there would be easier ways to do it.

Most independent veterinary referral centres have been approached for potential purchase by one of the corporate companies. Fitzpatrick Referrals presents a problem and a special case, because it's more than simply a referral centre. It comes with baggage – yours truly! I have an unusual media profile and a specific ethos, which is out of sync with the homogenisation of such large organisations. And so, although my facilities, colleagues, reputation and successes make Fitzpatrick Referrals an attractive acquisition, there's no doubt things would change drastically if such a merger were to happen. My ortho-neuro referral centre in Eashing has been approached by some of the big companies, and I've made it clear that I did not and do not want to sell my practice, which I consider my home, even though, with ownership of veterinary practices and referral centres confined to just a handful of large corporates, I knew that if I didn't sell then some primary care practices may be forced to block referrals to my services, thus potentially drying up my pipeline for cases.

I wish I could say that the existing veterinary business

ecosystem is one in which we can live and let live, but sadly it appears from the exchanges my team have had with the corporates and from what has recently happened that such optimism could be misplaced. However, I am hopeful that equilibrium can be reached over time by virtue of just consistently providing a good service which both corporate and independent primary care practices and families appreciate.

With fewer surgeons, and fewer of the easier orthopaedic and neurosurgical cases referred our way, we are in danger of being left primarily with a caseload of low-profit-making complex and revision procedures. Our clients come from all over the UK, seeking us through our reputation when no one else will help, but those clients within twenty miles of our practice often bypass us to attend other referral centres recommended by their primary care practices owned by the same corporate group for the more straight-forward cases.

The fiduciary responsibility of such groups is to make money for their shareholders, and I have no issue with that. That's business, and capitalism, for better or worse, is here to stay. I begrudge no one making lots of money, if they are honest, truthful and have core values that support society (i.e. if they are authentic). But there is also the potential for conflict of interest. The code of professional conduct for all vets in the UK states that *'veterinary surgeons must be open and honest with clients and respect their needs and requirements, must provide independent and impartial advice and inform a client of any conflict of interest.'* Can we honestly say that is happening if primary care practices and referral centres are owned by the same people, with one eye on the bottom line and one on their patients? The same code of conduct also states that *'veterinary surgeons and veterinary nurses considering offering or accepting any form of incentive, whether in a referral setting or otherwise, should consider whether the existence of the incentive gives rise to a real or perceived conflict of interest.'*

I worry that animals, and indeed love itself, are being commodified. I have seen dogs and cats referred to in paperwork as 'RGUs' (revenue generating units). This terminology for our patients is anathema to me. Many of the corporate groups also have as part of their portfolio crematoria, own-brand drugs, online pharmacies, laboratories, out-of-hours surgeries, locum agencies, and online or retail shops which they can market to the human families of their RGUs over their lifetimes. This is good business, but is it transparent?

I worry that the principles I hold so dear will fade away within a generation. People often think that I have a queue of vets wanting to train with me, but that isn't how it works in practice. Becoming a vet is always high on the list of aspirations for schoolchildren, especially young girls. And it's true that hundreds of children dress up as Supervet at school and write me letters saying how much they admire what I stand for. Many veterinary students do *say* they want to get experience at the practice. But when people see what it actually takes, it's a different story. Which, by the way, is entirely fair and reasonable. I work with animals to the exclusion of many other things and I work very long hours. I have not managed to have any balance with my personal life and I have no wife and children. I'm married to my vocation and not to a person. There's a reason I am good at what I do, and it's because of the deliberate choices I've made, but that has come at considerable personal cost. To be clear, I am not in any way complaining, but rather explaining that all is not as it seems.

Teenagers may say that they want to 'become The Supervet', but when they discover the reality of what that means,

I've not met one yet who actually really does. We've had more than a hundred vet students pass through the practice over the past few years, normally for a period of a few weeks at a time. They express an interest in orthopaedics and neurosurgery and spend time with my surgeon colleagues, all of whom are fantastic and do an amazing job. I invite these students into theatre with me at any time, with one stipulation – if they come in to learn, they stay until the end of the operation. Perhaps it's because my surgeries nowadays are complex and last a long time, but over the last three years only four students have taken me up on this offer. At such an early stage of my career, I would have gone without sleep, food and water to be in theatre with my mentors, trying to catch every golden nugget that I could see or hear.

Nowadays, there is a 10–30 per cent attendance rate in classes for first- and second-year vet students in some universities – it's easier to look at lectures online from one's home, even if one has paid the fees to attend. Of course, the SARS-CoV-2 pandemic hasn't helped in-person teaching. But this lack of participation will reap unintended consequences I feel. Similarly, by the fourth- and fifth-year clinical rotations, students are selling themselves short if they're not taking every opportunity that comes their way in my opinion. How authentic can new graduates feel on day one of their real-world practice, when they need to speak to clients and advise the best course of action, if they haven't exposed themselves to the rigours of long hours and the possibilities of failure under pressure? I do realise we live in a different world now than when I graduated thirty-two years ago, one where regimented working hours and work–life balance are prioritised to support mental health. I understand and empathise with this, but I remain vehement that the best carpenters work long hours with good carpenters and the best vets work long hours with good vets. One can't learn proficient skill sets for carpentry or vetting from a book or lecture. I know that many vets do make extraordinary effort and great sacrifice, and I don't want them to take offence at my observations. I really do applaud people making different life choices to me, and I'm in no position to lecture anyone on their priorities. But we should be open about the two-way street of effort and excellence. You can't have the latter without the former. The increasingly corporate structure of veterinary practices is more stable regular employment with clear progression and promotion opportunities and potentially less stress, which for the individual vet and nurse can be a very good thing.

Generally, after vet school, new graduates go into practice and learn on the job, with some courses and programmes along the way. They are labelled 'veterinary surgeons', and they can indeed operate straight away – I did when I graduated in 1990. However, it's not possible in vet school to equip graduates with anything other than a foundation on which they can build through experience. Through practice and mentorship from one's colleagues, one gradually gets better in one's chosen area of interest. It just isn't possible any more for vets to be all things to all people, just as GPs in human medicine aren't expected to repair a cruciate ligament, cut a tumour from a lung or perform spinal surgery, but to refer on for consultation elsewhere. General practitioner primary care veterinarians must know quite a lot about many things, but specialists like me know a great deal about very little indeed. Ask me to remove the ovaries and womb of a dog, and I could re-check the textbooks and do it, but nothing like as efficiently as a surgeon accustomed to such work. Ask that surgeon to perform a total hip replacement, my bread and butter generally in under an hour surgery time, or a decompressive spinal surgery which I perform regularly in less than fifteen minutes, and they would likely be at a loss. Even now, few members of the public know what any letters of degrees after a vet's name actually mean. Some have certificates in further education, some specialist diplomas in certain areas and some have academic qualifications like a PhD or professorship. All have different skill levels that are difficult for the public to decipher. For my own part, I'd rather buy a car that had been driven multiple times and refined by the engineer rather than one that the engineer had only ever drawn in a book.

Those who want to be trained to a higher level generally take an apprenticeship called an internship. In the past twenty years we have had an eight-to-one ratio of foreign to UK graduates applying for further internship training at my practice. And in 2022, it's incredibly difficult to get interns because fewer want to train and Brexit has made travel for work more challenging. Internship positions don't pay as well as a GP job and the work is more time-intensive. Corporate practice also makes the life of a GP more appealing, with generally excellent training programmes to set graduates on a pathway to improve their communication, alongside their clinical and surgery skills, in return for commitment to the organisation for a period of time. A norm has arisen in which new graduates can leave out-of-hours or weekend work to others. The idea of setting up one's own private practice is understandably unattractive for most graduates, so some corporates have good buy-in structures with support from their existing infrastructure. All of this is a way of saying that veterinary medicine, which used to be a vocation, is now, in my personal opinion, closer to a job for many. That perhaps sounds harsh, but I'm not judging. It's a reality borne out in recent surveys that the younger generation want a better work–life balance. When people are off duty, they protect that 'free' time vehemently.

For those who are vocational in nature, that's where a residency comes in. After a rotating general medical internship and a surgical internship, one can apply for a residency. This is a challenging three-year programme during which graduates work very hard indeed, dedicating long hours, before sitting an extremely difficult examination. Only the most diligent and talented pass. Though it's hard to hire interns, competition for residency training positions is fierce, because of the paucity of positions available. In my field of companion animal surgery, residents have effectively given up their social life, and perhaps family life too, for several years of work, study and paper publishing in order to become the real deal – an authenticated specialist surgeon. Most will be in their late twenties or early thirties, and the vast majority of veterinary graduates are female. Unsurprisingly, at this stage, starting a family becomes a priority for many. They have endured long days and endless nights and weekends of study, and hours of standing over operating tables with aching limbs and backs begging for release. So whatever perks may come with the job of being a specialist thereafter are well deserved in my opinion.

After residency training, specialist surgeons are on a lifelong journey to perfect and hone their craft, and are the cream of the crop professionally. Learning never stops – and knowledge will always be tested by inevitable complications. One has to be able to deal with the moments where the shit hits the fan, when the normal road map of blood vessels and nerves has been dramatically altered by trauma, cancer, previous surgical invasion, fibrous scar tissue or the debris from implants that have failed. This life, and this level of authentic expertise, requires supreme effort, which each and every specialist surgeon has put in.

Further to this, even after specialist surgical training with veterinary or human patients, to do what it is that I do with customised implants requires sub-specialist training and one cannot rest on one's laurels. The ego is there to be challenged and battle-tested. To be an authentic veterinary specialist one should not *have* to sacrifice one's entire life, but to be truly great, a huge price *must* be paid. Arrogant? Perhaps. Selfish? Sometimes. But with the goal of something more important than ourselves, which is the service of our patients. In the words of my countrymen, The Script, 'every day, every hour, turn the pain into power'.

The truth is that if I died tomorrow, most of what is in my head will go to the grave with me, because I haven't yet taught most of the customised surgery I perform to the next generation. Tackling such clinical challenges is a major undertaking for any surgeon, not just because a high level of surgical skill is mandatory, but also because one needs to be prepared to provide lifelong service to often challenging clients. This life choice is an ocean of pain in which precious few wish to swim. Even when one thinks one is a good specialist surgeon, one's ego is severely dented by sub-specialisation and navigating uncharted waters with custom implants for deranged anatomical situations, which are different every time. Sub-specialisation in ortho-neuro surgery is as different to being a specialist surgeon as Formula One is to rally car driving. Both drivers can be excellent at what they do – but it's a completely different circuit, road map and skill set. This sounds like an arrogant thing to say, but I know, because I have been a GP, a guy who performed 'a bit of' surgery, a guy who went off and pursued acting for a while and then a guy who paid the price for giving up any social life to take specialist exams twenty-three years after qualifying, before embarking on the most challenging training of all – to work on a daily basis with custom implant surgery, where every single case has its own unique intrinsic challenges. I drive Formula One every day of my professional life. I have no desire to drive a rally car, even if rally car drivers are superb and the sport is fun. If my team in the pit stop and radio gallery are not in tune with me, then I will lose the race. Every surgeon is wholly dependent on the support team, whether that's in a university clinical department, a travelling specialist, a non-specialist in a primary care environment or a specialist in a referral centre.

Thankfully I am now working with a small group of highly motivated specialists who genuinely do want to learn how to perform some of the operations I have invented and techniques I have pioneered. The plan is to pick the procedures and teach them one by one and all I can do is continue to strive with authenticity, and hope that I don't run out of steam or financial wherewithal before I have empowered enough others to take over from where I will inevitably be forced to leave off with my life's mission. Having buried my mammy, I am very aware of my own mortality, which is why I find myself at a crossroads of what to do next with my life, personal and professional, and I also feel that the profession I love is at a crossroads of authenticity, which is why I absolutely feel the need to talk about it.

Not for one second do I think that individual vets are compromising care for financial gain, but I worry that systemically we may inadvertently be de-prioritising our patients' well-being through the business structures we have created. I question whether, going forward, the profession I love may choose what is best for the animals or what is best for the venture capitalists. It seems to me that companies are quite openly 'built to flip' rather than 'built to last', in that the intention is to grow the assets and sell them with a profit for shareholders, rather than an authentic intention to build a lasting legacy for animals. My opinion is just that – my own – but I'd welcome a discussion of all stakeholders, including the families we serve, before we might go too far down the wrong road. I genuinely believe that the vast majority of vets care deeply about their patients and want always to do the right thing, and our sworn intention at the time of our oath is to put the welfare of our patients above all else, but are we fostering the right environment to do that? We have a moral responsibility for the animals and for those who love them. Society expects this of us. I do not feel that the next generation will thank us if we lose sight of our authenticity, or allow it to be taken from us.

Every morning that I am lucky enough to wake up to Ricochet and Excalibur, these hairy harbingers of honesty remind me why I set out to put the welfare of my patients above all else, and why I am willing to risk the wrath of some to try to encourage the authenticity of many. I owe it to the animals. I cannot continue to live with my own conscience unless I stay true to my core truth, for the greater good of animals everywhere. I believe that authenticity in all of its forms is essential for peace of mind and for real happiness, which is ever more important in a world torn apart by war, greed and misinformation. I can only act and speak for the innocents who cannot speak for themselves, but if each and every one of us were somehow brave enough to risk censure or ridicule for a goodness we really believe in, the animals who inspire me to be the best I can be could make us all better, and could make the world better for all of the innocents – man and animal.

One morning recently, Ricochet, Excalibur and I had our habitual 'who's the biggest cat' game in the kitchen to the melody of the song 'All Along the Watchtower' by Jimi Hendrix. In this game, I go on all fours beside them, and we each stretch our backs upwards in the classical 'cat-cow' yoga posture to show which of us is the 'biggest' cat for the day ahead. The boys like to stretch in this way as they wake up. Of course, I never win this game! I was minded that Bob Dylan recorded this song in the year of my birth, 1967, and he said that there was too much confusion back then and he couldn't get relief. I feel the same. Jimi made loads of money for other people, left a legacy, but died too soon before he realised any of it, desperately struggling to be his authentic self. I fear the same. I will therefore risk absolutely everything I have ever worked for to be authentic and tell the truth as I see it.

CHAPTER 10

Trustworthiness

As someone in the public eye, I'm well used to all sorts of ever more bizarre rumours. It's led me to believe that you can't believe everything you read. However, recently I had an experience of just how rumours start. Ricochet was going through his grumpy period after the ear surgery as he had the 'cone of shame' on and did not like his antibiotic dose one little bit. So, each morning I split the antibiotic capsule, pouring the powder onto a piece of card, folding the card and tipping the powder into water in a syringe barrel, whereupon I popped in the plunger, shook it about and into his mouth it went. So, there I was, hunched over the sink in the kitchenette next to my bedroom at work, tapping out the white powder, poised looking down a syringe barrel right next to my nose, to make sure the powder could fit through the nozzle, when the door suddenly opened. My colleague walked in unannounced to drop something off, assuming nobody was 'home'. One can imagine the surprise – for both of us! It turns out that some-times *you can't even trust what you see with your own eyes.*

Trust is a quality we're all born with, but it's as fragile as porcelain. Once broken it's incredibly difficult to reconstruct. Like all innocent children, I trusted, but that trust was shattered by my abuser and later by bullying. Over the years, I've seen multiple counsellors, psychiatrists and therapists in an effort to understand my past, but I'm not sure I can be fixed. The cracks will always show, and trust will always be hard. Trust is the single most difficult feeling that I've had to contend with in my life. Of course, I've been close to many people. I've had the most precious romantic relationships and I have some very dear friends that I love very much. I've trusted as much as I can trust any human being. I have been a fairly closed book all of my life, but after the passing of Mammy and Keira, I have decided to open up in this book because I have a very acute sense of my own mortality and if I truly want to change the world for the better for animals, and trust enough to love and have my own family, then for me this is the first step, telling the whole truth as I see it about myself, my vocation and the world I live in. Sadly I have also learned during my periods of depression that I can't trust myself not to spiral into the darkness. During such times I have made mistakes in my personal life and I'm definitely no saint, but some of the rumours I've heard about myself frankly baffle me. I maybe sometimes even wish I was actually as 'exciting' as some of the myths suggest. Suffice to say, *you cannot trust everything you hear with your own ears either!*

I have trusted and loved animals, confided and shared comfort with them way more than I ever have with humans. The dogs and cats that I have loved have never betrayed my trust and have never had ulterior motives. They have accepted pure love and returned it unconditionally. For me, dogs and cats have been the ultimate anticoagulant for the soul.

231

Their non-judgemental and unconditional love has often been a stent past blockages in my heart and, in their presence, I can be my absolutely authentic self. Keira, Ricochet and Excalibur did not and do not care what I do for a living, how much money I have, where I come from, what gender or ethnicity I am, they just care that I have been and am there in the moment with them. In that moment of 'oneness', to which I have oft referred, I can transcend my situation, and even time itself, since love carries on even after time ceases to exist. I know that the love I feel for Keira is as real today as it was when she was physically here, and I'm sure it's the same for you and your loved ones, animal or human. In the love of an animal, we can reach a place of peace where what people think of us doesn't matter, where our social media feed doesn't matter and where even what we think of ourselves doesn't matter – because the only thing that does matter is that they trust us implicitly and we trust them, even when sometimes we might have lost trust in ourselves.

Trust is often used in the abstract – do we trust the media, do we trust politicians? In my world, trust is a much more visceral and internalised thing. It is central to what I do. A person looks into my eyes and they want to be able to trust that I'll do everything I can to give them more time with an animal that they love, if it's ethically the right thing to do. This animal might be the love of their lives and I do my best, day in, day out, to repay their trust in me. I always tell my clients the truth, no matter how hard that is to take, and I am always fair, transparent and act with authenticity and integrity. An animal looks up at me and my colleagues and they trust that we will be kind to them. In that moment, it's not about balance sheets or business models, it's about love and care. It's about sacrifice and hard-earned professional experience, which allows me often to take potential sadness and turn it into joy. This is an enormous privilege and an enormous responsibility.

However, sadly I have found that this trust is not always reciprocated. As I have mentioned, one of the unexpected challenges I increasingly face is when I cannot trust my clients to be respectful in return for me being honest and giving them hope – but never false hope. When things go right – when I operate successfully and our best hopes come to fruition – that's wonderful. There's no better feeling than watching a dog or cat that came in at death's door, exhausted of options, repaired and running towards his or her human companion, a long and fulfilling life ahead. But when things don't turn out as well as can be expected – when hopes are dashed – the results can be toxic.

I felt this quite acutely one evening not long ago. I'd come out of surgery, cleared the radiographic images, checked the patient was in the good care of the night team, hurriedly changed from scrubs to jeans and T-shirt and drove through heavy traffic to reach a rock concert, looking forward to two hours of blissful oblivion after a tough week. I hadn't yet found my seat when my phone went off in my pocket. A text. I could have ignored it. I wouldn't have blamed anyone in my position for doing so. It was likely to be from work – something that would require my attention and potentially ruin the evening. The sound engineers were preparing the stage and the band would be out soon. I'd be able to get a great seat. I *needed* this.

I pulled the phone out and read the message. It was indeed the practice. A lady had been screaming down the phone at my receptionist colleague, demanding to speak with me directly about her dog (we'll call him 'Frank'). I'd operated on Frank weeks prior, to give him a chance to walk again after

233

being hit by a bus. Our initial treatments had, sadly, failed, and his condition was deteriorating. I'd already spent nearly an hour talking to the lady earlier, thus delaying another operation and keeping my surgical team late, telling her that in my opinion she had done all a loving guardian could and that I strongly felt euthanasia was the kindest course of action. At the time she said that the other dog waiting for me in theatre was not her problem and that I should care more about her feelings. I went to the toilets in the venue and called her straight away. She accused me of betraying the trust she'd placed in me. I tried to soothe her, to explain, again, my medical and ethical opinion on Frank's poor prospects. By the time I returned to the concert, it was under way. I watched the band, trying and failing to lose myself, with the woman's words echoing in my mind. And that night, I did call her again, as promised, sometime after midnight, reiterating my position, commiserating with her predicament, before drifting into troubled sleep.

I understand grief and pain. I understand that it needs to be directed somewhere, and that I am the easiest, most immediate target when an animal in my care is suffering. My work is never finished and I can never switch off completely, no matter where I am in the world, because if I do, my team, in spite of their absolute best efforts, often cannot satisfy some clients. Every other specialist or primary care clinician that I know is able to go on holiday with minimal disruption and their clients seem to accept the views of their colleagues regarding treatment or trust the team if they say that one has reached the end of the line with a patient from an ethical perspective. People put their hopes in my expertise, but hope and my surgical skills sometimes aren't enough to provide a positive outcome and that's just how biology is. I know I've always done my absolute best, but a despairing client doesn't always see it that way, and sometimes my best just isn't good enough. In this particular case, my team and I had spent in excess of a hundred hours trying to help Frank. My personal mental health or that of my team isn't generally considered when clients are in this heightened emotional state. As one client described it, I had dangled a carrot in front of her family and I had unfairly given them hope. I slept at the practice when I got back from the concert. The lady called again at 8 a.m., still unhappy with my view that we had exhausted options for Frank. It was a Saturday morning. She demanded that I was woken up. I spoke with her and again explained the situation as kindly as I could. My opinion didn't change – the most ethical course of action would be to end his suffering. She demanded all of the medical notes. As is her right, she wanted a second opinion. Frank was subsequently put to sleep by another vet, but I received a vitriolic letter of complaint from his human guardian. She said she would be reporting me to the RCVS, that it was disgusting I cared so little, that my ego was bigger than my ability, that she didn't trust me further than she could throw me, and that I deserved, to quote her, to be thrown under the bus myself.

I can only see one way to trustworthiness and that is to tell the truth – always, unflinchingly, whatever the consequences. Being completely transparent. I will be the first to admit that this has been a journey of learning from mistakes for me, as I'm sure it is for most people. Authenticity and trustworthiness overlap, but they are not the same. Authentic people mean what they say – they live according to their own ethical code – but trustworthy people go out of their way to tell the truth at all times. To be authentic is to have integrity, following through on your reasoned goals – it's truth to oneself. Being trustworthy is acting with ethics and honouring the faith others place in you – being true to others. We hope to recognise authentic people, trusting that they'll act with integrity, and without ulterior motive, but sadly it doesn't always work out like that. The vast majority of clients, of course, are incredibly gracious and kind, regardless of the outcome of my efforts with their beloved animal friends.

Oscar, a gorgeous black Labrador, was six and a half years of age when I met him in early 2019 and his mum Anita has been patient and dedicated to his well-being to an extraordinary extent, believing in him quite literally every step of the way. He could hardly walk at all when I met him due to very bad osteoarthritis affecting multiple joints. He had already been operated on elsewhere, six times on one elbow due to developmental elbow disease, once on the other elbow and also on one knee for cruciate ligament and slipping kneecap (patellar luxation) disease. But no matter how crippled he was, he waddled up to Anita every day, wagging his tail and wanting to go outside.

Oscar's previous surgeons were talented and trustworthy people who had done their absolute best for him. Sadly though, by the time I saw him, his right elbow was riddled with moth-eaten holes, gnawed away by bacterial infection, whilst his left elbow was painfully rubbing bone on bone due to poor fit (incongruity leading to medial compartment disease) and was on the verge of catastrophic fracture through a big crack in the bottom part of his humerus (humeral intercondylar fissure), all of which was genetically predisposed. The bottom part of his right humerus was chronically and incurably infected. Full limb amputation was indeed a fair recommendation, but then he would not be able to have a good quality of life on his very painful and near fractured left elbow. It was theoretically possible to cut out the diseased bone and fill it with a customised titanium spacer, fusing the elbow solid, but this implant didn't exist, and many vets might consider such an approach unethical because of the risk of subsequent infection. Plus something would have to be done with the near-fracture of the humerus on the left side as well as ongoing elbow osteoarthritis. Euthanasia had been recommended by some vets already. They were kind and meant well, as were his surgeons before. But whom do you trust when a life is on the line and if you do trust, what if the surgery, which has never been done before, fails anyway?

One might be inclined to believe that trustworthiness might best be validated if groups of well-inclined people agree the best path forward. I felt it best to request an ethics review for Oscar's situation as I did for Bran, the German shepherd dog on three legs who needed a hip replacement. This was as a result of complaints made by other vets about me 'over-treating' cases on my TV show, pushing veterinary medicine too far and bringing the profession into disrepute in an unethical way amounting to malpractice, as I've already explained. I presented Anita with all of the options and prepared an ethics adjudication document for review by an external panel of vets. The RCVS replied several weeks later to say that they hadn't yet got an ethics panel that could help with such a case, just as they had previously with Bran's customized hip replacement. Meanwhile, Oscar continued to suffer. When I sought help with a veterinary school, they said they couldn't help me and it was up to me to take responsibility for my own ethics and not 'pass the buck'. Thus, I was caught between a rock and a hard place – being advised to seek ethics approval on the one hand and being told to take responsibility myself on the other. Taking such responsibility had in fact always been the case, as I regularly discussed patients with my specialist colleagues at the practice. I did this again for Oscar and we all decided that rather than euthanasia, it was appropriate to give him a chance, with the caveat that if he wasn't achieving a reasonable quality of life thereafter, he should be euthanised. It's hard for me to trust the veterinary system of which I am a part when I am judged harshly by people who have never performed similar procedures, and yet I'm told I'm somehow a bad person when I'm trying to save a life. To echo Sharleen Spiteri from the band Texas, I can 'say what I want' in frustration regarding people's judgement, but they'd likely 'still feel the same about me'. It's not an arrogance for me to say that I do however trust my engineering colleagues because we have performed hundreds of such procedures together.

Anita elected for surgical intervention. On the left side, because standard screws had already failed on the right, with my engineering colleague, Jay, I invented a custom-made, very large metal screw which was placed across the near-fracture in the bottom of the humerus and around which a biological substance called bone morphogenetic protein (BMP) was injected to facilitate healing. Osteoarthritis would be an ongoing challenge which Anita knew we'd have to deal with. Oscar recovered very well, and then in a second operation, I cut out the bottom third of the right humerus and all of the articulating surfaces of the radius and ulna of the right front leg and replaced them with a custom-designed titanium spacer which we'd invented, into which the bone would hopefully grow and the elbow would be fused solid at the standing angle (endoprosthesis arthrodesis). His recovery took a while, and we're still dealing with his osteoarthritis, but Oscar is still wagging his tail and gulping in every moment of joy more than three years later. Throughout the journey, both he and Anita have been magnificent in our circle of trust. Oscar trusted his mum, she trusted and believed in his resilience and my willingness to design implants and perform operations that had never been done before, and I trusted her to do the right thing by Oscar if it hadn't worked out. This is the virtuous circle of trust that I experience with most of my clients, but not all.

Obviously all surgeons, including me, fail, which is absolutely no reason for people not to trust vets. The lack of trust for me arises if vets do not explain the facts, face up to the challenges, admit why things may have gone wrong and seek appropriate support. In the past year I have seen two very sad cases which, like Nora, Custard and Treacle who had disease of the knee which had been operated with suboptimal technique and implants, had been operated for disease of the elbow with exactly these same failings. In both cases the clinicians and the system failed to be honest with the clients, and trustworthiness was not central to their behaviour in my opinion. Both had forms of developmental elbow disease and humeral intercondylar fissure like Oscar. Let's call them Simon and Brandy.

Brandy was an adorable four-year-old cross-breed dog affected by osteoarthritis of his elbows due to developmental elbow disease and had been operated on by a surgeon using an implant system which his notes called 'experimental' and 'in development' to replace the part of the elbow which had been worn away by friction, a partial elbow replacement. Brandy's mum, Joan, trusted both her primary care vet and this referral vet. The referral centre and primary care vets were owned by the same company. Joan did not know this.

Nor was she made aware that the referral surgeon was not a specialist. As I've said, non-specialists absolutely *can* be excellent surgeons – I was an operating non-specialist for twenty-three years. I've already stated that, in my view, it is entirely legitimate for any qualified veterinarian to take a course and put in an implant as long as they inform the client regarding their skill level, alongside the evidence and efficacy for the implant system they are using. It most certainly is not all about exams, but it is about knowing your limitations and doing the right thing for the animal regardless of the financial implications for oneself or one's practice. As I've intimated previously, what one can't do is learn how to be a surgeon from a book. One can watch a video tutorial on carpentry, but it's unlikely to result in a well-turned wooden chair. The difference is that a shoddy chair is obvious, but shoddy surgery is harder to discern under the skin. Clients take it on trust that the surgeon is well prepared and experienced. It isn't until things start to go wrong, often much later, that suboptimal treatments are revealed.

When I was a trainee surgeon, I was always 100 per cent honest with people regarding my experience, success and failure to date, such that people could make up their own minds whether they wanted me to operate or not. Joan didn't know anything other than what she was told – that the surgeon was the best. The surgeon didn't meet her much at all, because Brandy was often transported by ambulance as a 'service' between the primary care practice and the referral practice. Joan didn't question the advice she was given in person or remotely by the surgeon. I have seen surgeons like this claim at symposiums (paid for by implant companies) that they have not experienced significant failures with their products, that I myself have performed revision surgery on. Joan and

Brandy, like many dozens of other surgical disasters I have documented over the past few years, were in my personal opinion deceived. Their trust was abused.

As for all veterinary implants in the UK, no certification or publication of trial results is required before widespread release, as I've alluded to already. I myself have never yet commercially launched any of the implants designed and fabricated by my company, Fitzbionics; this despite having spent a couple of million pounds on research and development, and on free or reduced cost, long-term follow-up for patients. I do this to provide evidence for efficacy in an ethically robust framework. I do not know of any corporate veterinary practice or implant company in the UK that does the same.

Implants are regularly deployed in dogs and cats in many countries, including the UK, without any strict quality control of either the implants or the surgeons putting them in, but the public are not aware. I am not aware of any surgeon other than myself who has been asked to submit ethics adjudication for either routine or advanced customized implants. I believe that the consumer has a right to be part of the ethics adjudication process for the animals they love. After all, they pay the bills. Uniform equitable regulation is in my view, the best way to protect the public interest and the interests of animals.

Implant companies, like primary care practices and referral centres, have also been consolidated. Now one company owns many of the biggest implant suppliers to the UK and much of Europe and the USA. They have certain profit margins and the need to sell products to satisfy shareholders. Tighter regulations would likely dampen those profits. I question whether the current paradigm is in the best interest of animals like Brandy. Joan happens to be the leader of an independent group of homes for elderly people – another area of business where venture capitalist money has been invested widely in the hope of handsome profits, so she is no stranger to the effects of making shareholder return a priority. Hers are among only a handful of homes for elderly people that are voluntarily regulated for standards. I am minded of Matt Bellamy's Muse song 'Uprising' where he bemoans a world that tries to keep us all uninformed in the hope that we'll not see 'the truth around'.

In my opinion, the degree of Brandy's original disease did not warrant the procedure performed in the first place, even if the implant may have been 'fit for purpose'. I saw radiographs of his elbows and videos of his walking pre-operatively, and determined that I personally would not have performed this surgery, with this implant system, even if I had been trained to do so. But I accept that different surgeons will have different opinions while believing they are doing the best for the animal. In this case the implants were applied with very poor technique. At all times, Joan was reassured that everything was going to plan. She trusted the source of this information.

In the first six months of 2022, as I have referred to already, I have attended more than a dozen unequivocal surgical disasters performed by surgeons within corporate veterinary systems that, in my view, permanently disabled some dogs. These dogs deserved better. The families that loved them deserved better. Can it be right that patients are so often not given an option of a referral provider external to a particular veterinary group? Or that implants are unregulated except for standardised manufacturing practice? So often clients don't know they have a choice.

None of the rehabilitation practitioners working on Brandy for many months after his initial surgery said anything direct to the surgeon about how badly things were going. I don't know why, but I expect that it's a certain misplaced respect for authority, a fear of criticising more senior veterinarians. I have also experienced a 'them and us' mentality among some vets, who sometimes only call on physiotherapists when things aren't working, rather than to orchestrate a cohesive plan for the patient. I don't find this approach to be either trustworthy or ethical. Nine months later, when I met him, Brandy was still non-weight-bearing on the affected front leg, with considerable muscle wastage, extreme pain, collapse, the implant loosening, plus likely infection inside the dysfunctional joint. Full-limb amputation wasn't advisable because of osteoarthritis affecting the opposite elbow – dogs can manage without one front leg, but generally not two, unless they're in a trolley permanently. Full elbow replacement wasn't advisable either because I have personally experienced a high failure rate of commercially available total elbow replacements and don't use them any more. They were launched without any requirement for ethical guidance or longer-term follow-up before widespread release, as was the partial elbow replacement implants used in Brandy. Further, I would not consider a custom elbow replacement in the face of possible infection and profound disruption of the ligaments around the joint.

Broadly speaking, there are three kinds of implant complications: those related to poor or inappropriately applied implants; those related to a surgeon with suboptimal training or technique, or who has made a mistake; or just, bad luck, where biology doesn't 'smile'. The last is the hardest to quantify. For example, an unfortunate infection might take hold in spite of all reasonable precautions, or the bone might not grow onto the implant properly, or the patient's family aren't sufficiently compliant with post-operative instructions (e.g. exercising too soon). I have seen all of these categories of complications in my own cases and in those of others. I think it's vitally important to look in the mirror and truthfully take moral responsibility.

The second dog, Simon, was a spaniel who had been operated on both elbows with poor choice of implants and poor technique. He had been crippled for months, with one elbow falling apart and the other non-weight-bearing and unable to extend at all due to contracture and infection after botched fracture repairs on both sides. Simon's character had completely changed. Once he had been the gentlest dog and companion for his family who loved him beyond words, the epicentre of their world. Now he was irascible all the time because of hopping around on one very painful leg and holding up the other. All of this pain had been avoidable with more appropriate technique. His family were understandably distraught.

Around the same time, I saw a third dog, let's call him Martin the bulldog, who, like Oscar, suffered an unfortunate elbow fracture and had already been operated on three times by a talented, well-meaning surgeon with reasonable implants, but he'd been unlucky and the surgery had repeatedly failed.

I had Covid for the fifth time in early 2022, and in five days of isolation I spent forty-two hours writing ethics adjudication applications to the RCVS for Simon and Martin, in order to see if they now had a system in place that might be able to help wade through the ethical quagmire of such complex cases, which had already been operated on multiple times by other surgeons with failed procedures. The remit of the RCVS is to protect the welfare of the animal and to oversee the fitness to practice of veterinary surgeons. The reason I asked for ethics approval is that, as I've mentioned,

I had been advised to try to protect myself from persistent vexatious claims of malpractice because I am on TV.

To be fair to the RCVS, they had done their absolute best to formulate a system which might provide guidance to vets performing complex surgeries with customised implants since the time of Bran, the 'ice-cream scoop' hip dog, and Oscar, the endoprosthesis elbow fusion dog, a couple of years earlier. The problem was that the RCVS were now caught between my opinion and the opinions of other specialists who ostensibly had not performed the types of surgeries I was proposing for Simon and Martin using customised implants. I have considerable sympathy for both the RCVS and also for the clients and animals caught in the crossfire between the past and the future. In the ethics adjudication paperwork that I got back for both dogs, I was informed that some of my ideas were 'perverse', 'unethical', 'fantastic novelty' or 'not recognised veterinary practice (RVP)' in the UK. These words seem somewhat egregious and unnecessarily confrontational to me, especially given the ready availability of 'novel' implants which one can simply buy from various companies. One of the challenges is that the patients who present to me often don't have any options within existing 'standard' veterinary practice, aside from amputation or euthanasia. Innovative, custom solutions, although based on my previous experience of more than one thousand such cases the years, are always 'novel' by nature of their rarity.

I want to emphasise again that I feel the RCVS are trying to do the best job they can – they are trying to allow vets of varying skill levels to perform all kinds of different operations with all kinds of different implants. I absolutely do not wish to patronise, but a high-street motor mechanic, while honestly helping thousands of motorists with their cars, would be lost if asked to fine-tune the Formula One car I mentioned before. It's just *not the same thing*. In the interests of fairness, a high-street mechanic can indeed train to be an F1 mechanic if they choose to study and apply themselves for many years. Sometimes guidance of other clinicians may be given authentically, but I do not feel it will work for my patients. Therein lies the subtle but profound difference. This is not my arrogance, though I have no doubt that some other vets may perceive it as such; this is life or death for the patient.

I proposed a custom elbow fusion plate and screw system that I had invented several years previously, for Martin's elbow and for one of Simon's elbows. This implant would be simpler in design by comparison with Oscar and similar to that I had designed for Barney the dog with the broken elbow at the time of Mammy's funeral. I had already fused more than a dozen elbows with conventional off-the-shelf implants for which complications and failures had prompted the design of these new implants. For Simon's other elbow, I proposed a customised plate and the 'Rita bolt' device that I had developed previously for Barney. I categorically did not feel that off-the-shelf implants would work and I felt a moral imperative to innovate. The respondent expert assigned by the RCVS entirely disagreed. They said that I should *not* use the custom implants I proposed, but instead use one of the many commercially available plate and screw implant systems. Their argument was that these implants have been 'tried and tested' in veterinary orthopaedic surgery. I was steadfast in my view that such implants would likely fail, and given the previous track record of off-the-shelf implants in these patients, the clients didn't want me to use them either, which is why they had sought my advice in the first place. I offered for the expert to come and review the cases in person, but the offer was not taken up.

The irony was not lost on me. None of these off-the-shelf implants had gone through ethics approval or regulatory oversight beyond manufacturing standards. They had already failed, yet I was being advised to employ such techniques again; to repeat the mistakes rather than to innovate; to likely condemn both dogs in my opinion to more pain, suffering and, ultimately in Simon's case, euthanasia. My critics accuse me of employing untried and untested implants or performing a 'surgical experiment', although I've used custom implants with small incremental improvements each time for many years, whilst any veterinary surgeon in the UK can apply so-called 'tested' implants and have no recrimination if they fail, even when they're suboptimal. The customised implants I was proposing were deemed not RVP, whilst any off-the-shelf implant was in fact considered RVP, even though I didn't believe it would work. The public in general have no idea what RVP even means – they just assume vets are trustworthy and everything they do is 'recognised'.

For Martin, the recommendation from the expert was that I remove the dog's broken implants and leave the elbow fractured so that a kind of 'false fibrous joint' would form. It was suggested that the resultant pain could be 'adequately controlled medically'. Though I disagreed, this was the only occasion in my entire career that I did what was recommended by the ethics reviews, against my own personal professional judgement. The poor dog remained in pain with a floppy leg that he couldn't bear weight on, as I'd anticipated. So, I took remedial action, fusing the elbow solid with the custom system. The same expert suggested that I might consider a total elbow replacement in spite of the fact that one didn't exist for a patient of Martin's size.

Meanwhile, I was asked by the adjudication expert(s) to provide all kinds of details for the custom implants I was proposing: but no such requirement exists for any other implant launched by any other company in the UK.

To be clear, my argument is not that I, and the implants I use, should not be regulated. Quite the opposite. But if these hoops are going to be erected, everyone should have to jump through them equally in my view. Complete transparency. If trustworthiness of optimal care is something we *genuinely* want to foster, perhaps we should define what an 'advanced' surgical procedure actually is and ensure that all advanced surgeries are carried out only by veterinary surgeons who've undergone formal training with established mentors for a designated period. This is an absolute requirement for a human orthopaedic surgeon in the UK. I feel there is also a desperate need to define for the families of animals what is and is not RVP.

RCVS and the expert adjudicators undoubtedly want to do what they feel is best for the animal, just as I do. But in my view, because the number of complications is dramatically higher overall for routine implants than advanced implants, these too would warrant regulation in such a fair and transparent structure. It has been suggested that I should have an experimental animal licence, though I am *never* carrying out an experiment, and those who already carried out the original procedures on Simon and Martin needed no such licence, despite frequent failure with unregulated implants. It has further been proposed that the ethics panel should include an ethicist and someone involved in animal experimentation. However, I had experienced before with Bran where an arbitrary finite time point of six weeks to recover satisfactorily or be put to sleep was the guidance offered. I do not believe that companion animals should have the same clearly defined end points of euthanasia as laboratory animals, as I've mentioned in Bran's case . . .

All of these people, an alternative specialist surgeon, ethicist and animal experimentation expert, would undoubtedly be worthy of trust from their perspectives, but I was not prepared to compromise my own ethical boundaries to acquiesce to what I perceived to be ethically dubious recommendations for my patients. For Simon and Martin the RCVS returned similar verdicts, that '*if a veterinary surgeon decides to proceed, as he is entitled to do when carrying out an acceptable treatment in the best interests of the patient, then any deviation from RCVS authorisation and its opinion will have to be justified e.g., at a DC hearing.*' In other words, to proceed with treatment for Simon and Martin with implants I felt most likely to succeed, I may have been putting my licence to practise on the line if there were yet another accusation of malpractice and yet another incredibly stressful and time-consuming legal process to defend myself, when all I was trying to do was help – and I had the family's blessing to do so. As such I proceeded with what was deemed not an act of RVP for both Simon and Martin. I have considerable sympathy for the RCVS in this regard, because there is indeed a grey area between what may be considered 'acceptable treatments' and what they call 'recognised veterinary practice' – i.e. what most vets do. The guidance seeks to protect animals but it makes innovation more difficult, and may also result in a very poor outcome in my experience. As such, trustworthiness in veterinary surgery is *much* more challenging than any guardian of any animal might ever imagine. In the words of the Irish band Inhaler, one would like to think that 'love will get you there', but in the case of these difficult ethical issues, it appears that 'love' alone just isn't enough – for the family of the patient or for myself.

By the time it came to considering operating on Brandy, he was in extreme pain for a very long time and something had to be done. I seemed to be speaking an entirely different language to those reviewing my elbow fusion proposals for Simon and Martin and I would propose the same for Brandy, so I did not feel such dialogue was in Brandy's best interest. I wanted to go to the moon and I was going to be offered a 1980s motorbike to do so. I genuinely respect the opinions of all of my colleagues and peers; they are good people trying to do the right thing; but their opinions can only be based on their experience, and my experience has been different to theirs. I am by no means always right and there are surgeons who are superior to me in lots of different surgeries. Also, there is no question that different implant systems can both produce excellent results, but for Brandy, I was as sure as I could be that a customised implant system would likely yield a superior outcome by comparison with off-the-shelf implants. Those asked for opinions gave them in good faith and with good intent, but their firmly and sincerely held 'truth' wasn't my truth and therefore I couldn't trust it. I proceeded with a custom elbow fusion system for Brandy as quickly as I could in an effort to get him out of his miserable pain.

Simon, Martin and Brandy were not straightforward patients for surgery or for rehabilitation. All had chronic scar tissue, disruption of the positions of nerves and blood vessels, poor bone quality and underlying infection in two of the three, after all the repeated surgeries. Simon and Brandy required post-operative antibiotics to treat infections, which had been there before I became involved. Infection is incredibly difficult to eradicate in the presence of a large volume of metal because bugs can hide away in the nooks and crannies and form a kind of umbrella called 'biofilm' which fends off the antibiotic, such that infection may come back at a later date. There were also significant mechanical challenges with all three dogs due to nerve problems, poor muscle mass and as I've mentioned, poor bone quality. Nevertheless, at the time of writing, all three are happily walking, swimming and even running on four legs without pain. There is a mechanical limp one would expect from an elbow fusion, but they are all back to their former joyful selves, as are their most grateful families.

Sequentially over more than two dozen cases of customised elbow fusion, the implant systems have incrementally got better and better, building on successes and learning from challenges to maximise healing and minimise the risk of fractures by distributing load more evenly throughout the three bones of the elbow – humerus, radius and ulna. Like all innovation, success comes from taking 'baby steps'. Ostensibly, none of this has been RVP, but loads of dogs' limbs have been saved and I am 100 per cent certain that if I hadn't innovated, and if I had *trusted* the guidance provided, Brandy, Simon and Martin would not be walking today. These examples represent a massive challenge for the profession I so passionately love going forward.

For my part, I simply do not have time to submit eight to twelve hours of paperwork with each case I'm asked to perform advanced surgery on, on top of time spent designing and planning and carrying out surgery. This seems especially challenging when it's not universally required of all surgeons carrying out similar kinds of surgery. That's not being disrespectful, but practical. I am fifty-five years old, and I only have a certain number of operating hours left. That's just how it is. So, I have made my decision. I will carry on and treat the patients to the best of my ability. If the RCVS wish to encourage innovation in my profession then they will, in my opinion, need to create a level playing field for all surgeons, all animals and all the families who love them. They will need to look to the thousands of surgeries performed annually with unregulated implants and sometimes under-skilled surgeons. If other veterinarians wish to take me through an exhaustive legal hearing to justify my actions with advanced customised implants as they have done before, then I have no choice but to fight for the animals in a public arena and compare my complication rates to the thousands of vets operating with regular implants and those operating with 'novel' implants that any vet can order on the internet. RVP remains a grey area which has thus far not been defined for either 'regular' or 'advanced' surgeries performed by any surgeon of any skill or qualification level. But if I become a scapegoat for an unwillingness to treat all animals, all families and all veterinary surgeons equally, and if one day the tide of opinion turns against me, then I may indeed cease to be a vet and there will be no 'Beyond Supervet'.

I have shown operations on *The Supervet* TV show that are more advanced than many I have seen in 'state of the art' lectures at symposia but I feel it's essential, in conclusion, to state I vehemently believe that all surgeons, including me, carrying out any advanced procedures should be tightly regulated, as should the implants they use. Every surgeon and every animal should be treated equally – same rules, same respect, same dignity, same integrity of purpose. I feel it would be helpful if the RCVS developed clear and transparent guidelines of what is and is not 'acceptable' regarding techniques and implants at all different levels of the profession in consultation with the guardians of animals about what they really want, and then meeting with all relevant groups to try to formulate a better way to 'do business'. This is undoubtedly challenging, but then everyone – vets and clients – would know where they stand, and nobody would be asking to do anything that wasn't perceived to be 'acceptable veterinary practice'. The rules would be super-clear for all to see. All of us want the same thing in the end, which is the best possible outcome for the animals we serve and love. I'm willing to risk everything I have worked for over three decades since I became a vet and all that I am as a person to do what I feel in my heart is the most trustworthy thing for my patients. And if Fitzpatrick Referrals ultimately folds as a result, I will have gone down with the ship, but with my conscience clear.

Everyone, including me, would like to be accepted by the 'tribe' they have chosen as being worthy and worthwhile of a vocational commitment. It's difficult to strive for advancements in veterinary surgery for the benefit of patients that your tribe doesn't respect or appreciate. I have no desire to become a poster child for any mental disorder, but constant criticism by colleagues in my profession from behind closed doors or sitting at keyboards has significantly contributed to poor mental health for me. I believe that my profession has a duty of care to all veterinarians to be mindful of this. I respect all opinions, to which people are entitled, but I feel there are better ways to go about looking after the welfare of companion animals in the UK than vilifying some bloke on the telly. To emphasise again, however, no surgeon should be above constructive criticism and should welcome it as part of their journey, which I would, if I felt it were fair, transparent and collegiate. Like many people who spend long hours doing something narrowly focused, and who give up much of their life for their art or their work, I am on the autism spectrum, displaying traits of Asperger's syndrome, and also obsessive–compulsive behaviours. This has been apparent to me for a long time, and diagnosed late in life. I've learned like many others to live positively with my condition, empowered rather than hampered by my unique mental wiring. Being 'wired' is not being 'weird'! I think this is one of the reasons I've always loved superhero comics and characters – they're often people whom society might view as physically and mentally damaged, but capable of great feats. The X-Men are also known as 'mutants'. They're outsiders, misunderstood and even feared by society.

I'm an outsider. I know it. Others have told me I'm 'different'. I'm not a fan of small talk – my conversation always drifts to bigger topics. I've even been called a 'madman', both fondly, by friends, and by those not so kindly disposed. I'm quite sure no one fears me, but it's fair to say there are plenty who misunderstand my motives. I make no apologies for who I am. I can be intense and emotional – I wear my heart on my sleeve, because I don't believe in hiding it away. I will always speak the truth as I see it. You can take me or leave me. I won't allow myself to be hard-wired into the system. As I alluded to earlier, I have realized that if I constantly seek my worth from outside, I will always feel worthless inside. The goal must be to always be true to my heart and to be answerable to that truth, rather than what people say, and with whatever motives they say it. To truly be trustworthy, one must first have trust in oneself.

It's no exaggeration to say that we're at an existential

crossroads for humanity and our planet, with global warming and decimation of habitats and species. I believe that our love for companion animals could translate into love for all animals, and humans, and this truly would make us the best we can be. But only if we make really brave choices and if we trust that love can save us. I find myself in a bit of a difficult spot, because this message, indeed my life's mission, might look to some, on paper, as a bit, well . . . *grand*. But here's the thing – I honestly believe in the vital importance of my profession as a leading light for goodness and trustworthiness in society and the real world. I have insisted that every episode of *The Supervet* must have some important core messages, and the same is true of this book. All I ever set out to do was to try to make the world better, one animal at a time. To paraphrase Metallica, I 'seek trust' and I have found it in my animal friends and their families. Every day they teach me 'something new' and open my mind for 'a different view'. I absolutely know that, for me, 'nothing else matters'.

As a final thought – I would like to address the RCVS and all my fellow veterinary professionals.

RCVS states that:

> *Our aim is to enhance society through improved animal health and welfare, by advancing the educational, ethical and clinical standards of the veterinary profession . . . (with) . . . our committed caring and compassionate team and a working culture that liberates our people to look for, and act on constant improvements.*

We have a choice about how we wish to progress and how such progress is policed. Change will happen, but real progress requires us to be very brave indeed. Human medicine will advance anyway, often experimenting on animals supervised by vets to do so. Do animals not deserve the same advances in drugs and implants for which the lives of their kin are sacrificed? I believe that to maintain the trustworthiness of the veterinary profession, transparency, integrity and regulation are paramount alongside compassion and care for all animals and for all fellow professionals on the journey. I believe that we need to be authentic, compassionate, trustworthy advocates for each and every animal, and we need to do the right thing by them. That's why all of us signed up in the first place. I do not believe that the veterinary profession has the right to withhold choice from the consumer. If there is no choice, there are no ethics, no morals, no fairness and no trustworthiness. I believe that the public deserve truth and honesty about what they are paying for in private healthcare for their animal friends, and I believe that our profession has a moral responsibility to actually advance the level of care we provide, and to offer all of the options to all of the families all of the time within a robust, sensible and ethical framework. How can we expect them to trust us if we do not?

CHAPTER 11

Creativity

I have performed castration hundreds of times, since I was a young teenager on the farm with lambs and calves, but when the bullock is nearly fully grown, it's a different matter. The head of the poor beast was held in the gate of a 'crush', like the one we used when I dehorned bullocks with Daddy. The farmer was holding tongs in his nose, as I had done myriad times in my youth. I instilled the local anaesthetic and with one swift thrust of my scalpel blade, I cut into the bullock's scrotum. My patient, understandably but unexpectedly, objected with the most sudden and almightiest kick which caught my right arm with his hoof, knocking it towards my left forearm, where the razor-sharp blade sliced through the muscle. I knew at once it had hit an artery because blood began to pump out like a high-pressure hose. The farmer recoiled in horror, dropping the nose tongs as I flailed backwards. He was well accustomed to blood from his animals, but not pouring from the visiting vet.

I landed on my arse in the mud behind the bullock and

assessed the situation as calmly as a man can when blood is spurting into his face from his own arm, but nothing in my twenty-four years on earth had quite prepared me for this. The doctor probably wasn't in town as he was frequently drunk, and the hospital was miles away from the farm we were on. The gushing artery would require some creativity.

'Let him out,' I shouted towards the farmer. The bullock could wait. 'Have you got a rubber band?'

'No, sure, I don't,' came the reply.

Just holding something against the wound was a waste of time, even if I'd *had* something clean, which I didn't. As I grasped my left elbow from the front, squeezing with my right hand, I looked around for anything I could use as a tourniquet to wrap around my upper arm to stem the flow. The rusty wire hanging off a nearby hay-making machine wasn't an appealing possibility. I could use baler twine, I thought, but rubber really would be best. And then I saw it. Leaning against a stone wall on the far side of the yard – a bicycle.

'Get the bike,' I said.

'It's no use me cyclin' anywhere,' replied the farmer.

I'm used to similar mystified expressions on the faces of my colleagues even today, when I ask for some oddment from Narnia during the course of an operation. I explained quickly that I didn't need him to ride the thing, but that I also needed a spoon. He flipped the bike onto its saddle, then ran into the kitchen of the adjacent farm cottage, returning quickly with a nice big spoon, using it to prise the tyre off the rim of the upturned bicycle wheel and pull out the inner tube. Perfect. I wrapped it round my left arm above the elbow and tied the bow with my teeth. Not the easiest manoeuvre, but I wasn't letting his muck-covered hands anywhere near me.

With the blood flow now just a trickle from the gash in my arm, I asked him to boil some water and he brought the steaming kettle from the farm kitchen to the back of my car where I was busy looking for a suture needle. *Damn!* I'd done a cow Caesarean the previous day and had left all the kit in sterilising fluid at the practice. So, no suture needle, but I did have a spool of large gauge (thick) nylon which I used for stitching cow's skin. Luckily, I did have some more large syringe needles for administering anaesthetic, which sadly didn't appear to have worked well enough on the bullock. That would have to do. I splashed some hot water and iodine solution on the gash, then sprayed some local anaesthetic and waited a couple of minutes. I pushed the injection needle through each side of the gash and threaded the nylon through the sharp point, then pulled the needle backwards with the suture following. I did this four times and then tied each suture with my right hand and teeth in neat knots. I trimmed the ends myself with a pair of scissors that the farmer found in a drawer in the kitchen. No more blood. Job done. I still have the scar, mind you.

More than three decades later looking back, it's clear to me that creativity has always been born of necessity for me – innovation from frustration. I have a few more physical scars from years of operating with sharp things. A scar on my right thumb from catching it on a piece of sharp wire sticking out from a bone, on my left palm from drilling through my hand when the drill bit slipped off a bone I was holding and on my left thumb from severing the tendons with a sharp knife in a meat factory whilst in vet school. But I also have some less visible emotional scars from my 'creative' thought processes. It's probably true of everyone who has ever created anything that their successes stand on the shoulders of their failures, and I have had very many of those. People only see the successes, but the inner scars from the pain of failure, especially where it pertains to life and death, run deep and last a lifetime. I know that some people believe we paint too rosy a picture on *The Supervet* TV show, but I have always felt strongly we need to show our failures. As I've mentioned earlier, it's understandably hard for people to have the death of their animal friend, and their own pain, shown on TV. It's an intimate moment and we're loath to relive it, and share it with others. But with the programme I have fought hard to show failure, as I have fought to show my fallibility and mistakes in this book. It's easier to write a book or make a TV show about only the heart-warming stories of miracles and cute fluffy animals, but while that is certainly entertaining, it's not real life. Real life is about coming to terms with failure, so the successes mean more. It's just a fact of life that to open yourself up to deep love means opening yourself up to deep pain. Sharing this truth of the creative process is hard, but necessary. As David Bowie alluded to in his song 'Starman', sometimes there's the worry that seeing the truth might just 'blow our minds'. I get it. What most of us want is simple escapism, but I've argued from the inception of the TV show that we should show everything, although some people are understandably concerned that it might upset a number of viewers, especially children. I share Bowie's view, that it really is 'all worthwhile' and that young people are far braver and savvier than we give them credit for. I say, 'Let the children use it,' and I sincerely hope before I too rest among the stars, that someone wants to inherit what's in my head – scars and all.

The process of creating the TV show is quite amazing really and all the people involved do an awesome job editing many hours of footage into a couple of minutes of blood or science and several minutes of more palatable viewing. It's a show unlike any other. In veterinary orthopaedics and neurosurgery, in which I specialise, there are some medical challenges where it's not right or ethical to operate because to do so would prolong the animal's suffering. None of these make it on to the TV show and this can give a somewhat distorted portrayal of my day-to-day reality, which is easy for people to judge out of context. It should be noted that the majority of surgical challenges can readily and successfully be addressed using commercially available implants. But then there are those problems for which no tried-and-tested, cookie-cutter solution exists – no off-the-shelf implant, nor an extensive body of clinical literature. As you'll have appreciated by now, that's never been good enough for me. I have always thought we could do better and I am always thinking of ways to innovate new solutions. In dire need, we do all we can for human medical challenges, and I take the same approach to my animal patients. This forms the core of the One Medicine philosophy and if I'd wanted it any other way I would have become a human surgeon. It never ceases to amaze me how my critics are happy for animals to be sacrificed for human benefit in experiments but not happy for me to do all I can to bring hope to those who really need it. I'm still the only vet in the world performing certain procedures on dogs and cats.

To me, it seems especially wasteful, uncompassionate and lacking in any truly creative thought process that similar procedures have previously been performed experimentally in completely healthy dogs, to develop implants for humans. Dogs who *don't need* them get them because humans *want* them, whilst dogs that actually *need* them don't get them because humans *don't want* them to. This is absolutely wrong in my opinion. Yet, when animals who really do need such implants actually get them in my practice, I have sometimes been accused by my peers of 'experimenting' on my clinical patients. It's all the crazier because I would never have an animal suffer on my watch. But dogs have suffered and have been killed under the legally required supervision of vets, to develop versions of most implants for humans, but dogs in pain can't have them routinely today. Even though the technology has moved on considerably and is available, vets still say, 'I'm sorry, it can't be done.' The truth is a rather more prosaic, 'I'm sorry, we're not prepared to make it happen.'

Vets accept being second best to human surgery and accept failure with conventional implants sold to us by implant companies for significant profit as just a fact of life, when in fact more optimal implants could exist and might avoid such failure. The simple reason is money – care and creativity require significant investment. Neither human doctors nor veterinarians need to think of this painful truth on a daily basis. Instead, life goes on as it always has, with very few trying to find any creative pathways towards a more collaborative joined-up approach. If a human surgeon has tried and failed with a certain implant, I'd want to know about that so I might avoid a similar complication in my patients; I would like to think that the same would be true of human surgeons regarding my work. But, truth be told, for most, it's just a mild curiosity that someone tells them about on a TV show, and life goes on in medicine as it always has – we make the same mistakes over and over and we call it progress; we waste money on research that could be better spent elsewhere; we don't find cures quickly enough because we are not creative in our thought process. Harsh, yes; truthful, absolutely.

Joint replacements are performed commonly in man and animal. Nearly all of those that exist for humans were developed in experimental animal models, as required by law in most countries in the world for testing of safety and efficacy. Two good examples of where human and animal medicine could work better together in One Medicine are total shoulder replacement (TSR) and total knee replacement (TKR). TSR was performed in dogs in the 1940s as an experiment for humans, and yet when I performed the first TSR in a canine case that really needed it a decade ago, I was criticised by some and praised by others. We developed a plastic-on-metal socket for the shoulder blade and a new metal head for the humerus bone that fits into it. It wasn't that difficult really – the key was finding a way to preserve the mechanics of the joint so that it worked properly. As is often the case, it's relatively easy to conceptualise something on a CT scan inside a computer, but in real life one needs muscles, tendons and ligaments to move perfectly around the joint, and a blood and nerve supply to power it. Creativity requires the ability to think *around* rather than just *about* the subject.

I've only performed a handful of TSR surgeries, since it's not commonly requested, but my patients have climbed mountains when they previously couldn't walk in the garden for a pee, and have run for miles when previously they whimpered getting off a sofa due to painful debilitating shoulder osteoarthritis and deformity. Such patients are generally not referred for treatment because it's perceived by many vets that 'it can't be done', when in fact it's been around for more than eighty years. This is generally an innocent rather than malicious omission, because primary care clinicians aren't told about such options in their training. I have in fact published an academic paper on the fall-back position, which is fusion of the shoulder joint solid, which is also a really good way to get dogs out of severe pain. As with every innovation, I have ideas on how to make these operations better with every case I perform. Creativity is essential for progress and progress in turn feeds creativity.

It's often in adversity that the most impactful ideas are born – if you allow their gestation. When we invented a TKR that wouldn't dislocate, the basic concept came from my teenage self once nearly turning over a trailer with a load of barley in it. I'd had it in my head that I was a better tractor driver than I actually was. I drove the tractor out of the field, not recognising that you had to turn much wider with a trailer behind. The wheel of the trailer rode up on a low cement wall bordering the edge of a bridge over a stream, and the result was that the trailer was left perched precariously, rocking side to side on its back axle, held in place only by the strength of the tow bar anchored to the tractor. My father was absolutely livid as I could have lost several tonnes of grain. Years later, we developed a joint inspired by my memories of that axle balancing and held by a lever on the bridge. The axle in our 'rotating hinge' TKR goes through a spigot or pillar which protrudes upwards from the implant in the shin bone (tibia) and links via a plastic bushing to the implant in the thigh bone (femur), and so a knee that had blown out most of its ligaments and rubbed away its cartilage can still be saved. This joint replacement has now preserved the limbs of dozens of dogs and cats, whereas in many cases elsewhere the leg is still amputated or the animal euthanised without even discussing TKR or the fall-back position of fusing the joint solid. This is in spite of our publishing these techniques in academic journals. Most of the patients I see for TSR or TKR are clients self-referring because they have seen the procedures on my TV show, whilst vets still say it isn't possible or it isn't desirable for whatever reason.

It seems that creativity is slow to be accepted in veterinary medicine whilst in human medicine they now use a similar TKR in similar circumstances and there is so much we could learn together, but we don't. The very best creativity is in my view that of a team with a common goal, because many minds are better than one. And yet we don't escape the straitjackets imposed on us as Brandon Flowers from the band The Killers once asked, 'Are we human or are we dancer,' meaning, wouldn't we all be better off if we stopped being robot cogs in the system, let our hair down and danced. I know that there would certainly be many dogs and cats better off. I think it behoves all vets to accept that we are in a service industry and that 'all options' are in fact what the families of animals want. Denying choice is neither sustainable nor sensible if we wish to progress veterinary medicine in a robust ethical framework. Meanwhile the popular press sensationalises simple fracture repairs by referring to a 'bionic dog' or 'bionic cat', and as a profession we welcome this as free advertising. It is, however, misleading, because the very word 'bionic' infers replacement of a body part with something mechanical or electrical to replicate or enhance function. It is trite but true that not all creativity is *bionic*.

Truly bionic implants require bionic creativity and bionic engineering. There would have been no *Bionic Vet* or *Supervet* without engineer Jay Meswania, whom I first met in 2006. Jay is the kindest, most genuine, gracious and dedicated colleague I have ever had the good fortune to be on my journey with. I admire him and I love him as a mentor, colleague and dear friend. Over the years I have dreamed up many things, emailed him at 2 a.m., even at weekends, only to find he has woken at 6.30 a.m. and worked on an implant solution to send the same morning. We go back and forth a bit more and within days a cat or a dog gets fixed. Together we have created more than a thousand custom implants for companion animals. Sadly, our creative twinning was brought to an untimely and abrupt end just five days before my little girl Keira died in September 2021, when Jay plunged down the side of a steep ravine, rupturing his ribcage and fracturing his spine in multiple places.

Typically, Jay was selflessly trying to help another person at the time. Someone had slipped down the edge of an incline where he and his family were out walking. While trying to give them assistance, Jay lost his footing and fell many feet onto the rocks below. Impact to his chest fractured ribs and drove the broken bones into the lining of his chest cavity. Air rapidly built up inside his chest outside his lungs and he couldn't breathe. He was transferred to a regional hospital and then to the Queen Elizabeth Hospital in Birmingham. They performed a tracheotomy and put him on a ventilator. The surgeons could not operate on his spinal injuries for weeks because he was in an induced coma, with a slim chance of recovery. The man who had helped me to fix Keira after being hit by a van and who had helped save the lives of hundreds of my patients was now perilously close to death himself. Jay's family and all of us at Fitzpatrick Referrals were devastated.

Alongside Professor Gordon Blunn, at the Royal National Orthopaedic Hospital, Jay had helped Hermes, the first tortoise, and the first cats, dogs and humans in the UK to have bionic limbs. Without Jay, these particular implants would never have been possible for man or animal. At the time he was in hospital, I was due to give a lecture in support of the Humanimal Trust, about how creativity in human and animal medicine brings us together as one, and by doing the right thing and the best we can do each and every time, the cumulative effect is progress – not just in medicine, but in life generally. The lecture would also support the charity of my legal counsel who had helped me cope with the profoundly depressed days and nights during the long official investigation by the RCVS, prompted by four vets who felt that I should be struck off the veterinary register for 'overtreatment' of Hermes the tortoise by fitting three bionic limbs, which I described earlier. The vets felt that we had put Hermes through too much from a welfare perspective, causing unnecessary pain and suffering when in their view the most optimal 'treatment' was euthanasia. Yet he had been doing very well on his new leg implants until he later died of a suspected gastro-enteric issue. Clearly the opinions of vets differ vastly on the role of creativity in medical practice and where the ethical boundary is drawn for such advanced surgeries.

Jay and I firmly believe in ethics, education, efficacy and evidence – the four Es. We want to make things better for animals, just as human doctors and surgeons do for their patients. All that Jay had contributed was foremost in my mind as I walked out onto the theatre stage in Shrewsbury to give my talk. Jay had been the fulcrum of creativity and hope for our animal and human families, and it was now time for all of us to step up to the plate for him and his. The talk to more than a thousand people for charity would not have happened at all if Jay and I hadn't tried to help Hermes for free. The sad irony wasn't lost on me. Some of my talk was about why my profession doesn't investigate the frequent use of badly applied suboptimal off-the-shelf implants in relatively simple operations which causes avoidable pain and suffering and can result in both amputations and euthanasia, but most certainly isn't for free. As I discussed earlier, I often wonder where the ethical boundary is drawn by vets for these everyday situations, of which there are hundreds performed yearly.

Halfway through the lecture, I paused and asked the audience to imagine that each and every one of us was holding Jay's hand and thinking of him with all of our might for a minute – willing him to get well again. I'm a clinician, so magic isn't my thing, but sometimes one has to wonder about the power of positive creative intention. There are things in the endless creativity of our universe that we will never understand and perhaps we don't necessarily need to. The very next day, Professor Sir Keith Porter, who leads the trauma and orthopaedics unit in Birmingham, called to say that Jay had woken from his coma and things were looking up for the very first time. Soon, his team were able to fuse Jay's spine with similar implants to those he had helped me to design for dogs. I'm pleased to say he is now doing well. We shall be forever grateful to the wonderful team of nurses, doctors and surgeons who saved Jay's life. Professor Porter and his team were incredible, not least working under the terrible duress of the Covid crisis in NHS hospitals across the land. We are extraordinarily lucky in the UK to have the NHS providing state-of-the-art care for free, which would in many cases cost hundreds of thousands of pounds. In my view, our taxes could not be put to better use than funding this exemplary and deeply creative institution.

Devices like those Jay had to push and hold spinal vertebrae in place had also been developed and deployed by him and me for dogs who really needed them, rather than as experiments to develop the technology for humans. Our spinal distraction fusion system has saved hundreds of lives and I was most pleased that Jay could receive the same level of care for himself. It was the least that medicine could do for a man who had dedicated his life to developing creative solutions to recalcitrant problems. We manufactured a titanium screw spacer shaped like and inspired by a Christmas tree (called FITS devices – Fitz intervertebral traction screws). These are held in place in the neck of a dog by saddle-shaped plates inspired by a saddle of a horse combined with dumb-bells and screw clamps inspired by a trip to the gym. Creativity requires paying constant attention to the world around us – ideas are everywhere if we choose to let them in.

Charles was a Great Dane that had his entire neck fused by 'Christmas tree' spacers linked with saddle clamps and dumb-bells to treat a condition which is a form of 'wobblers disease' (so called because of the dog's affected gait). The medical term is osseous-associated cervical spondylomyelopathy, or osseous-associated wobblers syndrome (OAWS, an acronym I coined many years ago). The bones of his neck had grown abnormally from puppyhood and were squashing down on the spinal cord and the spinal nerves. The conventional procedure, which was to try to remove the compressive bone, would likely not have worked for Charles because every junction of his neck vertebrae was affected and so his spinal column would have been rendered dramatically unstable. He was only two years old and the only option offered to his family had been for him to be put to sleep. They were truly devastated, but following surgery which fused all of his neck from just behind his skull to the entrance of his chest, Charles went from barely being able to get up at all, in considerable pain and falling flat on his face all the time, to running around with a stick in his mouth. As his family have said to me, if these implants didn't exist, Charles would be 'ashes on [their] mantelpiece now'. Instead, he is chasing other dogs, the 'life and soul of the dog field'. Most vets deem it fantasy to think that one could fuse solid the entire neck of a Great Dane, that it would put them through too much suffering and that it couldn't possibly work, but as it was, Charles was suffering every day and all my profession offered him as an alternative was death. Sometimes to be creative one has to overcome not just the challenges one is trying to solve, but also the minds of others who refuse to open to possibility. In general, the families of animals who watch *The Supervet* are far more receptive to possibility than some in my profession; for them, once you know something is possible, it's impossible to believe it's impossible ever again.

Brenda Lou was a three-year-old Labrador retriever who came to see me from the Netherlands with severe pain affecting both back legs due to a degenerative condition in her spine called degenerative lumbosacral stenosis. The furthest down disc at the base of her spine had dried out, and, along with new bone formed around it (spondylosis), squashed the origins of her sciatic nerves. I see a couple of dozen such cases each year. I empathise because I am affected by this condition myself, suffering from lower back pain every day of my life, sometimes to the point I can't stand up to operate. My posture as a surgeon, as I have spent thousands of hours saving dogs from pain, has ironically contributed to my own pain. Brenda Lou wasn't unusual in that she had been previously operated on using only bone removal techniques. This often fails in my experience in particularly severe disease like hers. Taking off the roof of the last lumbar and first sacral vertebrae (a dorsal laminectomy) does not address the new bone squashing the nerve roots at the sides, whilst widening the holes through which the nerves come (foraminotomy) may also fail, as it did for Brenda Lou. So, I invented a way to pass the FITS device past the nerves from the top to the underside of the spine to push the vertebrae apart and then with screws, clamps and rods, to fuse them solid.

We've had great success with this procedure across more than a decade, but it was rejected for scientific publication when I tried a few years back, even though I've used this to revise many failed techniques that are published, as for Brenda Lou. Infection or mechanical failure can occur, but they are rare and it has removed pain and allowed quality of life for hundreds of dogs I've operated on. Such are the vagaries of academic publications. Like television commissioners and movie producers often want versions of hit shows and films that have already been made, and record companies want clones of musical artists that have already made it, so too do medical journals more readily accept techniques that are derivative and closely related to precedents. If you want to be James Cameron and re-define cinema or Elvis with your inimitable voice and hip-shaking prowess, and if you want to change the entire paradigm of how things are done, then early publication in an academic journal is unlikely. I'll try to get it published another time and hopefully it will be accepted in the future, but one thing's for sure – without creativity, Brenda Lou would not be with us today.

'What have we done with innocence?' asks Dave Grohl at the beginning of Foo Fighters' song 'Monkey Wrench', and this is the single most pervasive thought I have in the midst of the uphill struggle to open vets' minds to creativity so we can make things better for our animal friends. And yet, I have never met a guardian of an animal that isn't innocent in their hope for a creative solution for the suffering of their friend. I understand that there has to be a consideration of ethics and what's in the best interest of the animal, but we need to strip back egos and vested interests of any kind, because a childlike innocence is essential for creativity. Most musicians will tell you that their best songs just fell from the ether into their mind, voice and fingertips. The same has been true for Jay and me. I will think of possible solutions to problems at the most unexpected moments and, as the other member of my band of only two for a very long time (some more have joined since), Jay and I would make a beautiful melody together that would actually heal an animal, again much like music heals the soul. I have often seen and appreciated our process in those terms and in fact when I am performing the procedure I described for Brenda Lou, which is called lumbosacral distraction fusion, I see the nerves to the back legs, urinary bladder, anus and tail every single time looking just like finely tuned guitar strings side by side, as I did for Stevie when I mended her fractures. I very delicately nudge them aside as I put my FITS device in the perfect spot, trying not to strike a bum note. Dave Grohl likely misses drummer Taylor Hawkins from his band like he misses his right arm, and I would have been the same with Jay. There will never be another Jay and my music would be unimaginably different without him. He can hear the beat of my tune and start playing it even whilst it's still in my head.

There isn't a greater example of this than with some of the prostheses that Jay and I have developed to replace parts inside the body. For example, I commonly replace bones affected by tumours with a metal endoskeleton, so that we can keep the lower joint and foot on a limb. One instance where I commonly perform this surgery is to replace the forearm of a large or giant breed dog, when I cut out primary bone cancer. I did this for both Dimitri, the Russian black terrier, and Frieda, the mastiff, in an earlier chapter. I need to be able to link the wrist (carpus), paw (metacarpus) and both bones of the forearm (radius and ulna), but the angles at which they fit together are always different, whether because of the breed of dog, or how much of the tumour bone I've had to remove.

What I needed was a 'jigsaw' of different pieces that I could have ready on the shelf, which when put together could fit any dog from a 30kg German shepherd to a 100kg mastiff. I wanted to be able to perform the surgery in the same week that the dog presents, so as not to waste valuable time – these tumours spread fast. The off-the-shelf tumour replacement implant consists of a chunk of metal and a long plate which bridges from the forearm to the foot. When I used it, the screws in this system came loose and bone fracture was common, so I won't use this implant in my patients any more. But I was stumped as to what might be better.

About ten years ago, having performed full limb amputation on a giant breed dog, I was upset that I didn't have a better option to offer. Many dogs will run around absolutely fine on three legs, but this poor dog was really struggling without a front leg. I was rushing towards my local train station and a 'lollipop lady' stepped out in front of me to stop traffic. I was annoyed at the delay as I was already close to missing my train, and I was en route to London for an important meeting to try to borrow yet more money for investment in the practice. My foot was quivering on the accelerator ready to take off. I stared at the lollipop with intense frustration for what seemed like an eternity. When she eventually let me pass, I sped off, quickly parked the car and squeezed through the train doors as they closed. I slumped in a chair, sweating and panting, and closed my eyes.

When I opened them again, I was momentarily blinded by a shaft of sunlight through the carriage window. I flicked my head away and my eyes fell on a giant engagement ring on the hand of the lady in the seat opposite, sparkling in the spring sunshine. I closed my eyes again, and as the gentle rocking of the train nudged me into a kind of reverie, there it was – an engagement ring and lollipop 3D linkage system!

Jay and I developed a ring with a nut like a diamond which threaded on a shaft attached by a plate to the radius in the forearm using locking screws that don't loosen, which connected to the pole of a lollipop, of which the circular bit attached in any rotational position to a plate on the ulna bone. *Voila!* A system that could work for any dog with any length of bone removed. The shaft slotted like a tilting 'telescope' onto a titanium body, which was linked to the wrist (carpus) by a forked plate stretching down to two palm (metacarpal) bones in the foot. All the cartilage of the wrist bones was removed for fusion and the titanium body and the plates all had specialised bone-on-growth surfaces so that the metal endoskeleton would become a permanent part of the body. Around the telescope the paw could be connected at any external angle of rotation to best suit the dog. This is the modular radius-ulna endoprosthesis implant system that I placed in the legs of both Dimitri and Frieda, which allowed them to run around happily on four legs for the rest of their lives. I've put a photograph of this construct in the picture section to demonstrate.

Throughout my life, I have found that creativity can strike at any time and requires an intrinsic innocence to put what may appear at first to be incongruous thoughts together in a novel way and to avoid thinking only in straight lines. I suppose it's my equivalent of songwriters who constantly jot down fragments of lyrics, waiting for the right moment for the right melody to make them into a song. You can't just write the same songs as everyone else if you want to change the world. Luckily for me I have had the greatest bandmate ever in Jay. Our relationship of creativity has actually changed the world for hundreds of animals and the families that love them. Jay will soon retire and in many ways this is my song of thanks to him. I shall think of him every day, even with the new musicians in the Fitzbionics band, and as Dave

Grohl says in 'Everlong', I shall hope that when he 'breathes out', even from afar, I 'can breathe [him] in'. Thank you so very much, Jay, for being the greatest 'medical musician' of all time.

Creativity in medicine has no room for solo musicians – it's a band effort or nothing at all, and there's no room for big egos and arrogance if one wants to do the best for the patient. When something that looks like a bone tumour is eating the inside of the bone away (osteo-lytic) and producing a bony reaction around it (osteo-productive), vets need to act immediately and start working together as a band of brothers or sisters, as do our human medical colleagues for their patients – imaging, pathologist, medicine, radiation therapy, implant manufacture and surgery, hand in hand; just like drums, bass guitar, electric guitar, keyboards, instrument tech and singer – all necessary to play the right tune. Creativity in curing cancer requires planning and teamwork to realise the best outcome. It also requires an ability to solve problems and force solutions into existence. Jay and I have been able to do exactly that with our implants. However, when it comes to improving chemotherapy, I have not been able to contribute to any change at all.

Most of my patients die within about a year no matter how good my implants are to replace the primary tumour. We need better therapies for the metastatic cells that spread from the primary tumour and ultimately kill both dogs and humans – and we can only find those treatments by cooperating through the philosophy of One Medicine, in my opinion. Late diagnosis, such as assuming the dog is lame because of a sprain, or some such, is also frustrating, as is taking a cut-in biopsy, which precludes my ability to save the leg due to contamination of the surrounding tissues. My greatest frustration, though, is that I strongly feel that my profession has no right to tell you what music to listen to – you should be given all the options – pop, rock, jazz, whatever – and the decision about what to listen to for the treatment of your best friend should always be yours.

There's no doubt that I have marched to my own tune throughout my life because I am absolutely committed to offering families all of the options all of the time, which I truly believe the animals who love us and are integral family members actually deserve. I'm thankfully getting to the point in my life where those who want to listen to my band are most welcome, and those that want to listen to something else have begun to bother me less. One of my musical heroes, Prince, once said that music is healing and holds things together, and thus it has always been for me and my band. Fitzpatrick Referrals is the only 'band' in the world that truly offers all of the orthopaedic and neurosurgical options for our patients, because we have invested in our own custom solutions. However, it's not an easy band to play music in because we are thereafter married to the cases on which we perform our procedures, in terms of aftercare and maintenance forever, as I relayed in an earlier chapter, so when original band members leave, generally I have carried on whistling the tune as best I can myself. Sometimes that's a quiet and lonely tune. It was at one of those particularly lonely moments that I met Angus, who didn't listen to hollers or whistles of any kind to come back to his family as he convinced himself he could fly and ran hurtling off the edge of a steep ravine in a moment of exuberance, crashing into the rocks below, much like Jay had and with similar chest injuries.

Angus was an effervescent yellow ball of golden retriever puppy fluff, and by the time I met him he was dragging a lifeless left front leg. He hadn't fractured his spine but the nerves in the brachial plexus of this left front armpit had been ripped apart (avulsed) and there was no question this leg had to be amputated. But in addition, the wrist (carpus) of his right front leg was badly collapsed, its ligaments shredded, and so I needed to fix this in order for him to bear his body weight. Historically I would have used one or two plates to fuse the wrist solid after removing the cartilage from the bones, but I felt we could do better for Angus. So, Jay and I designed a new kind of plate. It would be low profile to fit under his tight skin, but would be strong where it needed to be over the carpus (wrist) and taper gradually at the top of the radius bone and on two metacarpal bones at the bottom to avoid stressing one area of bone too much, which might result in a fracture, especially as he would bear all of his weight on one front leg thereafter. The plate worked brilliantly for Angus and after amputation of his opposite leg, he runs around happy and is still the king of mischief two years later.

Jay and all of the animals he has helped to fix continue to be inspirational to me, even on days when creativity seems very far away in the midst of all the other stresses. Angus has also been an inspiration to his human mother Zoe and her four children while going through her cancer and their own difficult times. Zoe's little boy Bertie was crying sometimes and because I didn't get many hugs when I was his age, it was painful for me that I couldn't hug the family to try and comfort them when poor Angus was going through very challenging circumstances, that were often life or death, because Covid restrictions were in force at the time. Zoe and I had many conversations about whether it was ethically appropriate to keep going with Angus, especially after his amputation wound became infected, but Amazing Angus pulled through and I pulled his final drainage tube on my birthday in 2020. I could not have wished for a better present. Through our journey together, Angus never allowed me even once to whistle a lonely tune.

Creativity is a gift that animals have given me throughout my life. After all, what is creativity but a refusal to live as things are and a choice to try and live as things could be. I have seen many hundreds of animals for whom an off-the-shelf implant would likely have failed or for whom conventional treatment would have been putting them to sleep, because it could not be imagined how they might live with any quality of life. And yet there they are, bounding after balls and sticks, curled up in laps or on the end of beds, many thousands of hours of extra life and happiness radiating out there in the universe.

Angus was one of the most 'creative' dogs I have ever met. He always found a way to snaffle an extra treat from the nurses at the practice, whom he wrapped around his remaining front paw. At home he remains a mastermind of the sandwich heist when the children aren't looking. He was also found by two policemen on bonfire night when he ran off. They brought him home through the serendipitous guidance of some neighbours. A very stern policeman knocked on the front door of his house, looked at Zoe, gestured towards Angus and said, 'Madam, don't you think he's missing something?'

Zoe looked right back at him and bemusedly and quite innocently answered, 'A leg?' The policeman didn't even crack a smile. With a completely stoical face, he glared back at her and said, 'No, madam – a collar and a tag . . .'

It doesn't matter what you're missing, you can always be creative.

CHAPTER 12

Love

Oz was a tawny four-year-old tabby cat who had an unknown accident almost six months previously when he suffered an explosive fracture of his left ankle (hock joint). The primary care vet had done the best they could to salvage the situation but all they had access to was a system of external skeletal fixation, placing pins into the bones and joining them together with rods and clamps on the outside. This can in fact work very well in some cases, and I have used it often for injuries such as when the leg of a dog or cat has the skin and muscle sheared off under the wheel of a skidding vehicle. However, it requires meticulous drilling away (debridement) of the cartilage and packing with bone marrow, usually collected from elsewhere in the body, in order to get the joints to fuse solid. Unfortunately, the previous surgical effort hadn't worked and Oz was left with a very painful and unstable bone-on-bone joint and a bad limp, for which the only option seemed to be amputation.

But the universe, via Harry Styles, had other ideas.

A week before, I'd been standing in the Brixton Academy, waiting for Harry to come on stage for his 'Love on Tour' show. As ever, I had kept my hoodie hood up until the lights went out – most people don't recognise me out of scrubs anyway, but I like to try and take a break from being the Supervet at gigs and lose myself in that magical feeling of connectedness between the performer and audience. As I've mentioned, it's my form of therapy and has served me very well down the years.

The show was awesome and as I was slowly making my way out among the excited hordes, a young woman shyly tapped me on the shoulder and asked if I was the Supervet. She introduced herself and explained that her cat Oz was about to have his leg amputated in the next couple of weeks and that this was considered the kindest option. Of course, my belief and experience is that if the blood and nerve supply remain intact, and if it's ethically in the best interests of the patient, the functionality of the majority of legs can be saved in one form or another, so I agreed to take a look as soon as was feasible.

It turned out that the young lady was the sister of Harry's drummer and it's fitting that I met Oz because of music. Music transcends all boundaries and a melody can evoke within us feelings of a primal, transcendental connection to something beyond ourselves, as I had discovered aged ten with my first transistor radio. I truly believe that our love for animals operates in the same way. Both strip us of self-consciousness and reveal our true inner core. If we were being completely rational, why would a song describing a stranger's life cause us to cry, just like the death of 'just' an animal? The answer is that we are thankfully not just rational creatures. These connections of love are both ineffable and ethereal. They defy rational explanation, as does all of love really – you can't explain it, you just feel it. For me, the music I listen to and the medicine I practise daily for the love of animals both gift me a profound connectedness to something much bigger and more important than me – a kind of universal oneness that isn't made of the stuff of conscious thought, a sense of belonging and joy that has brought me considerable peace down the years. I've referred to this in an earlier chapter and I see this light in my consulting room every single day when people are elevated in the love of their animal friend such that many of life's other worries seem to matter less, as I expect a music artist experiences when people leave their troubles outside the room and are lifted up on their music. It's the same currency in different languages – and that currency is love.

When one feels unconditional love, it's like plugging into an electrical socket. Everyone has the potential to be an amplifier for this current. Just like a crowd of strangers singing a song they love together, each and every one of you reading this has the ability to feel unconditional love. We can choose it for a child, a parent, a dog or a cat. It's a choice to let that love in and to amplify it. If everyone plugged in, we could actually change the world.

Unconditional love is extraordinarily rare between two humans in my experience, but actually very common with a dog, cat or other animal friend. No matter how sad, angry or grumpy we are, a companion animal will selflessly seek to make the world infinitely better for us in that moment. It makes me think of the line Florence Welch sings so memorably in her cover of 'You've Got the Love' – when life seems too much, we always have the love we need to see us through when we're friends with the animal we love. I have experienced true unconditional love only once with a human – with my dear friend, Philip, whom I am reminded of every time I see the spreading branches of the chestnut tree in the garden which I planted for him. But I have felt it many times with the animals I have loved and have been honoured to care for.

Music is made up of individual notes, which have different frequencies. Some of those frequencies work together and create something that sounds beautiful to us. We also each have a frequency ourselves and sometimes we find people whom we resonate with. I really think, more than that, we get back what we put out; it really is as simple as that. If we put out kindness, we receive kindness; if we put out misery, we receive misery; if we put out greed and selfishness, greed and selfishness will come our way in return. Love is special though. Putting love out into the universe means you are truly connected to that love and it's unique in its ability to amplify immeasurably each time it meets a similar frequency. In other words, you get back way more than you put out. In quantum mechanics, where scientists study the physics of particles and waveforms, there is something called quantum entanglement where two particles link together in a certain way so that no matter how far apart they are in space, their states remain linked. We are, all of us, made from elements born in the heart of stars. We are all one and all return to one. I believe that we are all connected and that it is through love, the gratefulness and joy we feel for each other, that connectedness finds expression. Earlier in this book, I called it 'a universal string of oneness'. It's immortal, transcends space and in its true form is eternal and absolute – there's nothing transitory, self-gratifying or convenient about love. The love of this string of oneness that Harry put out that night brought Oz and me together and when Oz came to see me, I desperately hoped that love would be amplified and I would be able to help him.

I operated on Oz in an effort to fuse all levels of his ankle, which is called the hock joint in a cat and comprises the tibio-tarsal joint, which is akin to a human ankle, and also the tarso-metatarsal joints, which is akin to the arch of our foot. A cat stands up on the digits or toes below the arch, which is off the ground, allowing a much longer lever for spring-like jumping. The operation of fusing is called an arthrodesis and because it's all of the ankle, that's a pantarsal arthrodesis. His family and I were well aware that surgery would be very challenging, that I might fail and that he could still lose his leg. When I opened up the damaged hock joint, there was chronic scar tissue built up over months of the shin bone (tibia) rubbing on the calcaneus bone. One of the bones in his ankle (the talus) had completely disappeared. I needed bone to fill the gaps and fuse the joints solid, so I removed the front part of the ilium bones of Oz's pelvis and used a bone grinder mill to mince it up, before packing it into the defects. I intended to use a plate I'd invented years ago, and the operation is normally very straightforward – but a very important artery was stuck down by chronic scar tissue and I had to carefully modify the plate to get around it. If that thread-like vessel were damaged then the underside of the foot would likely necrotise and die. I finally managed to get it all back together and the post-operative radiographs looked good. It seemed that Harry's 'universal string of oneness' might just have worked.

That very same week, I performed exactly the same surgery on a three and a half-month-old kitten called Pretzel. She came into my life at exactly the moment that I most needed her love, just as she did for a veterinary nurse called Nicole. Pretzel had been abandoned at a veterinary practice in Hampshire where Nicole worked. She was only five weeks old and had been born with significant deformities of her back legs, such that they were wrapped backwards and around each other in the shape that gave her her name. Her hock joints faced backwards rather than forwards, so that she was scooting along on the bottom part of her shin bones (tibiae) and rapidly wearing away the skin. She couldn't go on like that because her quality of life was poor and would only get worse. Euthanasia had been the only option offered to Nicole, by very well-meaning vets, who were doing the best they could, and Nicole felt utterly hopeless. She was desperate by the time she came to see me. As Jim Kerr says in the Simple Minds song 'Let There Be Love', love can heal and it sure can hurt..

Wary of the ethical perceptions of other vets, who may accuse me of over-treatment, I sent Nicole and Pretzel to get a second opinion from another specialist, who supported a potential route forward. Money was also going to be a big issue. From the beginning, Nicole and I both knew that it was possible that Pretzel might undergo more than one procedure to achieve a successful result and many rechecks would be indicated as she grew. It would cost a great deal to anaesthetise Pretzel several times, and to provide all the associated drugs, disposables and nursing care, in addition to all the implants which would be used. There's a big difference between cost and profit, and it would be a huge undertaking for all concerned. Then there were the challenges of the procedure itself, which definitely could fail. I would have to physically force all the tiny bones in her hock joints forward, with all associated ligaments, tendons, blood vessels and nerves – and somehow realign the tibia, tarsal and meta-tarsal bones using customised external frames. There was no precedent in the veterinary literature that I could find. Subsequently, we would likely then follow up with internal fixation using plates and screws as had been the case for Oz, since it was unlikely that the frame support would result in rigid fusion. While Oz could have had plates and screws as an initial option, I couldn't do this for Pretzel because the procedure would be too traumatic for the blood vessels and nerves in this dramatically deformed area, and Pretzel's feet were still growing.

Nicole started fundraising. As I've mentioned earlier, she couldn't refer to me or Supervet or Fitzpatrick Referrals as it would be unfair to others in similar need – or horribly, people using my name to defraud innocent donors. She posted pictures on social media and on lamp posts. Pretzel was a very cute fluff ball of black and white effervescent feline love, and once her picture made it into the local paper, people donated generously. Even though Nicole didn't know any of these benefactors, she loved them all. And of course, all of my team and I fell in love with Pretzel instantly.

With a tiny endotracheal tube, tiny doses of anaesthetic and a breathing bag, my team prepared Pretzel for surgery. I cut into Pretzel's hock joints, drilled out what cartilage I could from the tibio-tarsal joints and then slowly but surely twisted the tarsus, metatarsus and digits from backwards to forwards. I placed tiny wires through the skin and into the delicate bones in various directions to avoid where I estimated the nerves and blood vessels might be, and forced the hock joints forward with gradual pressure. Then I secured all of the wires onto an external frame by locking them down with bolts and nuts on a couple of small aluminium rings mounted on rods. This provided a scaffold in front and behind the hock joint and foot for both back legs. Because the frames were quite complex, I've shown the radiographs in the picture section of this book.

Pretzel was a truly remarkable kitten and walked on these frames the following day with her back feet in the right direction for the first time in her life. However, it became rapidly apparent that her tendons did not want to stretch with her feet, which were scrunched up, so I had to sever her flexor tendons, which is like cutting taut guitar strings. On one side they popped back up fine, but on the other they popped up too much, as the extensor tendons which pull the toes upwards stuck to scar tissue and became contracted. I built an extension on the front of the frame on this foot and attached a buffer made out of a piece of metal wrapped with foam to stretch the tendons by pushing the toes back down again. I found the foam in the 'Narnia cupboard' in my office, part of the plastic support boot I wore myself after my own ankle operations. (I like to think of that as a kind of quantum entanglement!) Like Oz and Pretzel, I also had bone transplanted from my pelvis to my ankle. I empathised with both of them.

Four weeks later, when I removed Pretzel's frames, it was apparent that the upper hock (tibio-tarsal) joints had fused but the lower hock joints (inter-tarsal and tarso-metatarsal) were predictably collapsing since they couldn't be fused at the time of the initial surgery. So, my colleagues at Fitzbionics and I manufactured two small custom plates to fit on the inside of Pretzel's hock joints. We attached these plates with tiny 1.5mm and 2mm screws to bridge between the shin bone (tibia) and the foot arch (metatarsus) on both sides. As with Oz, I packed the joints with minced bone from Pretzel's pelvis after removing all of the cartilage to encourage new bone growth for fusion.

Each night, after both surgeries, I gave Pretzel a cuddle whilst she stayed at the practice. I had to wash vigorously afterwards though, because as soon as I'd go back to my office/bedroom, Ricochet and Excalibur could smell if I had been 'having an affair' with another cat. Excalibur tends to sulk and ignore me, but Ricochet gives me an actual telling-off. Normally he jumps up on my knee when I sit at my desk and gives vigorous enthusiastic chin, nose and eye rubs, lying back in my left arm and demanding tummy rubs. But if he smells another cat on me, he prances over and plops himself on my keyboard in protest. I don't think he understands what my work is, but he knows I can't do it if he's lying there!

As I cuddled Pretzel, Ricochet and Excalibur, I was going through the most painful time in my professional career. The dream I had of building the four pillars of surgical excellence – orthopaedics, neurosurgery, soft tissue surgery and cancer surgery – was falling apart. I had personally guaranteed the entire business loan of a few million pounds for building and kitting out the soft tissue and cancer surgery hospital (FROST: Fitzpatrick Referrals Oncology and Soft Tissue Team). It wasn't possible for me to borrow more money when FROST had a tough time during Covid, and I was struggling to repay the loan when the revenue from my own hospital team (FRONT: Fitzpatrick Referrals Orthopaedics and Neurosurgery Team) dwindled. I'd lost five surgeons and work had to slow accordingly. There was a risk to the FROST business with me alone guaranteeing the funding, and sustaining the bank debt was becoming increasingly untenable. I searched high and low for other potential investors but nobody was interested, neither private individuals nor institutions. But then, I did have very strict criteria as I've already referred to. I wish to be transparent and to offer all of the options all of the time to all animals who come to see me. As I have alluded to, there is no amount of money that could force a tortoise to sell his shell.

My colleagues had to begin looking for other potential investors that they felt may be the best option for themselves to partner with. Quite understandably, any new partners can have advantages that I can't provide. I still deeply love all of the colleagues who I have had the honour of working with in the FROST hospital. They are incredible clinicians, nurses and veterinary professionals, and I respect them immensely, as I have always done, or I wouldn't have chosen to be on the journey with them or made the massive investment needed in the first place. They're also the very best humans I could wish to know. However, sometimes love of people, of a mission, or a vision, isn't enough in the hard practical realities of business. To echo Brian May and Freddie Mercury from the band Queen, I had a dream of 'One Vision', but it turned out to be a 'sweet illusion.'

I will be the very first to admit that being in business with me is challenging. My objectives for being in media and the public eye are very clear – I want to demonstrate that all companion animals who need medical help deserve all of the options all of the time, and a fair deal in gratitude for all of the love they give to us. I want to promote One Medicine by building a tangible bridge between human and veterinary medical practitioners. I want to explain to the world how man's responsibility for animals makes us the best we can be and importantly can actually make the world a more caring and kinder place for all. However, my media presence and *The Supervet* doesn't serve any business model in the direct sense. Everyone has to act in alignment with their own particular situation and ethical framework. In my eyes, medicine *is* love, but sadly it's also a business, and I had been somewhat naive in thinking that I could force my dreams of an oncology hospital replete with a linear accelerator to kill cancer into existence through willpower and hard work alone. I'd built the bunker for this machine but could not find financial backing to install the machine. This was in part because I am very determined to remain completely independent of any outside financial or business drivers. But, in reality, my big dreams in veterinary medicine require many people all wanting to pull in the same direction practically and financially and that just wasn't to be for me. My final attempts to get investors alongside me who fully shared my philosophy did not work out, and my business relationship with my colleagues would end soon thereafter with a management buy-out. By then all I could hope for my soon-to-be former practice colleagues was that they be happy, fulfilled and secure for their future, as anyone would want for friends one truly cares about. The song 'One Vision' tells me 'God works in mysterious ways,' so I'm holding on to that.

I wish them good fortune and sincerely hope that the legacy I helped to found in FROST will continue to help many more animals in the future. I had forced FROST into being by many trips to many financiers and banks, cap in hand, but now as my baby departed the cradle, which I had hoped would hold all of us for our lifetimes, I was wretched. After comforting Pretzel in the wards, I retreated back to my office and sent an email to all 250+ people in Fitzpatrick Referrals telling them how 'profoundly sad' I was about the separation of the two practices. The truth was that I was crying and utterly heartbroken. Soon the hospital which I opened with my mother by my side in her wheelchair would have a different name. It was the end of my 'big dream'. Freddie Mercury described best what I felt in his song 'Love of My Life', in that people will never really understand how difficult that kind of love can be or what it means to me.

Pretzel's mum Nicole and I shared a few things in common. From a young age we both wanted to be in the veterinary profession, and she shared her frustrations with me – that she was such a small part in the industry and could only save the lives with which she crossed paths and, even then, within the financial and practical limits of practice circumstances. There are so many other Pretzels out there, but she had only been able to save one. I feel the same every day. Nicole expressed to me how she was proud to work for an independent practice like ours. Our other commonality was that we have both had to take many examinations, some of which we have failed. Ironically, I failed a question in my specialist examination regarding the exact dimensions in millimetres of the fixation rings available for circular frames like the ones Pretzel had, in spite of having placed possibly a thousand such frames, and I still do not remember what the exact dimensions of all of them are. I just size them up next to the leg and crack on. As with any profession, there are some things you just do not need to know to facilitate a practical success, and that's one of the challenges with becoming a veterinary professional – practical versus academic acumen. One cannot easily examine the actual hand skills of a surgeon or the big heart of a nurse like Nicole. I would hire Nicole in a heartbeat, with or without her exams – and I would not hire plenty of surgeons who academically tick all the boxes. I think there should be some kind of in-workplace adjudication of compassion and care. Surely 'love' is the greatest prerequisite for all medical practitioners? I would absolutely hire someone for the size of their heart over the size of their head any day. Compassion over ego every time.

The American singer Phoebe Bridgers puts it best in her song 'Waiting Room', when she says that love both elevates and anchors – 'lifts you up and holds you down'. That's the kind of love I wish for all veterinary professionals, a kind of love for animals that allows fulfilment and happiness in your vocation but also one which is deeply earthed in the wellbeing of the animal above all things. I am genuinely worried about encouraging young people to be vets or vet nurses unless they know what our profession is really like now, in the sense that in my opinion there is a greater financial imperative than ever before and that it has become a job rather than a vocation for many. That's fine if you know it going in; it's just never going to be a job with limited hours of work for me personally. And yet I have great faith and hope in the next generation – I think that they are much more conscious about their responsibilities to society and to the fragile world we live in than my generation have been. I really do not want them to become revenue-generating robots, not asking any questions for fear of being criticised or ostracised. I do not want to work in a profession where the animals I care about are referred to as 'revenue-generating units'. I feel a profound need to tell the truth as I have seen it evolve in the past several years of my profession. I have seen many veterinary interns who would make fantastic surgeons fall by the wayside and never get a chance because they don't play 'the game' well, or ask too many big questions, or are not considered academically talented enough. I was that person in the early nineties. I am still that person now. I will not play 'the game'; I will ask too many big questions and I am *certainly* not academically talented enough. Nobody would hire me as a resident today, but if a solution doesn't exist, I'll do my very best to invent one if I firmly believe it's the right thing to do for my patient. Conversely, I will advise amputation or euthanasia if I think that's the right thing to do. Ultimately, I will always recommend what I believe in my heart is most morally right for my patient and their guardians, regardless of the earnest hopes of the well-meaning family, the finances involved or any well-meaning views of other veterinarians, because, though these are variables, which can be discussed or debated, at the end of the day, I can only live by my own truth.

In *To Kill a Mockingbird*, by Harper Lee, Atticus Finch, a white lawyer in 1930s Alabama, defends an innocent black man who is accused of beating and raping a nineteen-year-old girl. He says, 'Trying to do the right thing, is the right thing to do.' Atticus knows his client is innocent and knows that no one else will defend the black man, Tom Robinson, because of the colour of his skin. Atticus will not bow to peer pressure and does the right thing regardless in accordance with his beliefs and morals. He loses respect and friends along the way and his children are almost killed. When I was thinking about the stories I wanted to tell in this book, I knew that my own truth was the key. I saw this truth as fundamental to the thirteen traits I consider integral to a life which I hope to have fulfilled to the best of my ability in service of the commitment I made to the animals when I was ten years old. My truth was born in my dreams and readiness to be humble, passionate and thankful with complete openness and kindness in commitment to authenticity and trustworthy creativity, so that the love I have for animals can be translated into a tangible currency of hope for the world.

I have been honest in this book about sexual abuse, bullying and dark times in my life, and the long shadows that they cast. Harper Lee also said in her original book, 'Stand up for what is right, even if you are standing alone.' For me, absolute honesty is a manifestation of love and is the only way forward. The truth is the only way to the truth just as love is the only way to love. I love my vocation and my profession, and telling the truth as I see it, just like about my personal past, whatever the repercussions may be, is the only way I can find any peace of mind and come to terms with any future at all 'beyond supervet'.

As my original dream at Fitzpatrick Referrals was dramatically changing, the singer Ronan Keating brought his dog Aussie for a consultation. I hadn't seen Ronan for a couple of years, but it was like we'd only seen each other the day before. Aussie was in a bad way, heading towards paralysis of her back legs and Ronan was understandably very upset. But I was the one that started to cry. I was immediately embarrassed and quickly explained that writing this book was going to involve me talking about things I had never been able to before, and I was worried how people, the press and my profession might respond. Ronan had experienced the double-edged sword of the media and had many wise words for how I might approach trying to share my truth.

I operated on Aussie the following week with my colleague Joana, whom I first worked with as an intern and then a resident, and whom I have believed in from the start at Fitzpatrick Referrals. She is now, in my opinion, one of the most talented neurosurgeons at her stage of her career in the world. She loves all of her patients; she is a credit to the profession we love and she embodies my hope for the future of veterinary medicine, regardless of what course she chooses for her future career.

Aussie's spine was affected by multiple problems associated with obstruction of fluid flow and spinal cord damage contributed to by abnormal motion of abnormally shaped vertebrae. We knew that we could not reverse the damage which the disease had already caused, but we hoped we could stop her deterioration. She had a state-of-the-art spinal stabilisation procedure guided by computerised mapping of her 3D CT scan for pinpoint accuracy of implant positioning. At the time of writing, we do not know how Aussie will progress in the longer term, but like all of the families who come to see me, Ronan's family just wanted to do the right thing for their much-loved friend.

To come full circle with the 'universal string of oneness' which I believe joins us together through love in both music and medicine, my friend DJ Chris Evans and I sat on a bench quite a few years ago and talked about ways of sharing love with people through the things we were passionate about – he with cars and music, me with dogs, vets and music. And, thus, CarFest, DogFest and VETFest were born. It turned out that Ronan invited me to his performance at CarFest a few days after we met with Aussie. When we turned up, Chris was in a pickle because two of the acts had pulled out. Though he knew Ronan well, he genuinely did not want to put him in an awkward position by asking him to go on later than scheduled and with a longer setlist. So, I asked him, they chatted and all was well. Thousands of people were the happy recipients of the 'universal string of oneness' which had begun with a good intention in 2010 when Chris helped me get *The Bionic Vet* TV show, Aussie brought Ronan and I together again, and now more good intention came full circle as everyone sang along with 'Life Is a Rollercoaster' in the rain. Love indeed 'is a mystery', but you just have to 'get inside it'.

I genuinely believe that the universal string of oneness I've described, which brought hope for Oz, Pretzel and Aussie, could actually save veterinary medicine through this same love of animals if we always did the right thing for the right reasons without financial vested interest. Oz is lapping up the sunshine walking and jumping round his garden and Pretzel the impossible wizard miracle kitten is out of pain and running around on her beautifully straight back legs. Harry, Nicole and Ronan have shown us how to weave this string to make a better world through the love they put out. Together, we saved the limbs and lives of Oz, Pretzel and Aussie. If you believed in this string of medical music, you too could tune in to a better world for all of us – animal and human.

As some very wise men from Liverpool once said, the love you make really is ultimately equal to the love you get to take.

CHAPTER 13

Hope

Although this chapter is about hope, it's also about hope-lessness and attempted suicide. I have changed the names of those involved to respect their privacy but I know there will be some of you for whom this may be difficult to read. Please take care of yourselves.

Hope is the currency of my life every day. Fitzpatrick Referrals is the last chance for many patients, and their human companions, who come through my door.

When I first met Hero, a six-month-old red-and-white British bulldog puppy, I didn't know that his human parents Steve and Nicky and their son Brendan (names changed) were desperately looking for a solution to a far more traumatic problem than Hero's limb deformity. Steve confided in me later that Hero had been an extraordinary support to him, Nicky and Brendan during a horrific period of their lives. In many ways I am glad I didn't know this when I operated on him. There was so much more than Hero's quality of life on the line at the time.

The head of Hero's radius bone in one of his elbows was almost dislocated (luxated) from birth, and the growth plate of the other bone of the forearm, the ulna, wasn't growing as quickly as the radius, which pushed his wrist (carpus) sideways as he grew (which is called torsion and valgus). He was in a lot of pain, limping badly and getting worse quickly. Many consider this condition to be untreatable but I had developed a new technique to address it. Using a CT scan imported into a computer program, my team and I created a 3D printed guide mounted on pins to remove a chunk of bone from the radius at a particular angle, which allowed me to pop the head of the bone back into the joint, followed by placement of a new synthetic ligament on the side. With similar planning, I then cut the bottom part of the radius and de-rotated his wrist into better orientation. Simultaneous cuts in the ulna were followed by the application of a custom plate on the radius, which was designed such that the guide pin holes would be exactly the same as the screw holes in the plate. Thus the joint was reconstructed and Hero had a straight leg for the first time in his life.

This is a surgical revolution that we've now used on several patients. For the very first time in the history of veterinary medicine it is now possible to make a highly contoured custom-fit plate with threaded screw holes at any angle to match the guide pin holes, such that the plate itself realigns the cut segments and straightens the bone. This book is the first time that this has been documented anywhere in the world, and it's my hope that it will find its way into the textbooks of the future to give dogs like Hero a new lease of life. If we're open to it, the 'truth' is rewritten for medicine all the time as our understanding changes. What appeared to be an insurmountable challenge was overcome because of hope, a great team in my engineering and machinist colleagues, who deserve all credit, and a desire to do the best we could for someone we love.

Though their names have been changed, Steve and Nicky were in the middle of a painful struggle, and they wanted me to share their story in the hope it might help others. The first time their son Brendan had attempted suicide, Steve received a heartbreaking text from him explaining that life was too difficult and he could not continue. He wanted his parents to pass his love on to his brother and sister, and to say goodbye for him. By the time Steve and Nicky got to his flat, he was on the bed semi-unconscious following an overdose and cuts to his wrists. He was admitted to a mental health ward but, due to pressure for beds, he was released with little in the way of rehabilitation.

Suicide rates among teenagers are skyrocketing across the UK. Brendan is a sensitive, articulate and intelligent boy with loving parents, but afflicted by terrible feelings of worthlessness, anxiety and depression. In his state of mind, it was easy to succumb to so-called friends introducing him to drugs. Brendan found social media spiteful and hateful – folk behind keyboards not realising that their comments have real-life consequences. All sorts of prescription pills are readily available online and on the streets for anyone wanting to numb the pain of existence, and there are plenty of organised criminals making pills including anything from diazepam (Valium) to cough syrup containing codeine and other drugs (known as 'Lean') to benzodiazepines ('benzos'). In some places these pills are as cheap and easy to get hold of as ordering a pizza, and there are many vultures that circle the most vulnerable. Brendan began self-harming, and as the darkest clouds enveloped him, there was no hope of light shining through. Compounding their collective sense of helplessness, Steve and Nicky found NHS residential rehabilitation and aftercare services, in spite of best intentions, stretched to the limit. Following a second suicide attempt, when Steve himself desperately tried to resuscitate his son, crying, thinking he was gone, Brendan fortunately made it through again. But due to a vastly overstretched system, he still couldn't get access to a long-term mental health bed or appropriate rehab. Steve and Nicky felt hopeless watching the son they brought into the world, the boy they'd nurtured and guided with love and kindness, suffer so badly. They didn't have any answers at times to what felt like an impossible situation. However, amid the darkness, there was one ray of shining light and hope, and that was Hero.

Through his determination never to give into the hardships and pain of his own condition, Hero raised all of their spirits, even though he chewed every shoe, skirting board and bag he could get his teeth into. He even chewed the interior of the car door with a smile on his face – and he put a smile on their faces too. Taking him for a little walk brought them joy and hope, because Hero saw the amazement in the simplest things. He sniffed flowers and trees and was fascinated by birds and aeroplanes, parking his backside down and watching the world go by. When talking to Hero, the tears often flowed for Steve, as he was one friend who never judged and just listened.

Hero's resilience through his recovery from surgery and his patience with rehabilitation to eventually be able to run around happily without pain also gave Brendan hope. He had become agoraphobic and didn't want to leave the house or interact with the outside world. But Brendan loved Hero and Hero loved Brendan. No matter how low Brendan felt, a lick from Hero on the face or the ear, a wag of his tail and his inimitable doggy smile of absolute joy never failed to make him feel a little bit better. Hero gave Brendan a chink of light in the darkness – some small hope that he might pull through his illness. As Steve said, 'He had hit rock bottom, which is a solid foundation to start rebuilding from, brick by brick.' Steve also told me that it suddenly occurred to him that though he thought that they had all been looking after Hero, in fact it was he who had been watching over them, giving them more hope than they could ever have imagined.

For me too, the animals I have been blessed to know and love have held me together on so many occasions. Sometimes I've been in the grumpiest and most depressed state when Keira licked my face and cheered me up, or a patient I have treated that day has given me a wag of their tail as they awaken from my surgery in the wards. Nowadays, Ricochet or Excalibur jump onto my knee to tell me things aren't so bad. They are an extraordinary gift of hope. Other times, when the pressure has got too much to bear, as I've explained earlier, music has saved me. I have gone from the euphoria of achieving a good surgical outcome to profound sadness from financial pressure, business and staffing worries, and complaints about me from vets and clients in spite of my best efforts. Sometimes I do not have an animal friend to cuddle, and then luckily music has been my drug. Sadly, some of my music heroes have gone from the euphoria of being on stage to their own sadness, which ultimately ended badly for them – Kurt Cobain, Chester Bennington, Jim Morrison, Jimi Hendrix and Michael Hutchence, to name a few. I saw Chester perform less than two weeks before he took his life and he seemed so alive. One can never tell what darkness lies behind the euphoria. I start each day at my practice with a tune of some sort which helps give me hope for the day ahead. Like Chester, I do very much care if 'one more light' goes out and like Michael, I know that 'all you've got is this moment'. Each time I walk down the stairs to my consulting room past the memorial to Keira kindly donated by fans of *The Supervet*, I hope that I will save a limb or a life and I will bring redemption to a family, and usually that hope is enough to see me through.

Throughout my life, I have hoped that I might leave the world better than I found it.

Recently, though, when it came time to take off my black surgical scrubs at the end of each day – my Supervet 'cape' – hope has seemed in short supply. When no longer holding a hand or a paw, trying to alleviate the pain of an animal or their human companion, all I was left with was my own pain.

The trauma of my early years, compounded by the bullying at school, left wounds I have never addressed. Instead, I sought to bandage my profound sense of inadequacy, low self-esteem and hopelessness with work, running on an eternal treadmill to the next animal's crisis, forever healing any wound I could find – except those deep inside me. Back then I felt stupid and that I would make nothing of my life. Thereafter, there was no tiredness or emotional pain that I wouldn't endure, no failure too great, no criticism too harsh by comparison with my hidden darkness of betrayed trust and the pain of being violated. I have never come to terms with my sexual abuse, and the shame and guilt that came with it. Somehow back then it was – like the priest said – all my fault. I was an alien, alone and helpless. There was nobody I felt I could talk to or turn to, for fear that it would bring further punishment, either by God or man. When Daddy and Mammy had gone, when the door was closed and he looked at me with his tobacco-stained eyes, I was defenceless and hopeless. I closed a door inside myself too, never to be opened lest the terror escape.

For five years, between the ages of twelve and seventeen, I closed myself in the safe space of a room in our farmhouse where I studied night and day, emerging only to do whatever work was instructed by Daddy. This room was the only place I had control of anything at all – my homework. Even that was violated by the boys pouring milk on it and trampling it into the mud. I removed the battery from the ticking clock because I'd become severely noise-phobic, taking to wearing a pair of large blue earmuffs that one of the machinery drivers on the farm had given to me. Between midnight and 1 a.m. on a Saturday night, my schoolwork completed, I took them off to listen to *The Unforgettable Fire* album by U2 on an old black record player with a slightly broken needle. I lay on the floor repeating the line over and over again in my head about one man who came 'in the name of love', from the song 'Pride'. On Sunday mornings I went to Mass as an altar boy and felt sorry for the man born in Bethlehem who was now nailed to the cross before me with blood pouring from his hands. As I followed the priest carrying the golden cross or swinging the thurible, stopping at each picture depicting the Stations of the Cross, it seemed to me that the men around Jesus had been so very brutal – and yet somehow, he kept his hope and belief.

I really did believe that he had suffered for mankind. But in my own little world, it was the animals around me I felt were suffering and they were my friends. Mankind was not.

I suspect because of my childhood trauma that I have built a lifetime around control, making sure my conscious brain is in charge, drowning out the low humming of my desire to fight, flee or freeze. When I am in surgery, I can filter everything else. I had inadvertently turned my passion for working with the animals into a kind of addiction. The problem was that, over the years, there ended up being no me who wasn't the vet.

I am lucky in that I have wonderful, compassionate colleagues at the practice, but you have to be able to ask for and accept help, and I couldn't. The perpetual cycle of consults, emails, surgeries, reports and restless nights plagued by insomnia was slowly sucking the will to live out of me. I blame myself. This reality had been fuelled by my own dreams, and the position I found myself in was a prison of my own making. As head of Fitzpatrick Referrals, the buck stops with me. I'm often the only person who can answer client queries, carry out the surgeries in which I specialise or be there to pick up the pieces if things go wrong. It often felt like nothing I did was ever good enough. The constant cycle of financial pressures and vets complaining about my TV show added to the bubbling cauldron of my mind. The stress was making me physically sick, emotionally withdrawn, irritable and insular. I wasn't able or willing to speak to anyone around me that did actually care, because I was behaviourally 'shutting down' in a way I didn't understand. I was dying by a thousand cuts, bleeding inside but nobody else could see. I wasn't in any way feeling sorry for myself; in fact, I was sorrier for those around me because of who I had become. I was a scared and overwhelmed little boy again, wearing my blue earmuffs and trying to block out the world. Since I was twelve years old, I thought that the harder I worked, the more likely I was to be OK. I was working seven-day weeks but I was very far from OK. I'd been running away from myself all my life and yet it was me alone that I couldn't shake. I was terrified that my pieces were so broken that if I let them fall, I wouldn't have the courage to pick them up again. I had been trying to hold it together with the glue of constant action, but now I was finally beaten, and any moments of joy just weren't enough. When I wasn't saving an animal, I sank into not wanting to save myself. The endless anxiety of days melted into the sleepless depression of nights. Sometimes I couldn't sleep. I was crushed by fear, self-loathing and worthlessness. At the time, I had no hope and I didn't know I was at the edge until I fell off.

One night, I put on my running gear around midnight as I often do. The night nurses walking the dogs in the garden paid no attention to the sight of the boss jogging down the road into the darkness at midnight. It was nothing new to them. I know every step of my 10 kilometre midnight run by the feel of the ground on the soles of my feet, but I followed a different route that night, to the river near the practice. I waded out towards the deepest part. I stood there for a while, rocking back and forth with the current and the cold and I cried in the drizzly rain. Every vet has access to the drugs to end life, but I couldn't bring myself to desecrate with despair the cradle of hope that I had built.

In the darkness inside it seemed best for everyone if I just floated away. I wouldn't be hurting Mammy or Keira because they were already gone. Maybe even in my delusion, I thought I might join them, and that seemed a sort of blessing. It was just me, the darkness inside me and the river. When one is in that state of mind, one doesn't think about the effects on those you love, human or animal, those who love you, those who depend on you, or those for whom you are actually a beacon of hope – all I saw was pain and all I wanted was to end that pain.

I wallowed in my self-pity for a while, but in the end, some force outside of myself, I know not what, pushed me back to the side of the river, where I sat in the weeds for a while. Then I walked 'home' to the practice. The people around me are understandably concerned about me sharing my truths, but I cannot be silent anymore. I set out to write this book as I stood by the graveside of my mother, shovel in hand, on the exact spot where I myself will ultimately end up in the soil. It made me realise that life is too short not to act, and not to speak out. If I died tomorrow, I'd rather know that I've helped every animal I could, and maybe given hope to one person who felt hopeless. If even people like me, who appear strong and 'sorted' on TV, can also be insecure, scared, anxious and depressed, then maybe someone reading this might suffer less knowing that such feelings of worthlessness and isolation can happen and that it's OK to sit in the weeds for a while, but you can find hope and you can find a way through, like I did. Hope is not just a *want*, it's a fundamental *need* for each and every human being. A life without hope can lead to very dark places.

Exhaustion and insularity mess with your head, and they'd almost stolen every last reserve of my hope. But I am very much aware that it's all relative and that I know I am privileged by comparison with many in the world. Every single day I think of the pain of innocent fellow human beings in the world and I feel embarrassed for getting so low. But the reason I share my story with you is to explain that when one is in the sort of dark place I was, any rational thought can go out the window. I absolutely know that I am not trapped in my house, being shelled repeatedly by artillery in Ukraine, or being tortured in Yemen or watching my family slaughtered in Myanmar. Most of the time, when I'm being rational, I know I'm lucky and absolutely should not complain. But we can only lead our own lives, and I'm trying to help others to get some perspective as I have sought to. I did not know what 'neurodivergent' or 'being on the spectrum' was until I discussed it with professional mental health counsellors in later life. Neither sensory-processing disorder nor complex post-traumatic stress disorder even had a name in the 1970s in Ireland. My behaviour patterns have been rigid and repetitive, I battle against social anxiety and I find it difficult to interpret social situations, body language and sarcasm. But I have managed to cope reasonably well with communicating, mainly with animals and the people who love them and with musicians and actors who let the music and the drama do the speaking for them. In truth, as I've earlier alluded to, I haven't really allowed the psychologists and therapists I have seen to really help me as much as they could have, I suppose, reverting to my love of animals and music as my salvation instead. I'm also surprised by the stigma still associated with mental health issues among medical professionals, which resulted in one therapist advising me that 'one man's mental health issues are another's unfitness to practice'. I was truly shocked by this. I don't know many surgeons in high-stress environments who aren't a little bit divergent from the norm, as are most really talented musicians and actors. I think that sometimes being a little bit 'different' can be a useful perspective to actually make a real difference in the world.

As Rod Stewart once said, 'the first cut is the deepest,' but I was still really struggling with my mental health in mid-2022. I was crouched by a tree on the embankment outside the soft tissue surgery and cancer practice I had built with my colleagues, crying my eyes out. It had been a long Sunday a few miles down the road at the orthopaedics and neurosurgery practice, but I had come to say goodbye. I'd known the separation would be painful. Though the marriage was over, I had never fallen out of love with the people who helped me build the dream. I walked room to room, finally crouching by some old bits of furniture stored in the cement bunker. I had once planned for this space to be occupied by a linear accelerator cyber-scalpel to treat cancer with radiation, as I mentioned earlier, but that was one dream that I would never realise. As I've explained, I had tried many different ways to keep going, but the simple truth was I couldn't afford it. No amount of hope in the world can succeed in such a challenging situation, and I needed to reconcile myself with this truth as a management buy-out was underway. All I could do was go back to my orthopaedics and neurosurgery practice and continue to bring hope where I still could.

I drove tearfully back to that practice to meet an acute emergency. An eight-month-old Labrador called Ollie was strapped to a rigid board in the back of a car, distressed and panting. When I touched his head, he screamed. His mum, Sarah, was distraught. She had driven from three and a half hours away because her primary care clinician had called several weekend emergency and referral centres, but in all of England it seemed that there wasn't a specialist neurosurgeon on duty on that Sunday night nor any MRI scanner available for a dog with a broken back. Usually, an intern vet or a resident vet or a vet in an emergency clinic could see most cases at weekends, stabilise them and make a decision with a senior clinician on the phone or the following day. Most neurosurgeons, by the time they have passed their examinations, have earned the right to not work weekends or to work only the occasional weekend. I think this is entirely fair, when one has given up one's personal life to study for specialist exams. However, if much of the millions made weekly from veterinary care nationwide is truly being reinvested to provide the best care for the animal, as many claim it is, then it's more than a pity that there was no one available in all of England to treat a broken back emergency on a Sunday night.

The point is not whether Ollie was saveable or not, but rather that Sarah was left with no choice other than euthanasia by a system that in my opinion doesn't always prioritise the patient. Sarah and her husband Stuart simply wanted to know the facts before they decided whether Ollie could or should have surgery or not. They didn't want him to suffer for their sake of not being able to let go, but equally they did not want to let go if there was hope. It was an ethical dilemma and they were devastated. It can be argued of course, that if a spine is broken and the cord is badly squashed, one should put that animal to sleep because that's our 'moral' and 'ethical' responsibility as the advocates for the animal. Families may indeed be content with a compassionate hug, words of comfort and euthanasia, because 'nothing could be done' – but how could one know that if one didn't check the facts? Ethics is a tough subject and surgeons often have different views regarding 'hope'. Families have different views too, but my firm belief is that all diagnostic information should be provided so that families are at least allowed that choice. I have seen the consequences of profound regret carried for a lifetime by families when that choice isn't provided. In my view, at least a consideration of hope is the moral duty of all vets, rather than just dismissive acquiescence.

I explained to them that I had seen the radiograph taken by their primary care vet, who had absolutely tried their very best, and the outlook was bleak. Poor Ollie had run into the road and had been hit by a car. He couldn't feel his back feet at all. He was paralysed. By now, my colleagues and I had carried him into the hospital. His beautiful, gentle eyes looked up at me, pleading. We performed both MRI and CT scans of Ollie's spine. I couldn't tell for sure if his spinal cord was severely squashed or completely severed by fractured vertebrae, which were spiking sharp edges into the spinal canal. He had a very low chance of ever regaining the use of his hind legs or being able to urinate or defecate. If repair were attempted, nobody could know if the spinal cord might recover function or not, and furthermore, because few surgeons have ever tried, there is little guidance in the veterinary literature. Whilst Ollie was asleep on the table in my prep room, Sarah called Stuart. I sat by Ollie's side pondering 'the long wait', which I'd done hundreds of times before. The next time I saw Sarah, either Ollie would either be put to sleep or I would try to save his life.

I explained carefully to Sarah and Stuart that euthanasia would be indicated on the surgical table, as the only ethical option, if I found that the spinal cord was actually severed, and that I would recommend euthanasia soon thereafter if I could not get Ollie out of pain and provide quality of life. They also understood that even if the spinal cord appeared visibly intact at surgery, I still couldn't know if Ollie may regain urinary or faecal continence or recover use of his back legs because of invisible damage to the nerves inside the cord.

If the cord had been severed, I would have strongly advised and insisted that euthanasia was the only ethical option in my view as there would be no hope of urinary or faecal continence or ever getting the back legs moving again. But it wasn't. There was hope, albeit slim. If I could get the vertebrae realigned and stabilised then it would be down to whether the spinal cord nerves could recover or not. Nobody could possibly know and it was a very challenging ethical dilemma. Sarah and Stuart decided that if it were possible to operate, they would like to do so because Ollie was an integral family member.

With my dedicated colleagues at my side, we went into theatre just before midnight. It was easy enough to drill a window of bone out of the side of the broken vertebrae. I could then see that the spinal cord was visibly intact but haemorrhage was apparent under the meninges, which is the lining that protects the brain and spinal cord, but I could not predict if conduction would ever return for the nerves within. There was hope, albeit slim. I pulled the spinal canal back into alignment, drove stainless steel pins into the vertebrae on either side of the fractured bone, and then poured cement around the pin ends to hold three consecutive vertebrae together.

It would be some time before we'd know if Ollie had any real hope at all. He would stay in our hospital for a few weeks, with us managing his bladder-emptying for him and exercising his back legs as much as we could. Poor Ollie's recovery was frustratingly protracted, as we always knew it could be, but we met each of his challenges, always with his best interests at heart, and always in the knowledge that if he could not have a quality of life, then it may be kindest to let him pass peacefully away. Throughout all of this, Sarah, Stuart and I never lost hope because Ollie never lost hope. Every single day he gulped in the morning air when we brought him into the garden outside the practice, even though he still couldn't stand or move on his back legs, just extremely happy to be alive, sharing light, hope and frequent face-licks with all he met.

I often think of this light like that which Chris Martin from Coldplay sings about, when he 'tried his best' but didn't succeed and yet found a light to 'guide him home' and 'ignite his bones' because he tried to 'fix you'. Sometimes trying our absolute best is what we have to do and thankfully for Ollie, the light he shone out into the world every day did indeed guide him home. He is now able to urinate and defecate but sadly his back legs will never have enough nerve power to propel him around. However, he is now tearing around the park, in and out of puddles, in his back-leg-wheeled cart, affectionately known as 'Ollie's trolley'. Sarah and Stuart's thirteen-year-old son Joseph, who is autistic, is overjoyed to have Ollie back home. Ollie is Joseph's best friend and Joseph is his best friend. Joseph has taken to walking around on his bicycle, one leg on either side of the saddle, beside Ollie in his trolley, in deep empathy and extraordinary love. Sarah and Stuart are very grateful that Ollie has a quality of life and that they chose to give him hope.

All hope in medicine arises from the failures and successes of the past. I've had plenty of both. The truth is that hope often can and does follow despair if we invest our energy, and often our money, in progress – and if we truly believe that there is light at the end of the tunnel, no matter how dark it may appear at the time. Hope really is a choice we all have to make.

Soon after Ollie was safely back in *his* home, I was due to leave my *own* home for the first two-week period away from my practice for more than twenty years. It appeared that the universe intervened and allowed me to make this choice of hope myself – away from my mental and emotional struggles – by sending me to South Africa. I ostensibly did not have time in my work-life to go, but the visit had been arranged for ages and I knew in my heart that it was the right thing to do. I hoped to bring whatever advocacy I could to the plight of lions, tigers and rhinoceroses.

As I was getting ready to leave, I nipped out to say goodbye to Keira where she rests at the back of the practice. Some daisies planted around her resting place had recently bloomed – Mammy's favourite flower. I felt the love of them both, giving me hope for the journey ahead. As Mammy often said, 'It's never too late, Noel.'

Spending time with the magnificent animals of the savannah and their carers has been profoundly moving for me and, away from the travails of my own world, it has changed my perspective considerably for the better and imbued me with a new sense of purpose and hope. Here, I could see that the actual lives of both man and animal are on the line every single day. Poachers kill rhinos, tigers and lions to fuel an illegal market in horn and bones, which many cultures believe have medicinal properties and for which there is no medical evidence whatsoever. Rhino horn is no more than the keratin of human fingernails and horses' hooves, yet is valued on the black market more per gram than gold. A tiger skeleton can cost hundreds of thousands of dollars and be suspended in a fermentation tank from which 'tiger bone wine' is sold. It's hard to change any of this, the lion farms that actually legally export bones from South Africa, the substitution of lion for tiger bones which make more money, the big cat breeding farms in Africa and Asia, or indeed the pressures on people around reservations, parks and sanctuaries who have to put food on the table for their families and need to get money from somewhere. Here, too, there are many metaphorical vultures in the form of organised criminals exploiting the hopes of the needy, as well as real vultures who ironically are now an endangered species because of humans incinerating their brains and inhaling the powder, eating them or keeping the mixture under their pillow. Their excellent eyesight is deemed to bring foresight and good luck – but not for them. For criminals, neither human nor animal life have much value. They kill the animals and they exploit or kill the humans who stand in their way.

These animals can't rely on good luck, and it's up to humans to try to provide hope for their salvation. For example, significantly less than 10 per cent of the original rhino population remain on Earth and they could become extinct in my lifetime without intervention. As John Stuart Mill famously said, 'Bad men need nothing more to compass their ends, than that good men should look on and do nothing.' To bring sustainable hope in animal conservation, one has to offer people a genuine alternative. Animals can only encourage us to be the best we can be if we actually want to change – if we want to find hope for a better world. And, inevitably, that means making money somehow in a better way. We have to help find ways to make 'hope' profitable for the people living in these regions or it isn't sustainable. They can, for example, be paid through creating an infrastructure for 'sustainable tourism' to look after the rhinos rather than be paid by criminals to kill them for their horns, especially when culturally, they may just be considered an animal or just meat.

Unless one personally experiences the complex ecosystems and socio-economic circumstances of the environments in which these animals live, it's easy to pontificate on solutions. I do not eat meat, and I had a preconceived opposition to the hunting of wild animals before my trip, without any pertinent local knowledge. I am still absolutely against 'trophy hunting', but I have seen many places in South Africa where there would simply be no money to prevent reservations being turned into cattle farms without licences being issued for 'ethical hunting'. That's a really bitter pill for someone like me to swallow. The death of some specific animals, especially older ones past the age of breeding or on the slippery slope to death anyway, brings in money to look after younger animals properly and fund anti-poaching. Idealism has no place in this reality, and I must practise what I preach. Just as people form opinions about me and my work based on limited information and preconception, I am now aware that I don't know enough to formulate a valid opinion on the answers to the hard questions about conservation. To continue trying to provide hope and advocacy for the animals I care about across the world, I am committed to every day being a school day and to always being open to learning.

Back at my practice, a message came through to me that my surgical resident colleague Andi was operating on a Border terrier puppy called Kiera. I couldn't believe it.

Everyone from receptionists to nurses had been afraid to tell me because they felt it might really upset me after the passing of my little girl, Keira. Unable to help myself, I popped my head into theatre where Andi was operating. Lucky I did, because he too is always open to learning and asked for some help with the repair of a forearm fracture sustained when the seven-month-old puppy fell from her dad's arms.

I was a bit emotional as I walked into theatre scrubbed, gowned and gloved. The fractures of the radius and ulna were simple enough and Andi had already made good decisions, so I didn't have much to do. Operation completed, I pulled back the drapes and saw her for the very first time. She was the spikey-haired spitting image of my Keira. I was close to tears. I later spoke to her mum and dad and it transpired that they had seen *The Supervet* and knew about Keira's passing. Their own Border terrier puppy came along a couple of weeks later. Mum wanted to call her something else, but dad was adamant that he wanted Kiera, though spelt a little differently to my Keira.

When puppy Kiera woke up and was happy, I cuddled her tight, walked out to where my little girl Keira was buried and sat down by the gravestone in the setting sun. The tears that flowed down my cheeks were rich with renewed hope, and faith in the eternal cycle of unconditional love that I was blessed to experience every day of my life. I love my vocation and I am a very lucky man. The sun dipped in orange and red behind the trees at the back of the practice which is, and always will be, my home, where we try to give hope and healing to all who come. I hugged Kiera close, kissed her on the head, thanked her for being in my life and walked back inside full of hope for whatever the next day might bring.

EPILOGUE

Unbuttoned

In South Africa, I radiographed an old lion called Rici, whom I fell in love with. Rici had been rescued from captivity in Romania, where he had sadly been neglected. He was affected by elbow osteoarthritis and fore-limb deformities due to nutritional deficiency. Many of the wild cats at the sanctuary I visited were rescued from terrible situations with no hope at all. And yet they brought me more hope than I could ever bring them. I felt way more comfortable with the big cats than I ever imagined possible. It was as if I was coming home to the hope I'd had when I started the journey to be a vet in the first place. I felt a deep inner peace for the first time in many years and an extraordinary connected 'oneness' with all of creation. I was humbled and privileged by this immense gift.

All of the veterinary professionals caring for the big cats, and for the rhinos I saw earlier in my trip, were profoundly inspirational to me; all were hugely talented, dedicated, compassionate clinicians with a vast breadth of both general and specialist knowledge. In no small way, I felt I had come full circle from the farm animal vets who first mentored me in the early nineties, and who left an indelible legacy in my heart and mind. They taught me how to rely on my senses and develop an insightful clinical acumen. It was fantastic to be back in a similar environment again with my large animal friends and I rediscovered my love for the pure essence of my vocation.

When I came back home however, I had to explain to Ricochet that once again I'd 'had an affair'. Except this time, rather than with a tiny kitten called Pretzel, with a lion called Rici. Rici's mane was considerably bigger than that of Ricochet, who I also call 'Rici' sometimes. I suspect the latter. Needless to say, Ricochet 'had the hump' on my first night home – maybe because I'd been away and he hadn't had his dozen snuggles a day with mandatory nose nuzzling, or maybe because he could sense the 'guilt'. Either way, his full vitriol was released the following morning. I was again filming the TV show at the practice and went into the bathroom to change my scrubs because another cat had peed all over me. I detached the microphone I wear when I'm filming from my scrub bottoms and its lead was dangling down from my scrub top. I had no pants or trousers on when my 'Rici' jumped from my bed as I came out of the bathroom less than three feet away, with claws fully outstretched – ostensibly lunging at the dangling wire. Something else a bit more 'important' to me was also dangling! Inadvertently or not, Ricochet told Dada in no uncertain terms just what he thought of his 'affair' with a lion. I only narrowly avoided potentially serious injury! We have since reconciled, with many face rubs and an assurance from me that there's plenty of love inside me for all creatures who deserve their pawprint on Planet Earth.

The day before I left South Africa to return home, I performed athroscopy on a tiger called Laziz (Arabic for 'pleasant one') at the same wild cat sanctuary. This involved sticking a large needle with a tiny camera inside into the joint for diagnostic evaluation. He was affected by severe cartilage erosion on the inside of his elbow joint leading to osteoarthritis, like many thousands of dogs I have operated on in England. He was thirteen years old, and our objective was to provide the best quality of life possible for what remained of his days. Laziz had been rescued from a zoo in Gaza, where many of the animals died and were mummified in their cages during the human conflict. In my rush to pack, I'd forgotten my black scrubs and felt disconcerted needing to operate on Laziz without my Supervet 'cape', which was a kind of comfort blanket for me as a surgeon. However, on the morning of the surgery, my scrubs arrived in a courier package just in the nick of time, thanks to my new friend, Robin, chasing down the delivery guy in a remote South African town called Bethlehem. Robin had brought Batman his cape after all. I smiled as I recalled the Batman sign on my office wall, which was so clearly prescient.

Whereas my black scrubs had become somewhat heavy to bear in the months before my departure for Africa, they now brought me renewed strength in the very best way. In my familiar attire, I felt calm and at peace with myself even though I was in a very different operating environment, with unaccustomed kit and a team I had never met before, all of us in it together, devoid of vested interest or ego, trying to bring hope to a tiger and a lion. I treated both Laziz and

Rici with intra-articular injections (into the elbow joints) of a combination of platelets derived from their own blood and viscoelastic lubricant. We hoped this treatment would help because large cats are very sensitive to the possible side effects of the pain-killing drugs we use in dogs and domestic cats. I suspect, however, it will rather be a small 'first step' as it is for every innovation in my career. I expect we will be able to do much better over time by reaching out to colleagues and sharing knowledge, such as by possibly using anti-inflammatory stem cells derived from the patient's own fat, as we do in dogs – moving medicine forward for animals the world over and trying to give them what I've referred to as 'a fair deal'. In deeply caring about these wild animals, without any agenda or financial vested interest, my sincerest hope is to inspire the next generation to potentially be way better than my generation has been in looking after the well-being of all animals and our natural world. This is all I have ever wanted since I took the first step towards being a vet in that frozen field when I was ten years old, after the passing of my first lamb 'patient', and I wished I could become strong enough, brave enough, clever enough, skilled enough and powerful enough. I was still none of these things and my journey as a surgeon had shown me that I never would be, because biology would always humble me and I could always be better, but it turned out that this was very much okay.

All I ever wanted was to change the world for the better. Humanity will be judged by how we treat the vulnerable – children, minorities, old and disabled people, persecuted people without food or homes – and animals who depend on us for their survival. It's time we woke up and realised that we depend on them for our survival too. A major goal for me now is to translate the love we have for the companion animals in our homes into a broader responsibility for our home on this planet and all of the species in their homes upon it. If we love the dog and cat in our own backyard, can we extend that love to a rhinoceros, lion or tiger in the back-yard of planet Earth? Can we extend that love to our fellow man? Can we become better and more compassionate neigh-bours to all living beings? To echo my opening sentiments, many animals could live without humans, but without them and their ecosystems, humans will not survive. Man's hu-manity to animals could prove the impetus to assuage man's inhumanity to man if we allow it to. Unless we look after all animals and learn from the unconditional love they give us, we will never become the best we can be. And what's worse, we shall destroy what we already have. Unless we address global warming and the deracination of species of plants and animals, we shall all face the inevitable consequences of extinction.

And yet, I remain an optimist. I saw the light of hope in the eyes of students at all of the reservations and sanctuaries I visited in South Africa. I believe the generation after me are more cognisant of the direction our consumerist society is taking us. In the words of the singer Yungblud, 'there's hope for the underrated youth,' but so far, we have been 'so far from telling' them 'the truth.' They know that the Earth will burn, they won't have clean air to breathe or clean water to drink unless we become better stewards of the planet. We have to both *undo* the legacy of our actions and *do* better going forward. Fixing the problems we've caused and ad-dressing the ways we damage our environment will be hard, but in my life I have been told that most of my dreams were impossible, and yet many of them have already been realised. All potential is born in dreams and realised in effort, with a sprinkling of good fortune, the blessing of good guidance and of course all of the inevitable bumps along the way. This book has been my effort to share all of these parts of my life with you, the ups and the downs, the good and the bad, undiluted, with total honesty and no veneer – as life is for all of us, if we're truthful with ourselves.

I wonder what it's like for a tiger or a lion who has been suffering and hopeless in captivity to feel grass under their feet, to see the sky and to roam in relative freedom for the very first time. Do they have the capacity to reflect on *their* journey? I hope so.

As I sat at a desk in my room in South Africa writing this, I again reflected back on the themes of this book – the various dreams I'd had over the course of my life, my readiness to chase them, the humility, passion and thankfulness they have taught me along the way, the promise of openness and kindness I have made to myself, and my commitment to authenticity, trustworthiness and creativity, so that love and hope endure long after I am gone.

I stood outside my room, which was perched on a hill, gazing down at a waterhole in the valley below. I saw the shadows of animals melt out of the bluish haze of night-time to drink. They were all totally dependent on and attracted to 'the source', and in that moment I realised I needed to go back to my source too. In 1992, I left farm animal practice in Ireland with big dreams, thinking I would have it 'all buttoned up' if I just worked hard enough. But now, thirty years later, in spite of all the work, I felt like my professional and business buttons had come undone and my emotional stitching had unravelled. However, in the quiet solitude of my newly open and 'unbuttoned' state near Bethlehem, I looked to the dark clear sky, found the brightest star, which I had wished upon in a field in Ireland forty-two years earlier, and then, quite unexpectedly, I felt its light enter me. I cannot quite explain it in words but, in that moment, I felt that I had 'come home' and that the starlight really did bring me strength and bravery. As a somewhat lapsed Catholic in the aftermath of my childhood trauma, it did not escape me that the God of Oneness shone a star in Bethlehem to guide me home to my source. Amid all of the darkness I had felt consuming me, there was love and there was hope, as this brilliant light shone for me in the infinite darkness of the universe. I knew that this was where I had come from and to where I would ultimately return – stardust. As in the Book of Matthew from the Bible, I 'rejoiced with exceeding great joy'.

I went back inside, lay on the bed and closed my eyes. Then, quite suddenly, the lions started to call out to each other across the valley – bellowing, mesmeric, extraordinarily loud, echoing calls, full of hope and love. I felt like Rici was gifting me a little bit of his huge lion's heart. As I ran my fingers through his gorgeous mane during his recovery back in the field earlier that day, I remembered how, as an excited ten-year-old boy, I'd told Pirate the story of Vetman meeting a lion with a big heart and heading off on a journey to save the world. And so, I would start over, stronger and braver than ever before – with the heart of a lion and the light of a star inside me.

When I got home, I drove to pick something up that I had bought a long time ago. It was in storage waiting for the day I needed its light the most – which was exactly that moment, with the separation of my practices and the end of that part of my life. As I entered the outskirts of the town where it lay waiting for me, serendipitously, the rock channel on the radio played all seven minutes and fifty-five seconds of 'Stairway to Heaven' by Led Zeppelin. I sat in the car until the song ended and then picked up what was waiting for me: an original Led Zeppelin vinyl, signed by all four members of the band – my original musical heroes. This time, authentic. I have kept it by my bed since, to anchor me and to elevate me, like the best love does. Remarkably, Excalibur and Ricochet, who often chew old paper, seem to know its significance and reverentially haven't touched it. Music and the animals I love have saved me once more. As a child, when I first heard that song, I built a stairway to heaven right up to the star I had wished upon, and I had climbed it with Vetman, Pirate and a lion by my side. As I hid in my secret place, listening to my old radio, and I knew back then exactly what I still know today – and that is: if you do listen hard enough, the tune will come and 'all is one and one is all'.

I would soon embark on the road around the UK and Ireland in November 2022 to share some of the lessons I had learned thus far, in the hope of helping others, spinning the 'universal string of oneness' that binds us together with both music and medicine, through the journeys of the animals who truly can make us the best we can be. 'What does a vet do on a theatre tour?' I am constantly asked. The answer is simple. The same as I do in the operating theatre – try to bring love, hope and redemption. It's not called 'theatre' by chance. Music and medicine – always the same currency, even if in different languages.

For a while, I thought I had it all buttoned up, my focus firmly locked on the goal, and that everything would be okay – but I was mistaken. The fabric of who I really am came unravelled for a time. But the love I share with animals has mended my heart when it broke and stitched up the wounds which I have carried nearly all my life. I am a very lucky man. I now realise that keeping everything 'all buttoned up' is not the best way forward. I have discovered that I found *my purpose in my truth*, and *not my truth in my purpose*. I had been chasing a great 'purpose' in life for so long that I had forgotten my 'truth'. It was there inside that ten-year-old boy and it's there now. I absolutely know that if I stay true to my truth, I am unbreakable. So are you. As I 'unbuttoned', so I 'unburdened'. Maybe you could give it a try too.

There is more in giving than in taking, in helping than in ignoring, in progress than in apathy, in praise than in criticism, in love than in hate. It turned out that the animals were trying to teach me that all the light I ever needed was there inside me all along, and that the door I'd closed a very long time ago wasn't locked forever. In their own way and in their own time, they gave me the key to that lock at exactly the right time.

Talking to you in this book has also really helped me, and I hope that it's been an important journey for you, too. Thank you so much for travelling a little way with me. We are all of us magnificently unique in our potential for greatness and for failure, in all of our talents, in all of our genders, religions, races and countries, in all of our humanity and animality. We are all one and the time has come for us to stop messing around and act as such. Man, animal, the natural world. One Planet. One Love. One Medicine. We all have dreams and we need to be ready with humility and passion to seize opportunities and be thankful for the failures that lead to success, if we are open to change. If we are truly kind and committed to creativity in an authentic and trustworthy way, then I know with absolute certainty that love will find us and will light the path of hope for each of us to become the best we can be. I know this because the animals told me, and they know best. I have dedicated this book to them, for they are the innocents, and to children everywhere, for they are innocent too. If we could all be brave enough to try being a little more innocent ourselves, then we just might have a chance.

What's 'beyond' Supervet? Well, I've just taken the first step of this new journey, so I can't tell you for sure. What I can tell you, though, is that our destiny is not defined by our circumstances or challenges but rather by our response to them.

We all feel small some days – tiny specks of stardust in the enormity of it all; we may feel we do not have a voice. Well, my greatest teachers – the animals we have met in this book – had no voice too. But they were heard. In each and every case, the family who loved them responded to their challenges by doing the right thing. We can build a community of compassion, if we really want to – by doing the right thing.

The animals have shown me that it is through our vulnerability we find our strength, through our darkness we find our light, through our rawness we find our courage, and through our truth that we find our hope. Every day of my professional life, I see families at their most vulnerable, desperately seeking hope, just like all of us are in one way or another each and every day. The animals will always give us strength, light, courage and hope through their love, if we choose to see what has been there all along. But maybe we just didn't notice it until now.

I'm still trying to build a stairway to heaven. But I can't do it alone. I need and want you by my side.

Let's go.

ORION CREDITS

Trapeze would like to thank everyone at Orion who worked on the publication of *Beyond Supervet*.

Agent
Ciara O'Flanagan

Editorial
Anna Valentine
Jamie Coleman
Michael Ford
Tierney Witty

Copy-editor
Ian Greensill

Proofreader
Martin Bryant

Editorial Management
Jo Whitford
Jane Hughes
Charlie Panayiotou
Tamara Morriss
Claire Boyle

Audio
Paul Stark
Jake Alderson
Georgina Cutler

Contracts
Anne Goddard
Ellie Bowker

Design
Nick Shah
Chevonne Elbourne
Joanna Ridley
Helen Ewing

Picture Research
Natalie Dawkins

Finance
Nick Gibson
Jasdip Nandra
Sue Baker
Tom Costello

Inventory
Jo Jacobs
Dan Stevens

Marketing
Lindsay Terrell

Production
Katie Horrocks

Publicity
Francesca Pearce
Alex Layt

Sales
Jen Wilson
Victoria Laws
Esther Waters
Group Sales teams across
Digital, Field Sales, International and Non-Trade

Operations
Group Sales Operations team

Rights
Rebecca Folland
Barney Duly
Ruth Blakemore
Flora McMichael
Ayesha Kinley
Marie Henckel

Professor Noel Fitzpatrick is a world-renowned neuro-orthopaedic veterinary surgeon, the founder of Fitzpatrick Referrals in Surrey, the star of the hit Channel 4 television show *The Supervet* and author of the no.1 bestsellers *Listening to the Animals* and *How Animals Saved My Life*. Globally recognised for his innovative surgical solutions for animals, Noel has developed dozens of new techniques, including many world firsts, that have provided hope where none seemed possible. Noel lives in Surrey with his Maine Coon cats, Ricochet and Excalibur.